THE DEVIANCE PROCESS

Third Edition

THE DEVIANCE PROCESS

Third Edition

Erdwin H. Pfuhl and Stuart Henry

ALDINE DE GRUYTER
New York

About the Authors

Erdwin H. Pfuhl is Emeritus Professor of Sociology at Arizona State University. He has been affiliated with several universities in the United States, Canada, and England. His teaching, research and publications have focused on delinquency, deviant behavior, the sociology of law, and several aspects of the criminal justice system.

Stuart Henry is Professor of Criminology in the Department of Sociology, Anthropology, and Criminology at Eastern Michigan University. Dr. Henry has published several books and over 50 journal articles on aspects of crime, deviance, and informal social control. Among his books are; *Private Justice, The Informal Economy,* and *Degrees of Deviance.*

ALDINE DE GRUYTER
A division of Walter de Gruyter, Inc.
200 Saw Mill River Road
Hawthorne, New York 10532

This publication is printed on acid-free paper ⊗
Library of Congress Cataloging-in-Publication Data
Pfuhl, Erdwin H.
  The deviance process / Erdwin H. Pfuhl, Stuart Henry. – 3rd ed.
     p.   cm.
  Includes bibliographical references and index.
  ISBN 0-202-30469-8. — ISBN 0-202-30470-1 (pbk.)
  1. Deviant behavior.   2. Stigma (Social psychology)   I. Henry, Stuart.   II. Title.
HM291.P485   1993
302.5'42—dc20   93-2942
                                                         CIP

Manufactured in the United States of America

10 9 8 7 6 5 4 3 2 1

To our families

Contents

Preface

As with prior editions of *The Deviance Process*, the aim of this book is to answer the question "How is deviance created?" To provide an answer we offer students an in depth examination of deviance from the social constructionist perspective. From this perspective we analyze the process whereby morally condemned behavior or conditions come to be defined that way. We examine the process by which persons performing actions judged to be consistent with these definitions acquire a public moral identity and how they adjust their personal and social relationships accordingly, either accepting, resisting, or rejecting the definitions of others.

Our perspective regards deviance and its counterpart, respectability, as a human creation, generated by people interacting with one another in the context of the local and societal constructions of others. Deviance is seen, therefore, as the emergent outcome of antagonisms, contradictions, and conflicts in societies whose members identify differences between people, signify these as meaningful, and evaluate them negatively. Three consequences follow from our approach, which distinguishes it from other texts on deviance. First we believe that the process of constructing meaning, and the meanings themselves, together with the accounts used by people to explain their action, deserve serious attention. The explanations of those categorized as deviant are treated here as significant and purposeful and are not to be displaced by "expert" or authoritative commentary, where this fails to be grounded in an appreciative stance.

Second, we assume that people actively construct their own meaningful worlds (although they are not necessarily aware of this process). We reject the view that people are somehow inherently "bad" or "evil" in and of themselves. Rather than essential deviance we see people both as capable of being deviant, and of transforming their being. They are capable of creating deviance and of recognizing differences and imposing judgments about those differences on others; doing so gives the appearance of normality, abnormality, essence, and truth. Thus, approaches that buy into the preexistence of fixed, immutable qualities in humans as explanations for their behavior or their conditions, are critically scrutinized.

Third, and perhaps most important, because we take the social constructionist perspective throughout, we do not review the range of competing theories on deviance. Unlike the numerous texts that take a multiparadigm approach to explaining deviance, and as a result suffer from a lack of depth, our social constructionist approach draws on these other theories only where they are relevant to our argument. As a result, our analysis takes more from the theoretical traditions of social process theories (including symbolic interactionism, differential association, neutralization and social control, and labeling theory) and from conflict and critical theories, than it does from positivistic theories of sociobiology or structural functionalism and systems theory. We make no apologies for this. We believe our composite social constructionist approach has much more to offer the understanding of deviance than any or all of these alternatives. Moreover, by incorporating aspects of these other perspectives into our argument we believe that, while being focused, our approach is also a comprehensive analysis of the deviance process.

An implication of our theoretical approach is that we must temporarily suspend, for the purpose of analysis, our judgments about the morality of the behaviors that we examine. To appreciate the meaning and construction of moral identities in the social structure, we need to be sensitive to the moral relativism of everyday life. We reject arguments that suggest ours is an absolutist world, although many might like to see it as such. We believe, instead, that such claims are part of the politics of reality construction wherein internal differences and disagreements are subject to daily "spinning" so that they are either minimized, giving the appearance of consensus, or marginalized, giving the appearance of exception. Such ideology glosses over the naked impact of heterogeneity wherein few things remain sacred and unquestioned, where rules seldom go unchallenged, and where behavioral styles are defined and redefined regularly. In the affairs of everyday life, many of us behave ambivalently, believing that our own morality should be *the* morality. We ignore the moral relativism that this implies and either do not care what others think or else believe that "the majority" think like us!

Examining deviance as a human creation also requires that we study the phenomenon in political terms as a fundamental part of the business of making and enforcing public rules. While other theoretical approaches, notably conflict theory, focus on a discussion of the politics of deviance, many ignore it. They take for granted what counts as crime and deviance, how it comes to be defined in a particular way, and whose interests such definitions serve. In contrast we argue that deviance is partly an outgrowth of making, enforcing, and administering public policy, particularly through banning behavior, establishing norms, rules, and laws, and seeking to discredit categories of behavior and persons. Equally political is the process of resistance, whereby some people reject, modify, or seek to transform the imposition of stigmatizing labels on themselves. Whether they do this individually or collectively, the result cannot escape the observation that rather than dealing in truth the study of deviance is the study of contested terrain.

Finally, to study deviance as a process means to study changes in definitions and categories of meaning over time. Reflecting this, the chapters of this book examine analytically discrete aspects of an integral process. As a result, categories or types of deviance and their discredited status are subordinate to the social process whereby that status is constructed. They are drawn on throughout only to illustrate selected aspects of the process. It is recommended that students who require an in depth understanding of a particular type of deviance supplement their reading with ethnographic accounts and original case accounts contained in various collections.

Consistent with our perspective the book begins by introducing students to our assumptions about society, people, behavior, and the construction of meaning and structure on which our theoretical approach rests. In Chapter 2, Counting Deviants, we examine how official agencies produce statistical data that form part of the public knowledge of rule breaking and how these data are used as "measures" of deviance. Chapter 3, Breaking Rules, could have followed our subsequent discussion of making rules since, in many cases, rule making is the prior activity. However, behaviors that become deviant may also exist before they invoke the action to ban them. Here we discuss the meaning and reasoning that forms part of the motivational context from which individuals elect to act. Once they have done so, or even before that, audiences interpret the behavior, and seek to ban it. Such Banning Behavior is the subject of Chapter 4, where we examine how selected patterns of behavior come to be elevated into public issues as subjects of policy making and law creation. The role of moral entrepreneurs and the media in this conversion of private troubles to public issues is stressed. Once formal banning has occurred, control agency personnel employ everyday categorization techniques to identify and label a select number of rule breakers for official processing. The activities involved in this aspect of the deviance process are examined in Chapter 5, Creating Deviants. Such a process is not without effects and in Chapter 6, Consequences of Stigma, we discuss the theory behind labeling and give consideration to the personal and social consequences experienced by people publicly identified as deviant. Special attention is paid to the progressive reconstruction involved in the deviancy amplification process. Lastly, Chapters 7 and 8, respectively, focus on individual and collective attempts by those defined as deviants to cope, manage, or transform their stigma, through undertaking personal and/or political change. In Chapter 8 we give special attention to the political dynamics of how groups of deviants mobilize themselves through mutual aid to combat and ultimately transform their members' situation and also to the limits of that process for the transformation of society. We conclude with an Epilogue which draws out the central message of our analysis and returns us to the suspended moral question that, subsequent to an appreciation of the diversity of deviance, we are much better able to address.

CHAPTER

1

Studying Deviance

INTRODUCTION

There are numerous views of what deviance is, who commits it, what causes it, and what should be done about it. In the view of many lay people the term "deviance" applies to specific behaviors and/or conditions that are inherently dangerous, threatening and offensive; it is engaged in by "outsiders," "oddballs," "weirdos," and "creeps" who appear regularly on television talk shows and who, simultaneously, tantalize and outrage us. We pass laws, and establish police departments, courts, and prisons to protect ourselves against those we see as qualitatively different from ourselves. In short, most people perceive deviance as something that exists "out there" in the world.

In this book we take a different view of deviance. For us deviance is a social construction, created by a process engaged in by humans in their day-to-day interaction with one another. That is, for us the phenomenon of deviance depends on the interactive work of humans as actors and audiences; it is people's behavior, its interpretation, and evaluation that create and sustain the phenomenon of deviance.

That deviance results from the interaction of actors and audiences may be seen in the case of Ivan Boesky, who used "insider" information to gain financial advantage in stock market transactions. What did Boesky deviate from? Was his behavior different from all others who trade in stocks? If there had been no rules of fair trading, had there been a truly free market, his behavior may not have been deviant but normal (at least in terms of statistical typicality). Does this mean, then, that the creators of the rules of fair trading were, in some sense, a party to Boesky's deviation? We believe they were, just as all rule creators make it possible for others to engage in violations since, in the absence of rules there can be no rule violation. In short, actors and audiences (rule violators as well as ordinary citizens, groups, and/or organizations who are fearful or feel offended) "interact" to construct the phenomenon of deviance.

1

Deviance involves more than simple rule violations. Nor are behaviors or conditions deviant per se. Deviance is a matter of interpretive judgment occurring in an established historical, cultural, and situational context. Consider the matter of behavior regarded as being different vs. being deviant. Drinking alcohol in a bar is not deviant. Drinking tea in a bar is different—statistically deviant—but rarely is it seen as significant unless, of course, the tea drinker is a recovering alcoholic and that is why he or she is drinking tea. However, depending on who sees it and what state you are in, drinking alcohol in your car can be very significant. For fellow drinking buddies it may be acceptable, even normal and expected; for fellow state troopers, drinking a beer while on patrol might be an indication of social status, marking the trooper as "special" and above the law. For members of Mothers Against Drunk Driving (MADD) both of these acts are morally and criminally deviant.

Whether negative or positive, the significant evaluation of statistically deviant behavior in particular social contexts may also be accompanied by a stereotype that others construct of the persons performing the behavior in question. Often these people are not seen merely as behaving differently; they are seen as deviant types and are given a deviant identity. For example, whether a person smoking marijuana is seen as a "pothead" or whether a cocaine user is seen as a "crackhead" depends on many factors: frequency and amount used, motives for use, when and where used, who sees them using, at what period of history, and what is expected of the person on the basis of their other social roles. Contrast the college student in Ann Arbor, Michigan (where even now there is a negligible fine for personal possession only recently raised from $5.00 to $25.00) at a summer rock concert who smokes an occasional joint before the show to heighten enjoyment, with hospital registrars or emergency room physicians who regularly use marijuana to help them cope with the stress of their job. Moreover, whether either incident would be considered deviant would depend on the actor's ability to manage public impressions of self.

Nor is deviance confined to individuals. Corporations can be deviant, as with A.H. Robbins' negligent action regarding the quality control tests of the Dalkon Shield IUD birth control device or the alleged failure of Dow-Corning to adequately test the safety of silicon breast implants. Importantly, the question of deviance here depends on whether the corporation has been officially declared deviant by government agencies such as the Food and Drug Administration. Without such official declaration, lay observation of difference and evaluation of outcomes is extremely difficult; ordinary people are unaware of the complexity of the issues, are unable to distinguish between independent testing and company sponsored research, and are ignorant about what is the typical practice in these matters. In such cases lay people rely on specialized groups of observers, watchdogs, whistleblowers, and journalists for interpretive guidance. Each of these groups may either serve as "moral entrepreneurs" (Becker, 1973) and whip up support to ban behavior, or they may be used by other interest groups for this purpose.

As one might gather from these few pages, we take the view that we are all surrounded by, and immersed in, the deviance making process. In the following pages we will make a systematic, sociological examination of this process. This involves the identification of common elements among many behaviors and conditions regarded as deviant, arranging these in categories, and investigating our part in the social construction of deviance. We begin with a consideration of how sociologists view deviance.

A SOCIOLOGICAL VIEW OF DEVIANCE

While sociologists also have an interest in rule breaking, they approach the subject somewhat differently than lay people. Sociologists studying rule breaking are guided by one or more *models*, i.e., "conception[s] of the realm in which [they are] working, some . . . mental picture of 'how it is put together and how it works'" (Barber, 1973:2; Liska, 1987). These models influence what the sociologist looks for, what is discovered, and how they interpret the resulting information. Overall, models are intended to assist the investigator to understand and explain the world.

However, models also impose limitations because of the *assumptions* they make about people, society, and behavior. Because these assumptions differ from one model to another, it will be helpful to have an appreciation of the ones made by the model used in this book. Our model is called the "Social Constructionist Perspective" and consists of several elements, including a philosophical base, methods to be used to study the subject matter, beliefs about the nature of reality, of people, and of society, and, finally, some assumptions about the basis of human behavior. In the following pages we will consider each of these elements and their implications as "guides" in studying the deviance process.

The Social Constructionist Perspective

Philosophical Base. Quite commonly people believe that the universe is comprised of things that are *real*, i.e., stuff that is assumed to be part of the "nature of things" or that is part of "reality." For example, you often hear people talk about the world "as it is" or about things "as they are." You may also hear them insist that others "tell it like it is" or that the "facts speak for themselves." Though few ever hear a fact speak, these expressions suggest that the essential meaning of things is shared and understood by everyone, and that these meanings have a vitality independent of any person or group of persons. In other words, it is assumed that a "reality" exists above and beyond humans' conscious awareness; reality is taken to be objective. So, while they may disagree sharply over which conditions, persons, etc. meet their criteria, people take it for granted that qualities and social events such as deviance have an objective reality, i.e., exist in their own right.

The philosophical base of the social constructionist perspective proposes something different; specifically that names and meanings are very distinct from things. For example, by *naming* chemical substances "drugs," or *naming* different drugs by terms such as "acid," "uppers," "Angel dust," or "reds," people are creating *mental constructs*, concepts and words used to identify things perceived to have common elements and that are classified in the same category. Most important for our purpose is that *the names and meanings constructed, or the meanings invoked by naming, do not exist outside the human mind and should not be confused with the things themselves*. As war veterans know, a wound resulting in a return home may have a euphoric meaning, while the same injury sustained in a domestic auto accident may be given a dysphoric meaning.

This position regarding the difference between things and their names and how they are defined is useful in making sense of issues involving morality and immorality—deviance. Unlike models that suggest reality is "out there," our model suggests that "realities are achieved only when they can be imagined and labeled" (Inciardi, 1978:7). Using the same argument we used in talking about the names of certain chemical substances, we may say that while behaviors occur, names such as "misconduct," "crime," or "deviance" exist only insofar as (1) they are held in common by others, (2) a difference has been observed and judged significant, and (3) it has been assigned a name imbued with negative meaning.[1] Thus, by this definition men making sexual advances toward women in the workplace, people using mood-altering substances, limbs not working, and eyes not seeing are not deviant unless they are observed/defined to be significantly different and named accordingly. *Nothing is qualitatively deviant unless it is so named*, although it may be statistically atypical. Fuller appreciation of this calls for a brief examination of what our model has to say about the nature of reality.

Nature of Reality.   We have noted that some people think the world consists of things that are *objective*, i.e., entities that exist and operate independent of the mind (consciousness) of the observer (Zukav, 1979:29). They also assume these things have inherent meanings or essences, i.e., core properties (sometimes including a moral element), and that it is these things sociologists should study. That is, they believe sociologists should study *objective reality*.

The distinction between that view of reality and the one used in this book may be appreciated by recounting the tale of three baseball umpires, each of whom is describing how they approach their work (Henshel and Silverman, 1975:26). The first umpire says, "I call them as they are!" The second says, "I call them as I see them!" The third says, "They are nothing until I call them!" These umpires represent three major western approaches to knowledge. The first umpire sees knowledge as objective and views umpires as impartial reporters of things "as they are." The second umpire suggests that people's knowledge of the real world needs to be approached in terms of the categories of thought they create ("strikes" and "balls" being categories), and according to which they organize and interpret their world. Moreover, this umpire suggests that the categories people create "intervene" between themselves and their knowledge of this imagined "real world." The third umpire represents the social constructionist perspective. For this umpire, "strikes" and "balls" have no meaning other than that given them. "Strikes" and "balls" are mental constructs. Because we will use this position throughout the book, let us expand on these ideas and link the "three umpires" to the issues of ontology and epistemology.

Ontology is the part of philosophy that focuses on the nature of the world and how we come to know it. Put simply, this translates into the ordinary question: What is the "real" world like? The first umpire says the "real" world is one that operates according to the inherent laws or principles that people discover. Consistent with traditional western thought, this umpire implies that human reason is the principal instrument and final authority in the search for truth. Accordingly, this umpire simply discovers truth and "tells it like it is".

The second umpire is less certain about the independent existence of the world and what constitutes truth. By saying "I call them as I see them" (i.e., as I define them), this umpire acknowledges the observer's intervening role in naming, defining and classifying things. This uncertainty leads to a consideration of the role people play (their consciousness) in determining the verity or "truth" of their description of the "real" world. It also raises the possibility that there is a difference between *things*, on the one hand, and how people *name and define* them, on the other. This distinction prepares us for the views of the third umpire and the social constructionist perspective.

In saying things are nothing until they are named, the third umpire suggests that what people perceive and react to are not core properties or essences of things (which may not exist) but, rather, the names and meanings assigned to what is imagined to exist. That is, people respond to a reality that is a human or social creation, rather than one that is *objective* or independent of human consciousness. Moreover, this position suggests that *if* there is such a quality as objective reality, people do not apprehend it. This is because the definitions, names, and categories people employ to organize their world serve either as "barriers" between themselves and any hypothesized real world or as images or representations of what is imagined to exist. It is only these "barriers" that people apprehend. So, when the third umpire calls balls and strikes, or when any of us respond to "things" in our environment, we do so on the basis of their assigned meaning rather than their "inherent nature." In short, the third umpire is saying that the world is whatever people perceive it to be. Beauty and ugliness, morality and immorality, deviance and normality are terms reflecting observers' constructions and definitions. Accordingly, in response to the ontological question, the social constructionist perspective leads to the conclusion that the social world has no underlying objective character. There are no dirty words, only dirty minds.

Epistemology, another branch of philosophy, raises related questions: "How do people know about the world?" and "How certain is their knowledge of the world?" If the only world people have knowledge of is socially created, it follows that people are unlikely to have knowledge of an external, objective world. Further, even if there is an objective world independent of human consciousness, one wonders if people can ever have knowledge of its properties (Quinney, 1970a:138). People are unlikely to apprehend those properties because they are "encapsulated" in a world of socially constructed meanings. They are left with an awareness only of the meanings or properties they have assigned to things or to images that presuppose things; concerns about the properties of a supposedly objective world may then be dismissed.

On the other hand, to have knowledge of a socially constructed reality, i.e., how people create meaning in the process of naming, we must look to people themselves and focus on their social experiences, interaction, and discourse. This is the position to be followed in this book. Our goal, then, is not to search for or explain the "objective causes" of something called deviance. Rather, and most importantly, it is to *explain the origin of the meanings* of select behaviors and attributes (Freidson, 1970:215) and how people deal with these meanings. Because this goal will influence our method of study, we need to turn to that aspect of our model.

Method of Study. According to Western thought, the scientific method is the proper way to study the human condition and unlock the mysteries of a supposedly objective universe in which things are assumed to exist and to be related in terms of cause and effect. Researchers are expected to gather information in very specific and reproducible ways in order that they not influence or shape (bias) that knowledge (Brown, 1977:89). Like the first umpire, the role of the scientific investigator is to "tell it like it is." For example, if juvenile gang violence or illicit drug use rates seem to be higher in low income than middle and high income areas, the factor of low income (or something perceived to be related to low income) is likely to be regarded as having some objective (though perhaps unspecified) causal influence on these behaviors. Alternatives to cause–effect interpretations (i.e., different ways of perceiving relationships) tend to be precluded because it is taken for granted that things existing in an allegedly objective world are believed to be united that way (Kotarba, 1975).

Explanations of deviance based on these cause–effect ideas have been very popular in our society. Examples include the idea that "drug use and/or violence in the mass media cause crime," that overprotective mothers make boys homosexual, that "patterns of child abuse are passed on to children who themselves become abusers," and that "inequality (e.g., poverty) causes violent behavior." In each case, deviant behavior is seen as an entity *produced by* the factor correlated with and preceding it.

In contrast, our model suggests that the scientific method itself is no more than a concept, i.e., an idea developed and used by people to make sense of and give order to a world that is without essential order. It also suggests that these cause–effect statements reflect the observer's perceptions (constructions) of so-called "facts," rather than conditions/relationships existing in an objective world. It also suggests that variation in officials' and other audiences' responses rests less on variation in the objective behavior in question than on audiences' *definitions of the situation.*

The essential implication of these contentions is that, to a great extent, we have produced a sociology in which the *social basis of meaning* is taken for granted rather than being a process subject to investigation. A lack of concern for the social construction of meanings has produced a sociology in which the multiple experiences and common sense meanings of ordinary people are replaced by the understandings of the sociologist. As Howard Becker (1973:190) has noted:

> we [sociologists] often turn collective activity—people doing things together—into abstract nouns whose connection to people doing things

together is tenuous. We then typically lose interest in the more mundane
things people are actually doing, . . . ignore what we see because it is not
abstract, and chase after the invisible "forces" and "conditions" we have
learned to think sociology is all about.

As an alternative to pursuing these illusive "forces" and "conditions,"
the method of study proposed here is that we carefully and systematically observe the social world as it is constructed and experienced by
people in the course of their everyday lives. This way of doing sociology
calls for relinquishing the idea that things have intrinsic and fixed meanings. Instead, it calls for examination of how people create meanings
(i.e., their social construction), how these meanings are applied to
things in the environment, the consequences of applying these meanings (e.g., how things are then classified), how people respond to these
meanings, and, finally, how and under what circumstances these meanings change. Ideally, it requires that we participate in the scene of interaction to observe, first hand, how meaning is constructed.[2] These issues
will concern us in subsequent chapters.

Nature of Society.   One of the most important concepts in sociology is
that of *society*, i.e., prolonged relations between individuals producing
patterned cooperative and conflicting interaction and an identification
with a whole that is greater than its parts. For some time scholars have
debated over the nature of society, oscillating between "consensus" and
"conflict" models with respect to which best represents the social whole.
According to the *consensus perspective* society is perceived as stable, internally harmonious, with the bulk of its members exhibiting value agreement or consensus. Patterns of interaction are said to be repetitive and,
for the most part, predictable. In western industrial societies peoples'
roles in family, business, the professions, recreation, etc. are said to be
harmonious and congruent with one another since they are assumed to
behave and interact in conformity with rules, norms, and expectations
with which they are in essential agreement. This normative consensus is
taken as an index of the essential orderliness of society, an orderliness
rooted in nature and part of the objective or real world (Piven, 1981:490).
The essence of society is held to be orderliness.

The consensus view also implies that deviance arises either (1) as a
result of unintended conditions that are alien to the ongoing social system (such as the unintended blocking of people's opportunities to
achieve legitimate goals), or (2) because groups embrace values and interests contrary to those held by the "moral majority" or mainstream, or
(3) as a result of the way society established and/or maintained its moral
boundaries. Here deviance, and the subsequent creation of deviant cate-

gories, is felt to serve the purpose of integrating the group, community, or society in defense of those boundaries (Durkheim, 1895; Dentler and Erikson, 1959; Lauderdale, 1976).

In contrast, the *conflict perspective* views society as made up of classes, strata, or groups in a constant state of struggle. The nature of the relationship between these segments has no lasting character, and agreement between them is felt to be through domination of one by another, rather than as a result of value agreement. The root of the conflict is alleged to vary from differences in the distribution of economic wealth (as among Marxist theorists), to differences in culture or gender (as among culture conflict or feminist theorists), to matters involving status, prestige, religion, morality, etc. (as in more pluralistic versions of conflict theory). Nor is there seen to be value consensus within the social groups or classes.

The idea that change is everywhere and constant means that each element of society contributes to the disintegration of the whole *as it exists at any point in time*. That is, society is seen as dynamic and ever-changing, each element contributing to the instability and flux of the whole. As a result, the unity of "values" and "norms" assumed to exist by consensus theorists is said to be a fiction and should not be confused with expedient, short-term unity—as when groups are in more or less agreement with one another while pursuing shared goals. The appearance and taken-for-granted nature of such "small group" unity does not preclude the existence of widespread value disagreement or dissensus. However, such alliances quite often are matters of expedience and rest on the belief that they serve unique purposes for each group. Given its utilitarian basis, such "unity" should not be confused with "essential value consensus and stability." The more fundamental and widespread condition in society from the conflict perspective is value disagreement or dissensus.

During the 1980s a third view of society emerged that is more consistent with the social constructionist perspective. This view holds that society is an ongoing, constantly emerging outcome of human agents' interaction with one another. Some theorists saw society as a number of "links" in an endless series of interactions at the local level (Collins, 1981). Others viewed society as a composite mental picture taken to represent a reality assumed to exist (Knorr-Cetina and Cicourel, 1981; Giddens, 1984). This mental picture or representation is constituted through many individuals acting toward each other *as though* the institutions and the society they formed were real. When people approximated each other's pictures, they were able to assume a reality and identify with it and with each other, even though examination of their respective images might reveal major discrepancies of assumption and belief.

Enough was held in common to produce patterned behavior designated with institutional labels and that was further reinforced through repetition. This recurrence gave the appearance of social structure.

Where people were not prepared to let discrepancies of assumption and belief go unchallenged or, conversely, where they invested time and energy in restating and reaffirming their version of what was reality, conflict arose. Conflict existed between supporters of alternative truth claims, those who either wittingly or unwittingly exposed the process as a fabrication, and those who wanted it to be real.

The social constructionist view regards society as a grand or ongoing social construction, the medium through which individuals constitute their social worlds. Unlike the bifurcated vision of earlier perspectives, they see *both* consensus and conflict as simultaneously present as cocontributors to the illusion of the whole. Indeed, without conflict, consensus would be meaningless, as would conflict without consensus. Neither represents the truth in any objective sense; each is an exaggeration of integral aspects of the mental pictures people have of the world in which they live. This can be illustrated by focusing on one aspect of society germane to our discussion: morality.

While many people may claim to subscribe to a general or public code of morality, there is also a *private* morality that influences their everyday life and that consists of *situated moral meanings*, i.e., interpretations of abstractly conceived morals applied to concrete situations (Douglas, 1970:20). For example, in terms of public (abstract) morality such things as dishonesty are widely condemned in our society. However, not every "common sense" instance that reasonably fits legal definitions of dishonesty is perceived to be an instance of such behavior. That dishonesty is ambiguous and situationally constructed can be seen in the following illustration:

> The members of the jury were requested to complete claim forms for expenses they had incurred while fulfilling this civic duty. On filling these in, there was considerable discussion concerning which items could be inflated, such as mileage by car, and whether to risk the claim that by fulfilling their jury service they had lost their normal weekly wage. After payment had been made, there were comparative calculations on the amount of money that had been illegally obtained, or "spending money" as one of them called it. The money acquired in this fashion ranged from 3 ($6) to 25 ($50) pounds. No one condemned this practice or reported it to policemen on duty in the court; yet shortly before the same [jury]men had found an adolescent guilty of stealing items valued at 2 pounds 50p ($5), and had all morally condemned his behavior by agreeing with the judge's sentence of nine months in prison. (Box 1971: 63)

By recognizing the difference between abstract public and private situational morality, we are better able to "make sense" of the stuff of everyday life and reconcile what many people perceive as hypocrisy or the contradictions between people's behavior and their professed standards. The jury example is an instance of the inconsistency between behavioral activity and truth claims. People "preach" one set of morals, virtues, etc., on a public level and even act toward it as though it was real while practicing something very different in private. These differences are the stuff of scandals such as that involving televangelists Jim and Tammy Bakker and Jessica Hahn, the alleged sexual improprieties of members of the Kennedy family, the alleged marital infidelity of President Bill Clinton, check kiting by members of Congress, as well as innumerable cases of corporate and political corruption, fraud, and embezzlement. That people fail (or are believed to fail) to "practice what they preach" is not only an acknowledgment of the difference between public and private morality, but also confirms the socially constructed nature of society.

Another way of noting this difference is to recognize that as the level of abstraction or generalization of an issue rises, so does the degree of public consensus with respect to it. Conversely, as the level of abstraction declines and the issue becomes more specific, the probability of disagreement and conflict increases. For example, it is not difficult to find consensus among people concerning the *general* idea that "something needs to be done about crime." It is much more difficult to find consensus about what that "something" ought to be; what constitutes the proper response to *specific* kinds of law violation engaged in by *particular* segments of society in *specific* times and places. Everyday life clearly shows that *the meanings of things, moral and otherwise, have a contextual or situational base*. We will return to this point shortly.

Finally, the social constructionist perspective suggests that the formal, public values and interests that prevail at any point in time, relative to any specific issue, do so as a result of both coercion and consensus. For example, regardless of the outcome of present social conflicts over such issues as abortion, homosexuality, use of mood-altering drugs, and pornography, the views that "win" (i.e., prevail in terms of public law) will do so partly as a result of consensus among some people over the acceptability of the "winning" image and partly as a result of public and official condemnation and/or suppression of their opposite by force or the threat of force. Our perspective suggests, then, that conformity among representatives of "losing" interests reflects temporary assent, and coercion from the fear of the consequences that might follow if they dissent. In a variety of everyday situations, people's decisions and behavior rest as much on their understanding of the consequences of the unequal distribution and use of political power between various interest groups and individuals, as on any acceptance of the way in which an issue is defined and presented. We will return to this duality of conflict and consensus in the following sections.

Human Nature in Society.   Scholars who view people as basically conforming creatures have often adopted an "oversocialized" conception of humans (Wrong, 1961). This is consistent with a belief in an essentially orderly society. Further, these basically conforming creatures are often felt to be influenced or directed by "invisible forces" and "conditions" (Babbie, 1989:60–61), though they are guided and constrained by a superego or conscience. In turn, *conscience* has been defined as a consequence of people being *socialized*, i.e., having had the values, rules, and expectations of society "built into" them. People are felt to behave in the "right way" largely because they have been "programmed" that way; the values, rules, and expectations are believed to have a constraining influence. If people deviate it is because they are either unsocialized, undersocialized, or unsocializable and/or because of an "aberation" or "imperfection" in the social system. Basically, then, the notion of people as "essentially conforming" harmonizes with a conception of society as "essentially orderly."

Many scholars challenge the contention that humans are what abstractions such as "socialization" and "society" have made them. They contend that people are not validly described by the metaphor of a billiard ball or a hockey puck, i.e., things propelled, willy nilly, by external forces over which they have no control. Instead of defining people as *reactive* (i.e., responding mechanically to forces over which they have no control), our model employs a *humanistic* conception of humankind that perceives them as *interactive*. Accordingly, it focuses on people's awareness of self, the active part they play in shaping their own lives, their ability to make evaluations and judgments and consider alternatives, and their capability of breaking away from hypothesized social constraints (Quinney, 1970b:13). Moreover, it suggests that if people appear to be ordered and orderly it is the outcome of their own active concessions, their own contributions (unwitting or otherwise) to consensus. It is a view that regards people as conscious beings who interact to produce a meaningful environment. This leads us to a consideration of the basis of behavior.

Basis of Behavior.   The social constructionist perspective views people in humanistic terms, stresses the active part they play in shaping their own lives, and regards human behavior (rule breaking or otherwise) as the action of conscious beings. Logically, then, this perspective must explain that behavior on the basis of people's choices and reasons rather than constraining forces (Brown, 1977:84). This is necessary even where people appear to subordinate their decision to choose, or abandon the choice to others, which, as Illich (1981) says, occurs when they "connive at their own oppression." The reasons for such choices are to be found in the meanings (definitions) people create about the world around them. Such reasons explain rule breaking as well as conforming behavior since *both involve people behaving in ways meaningful to them*. Thus, the social constructionist perspective embraces the notion of *indeterminate social causation* as an alternative to the idea of determinism. In other words, people act on the basis of their own interpretations, definitions, and intentions. Conduct is meaningful in relation to people's *motives*, i.e., the meanings people use to make their behavior seem suitable and justifiable in their own terms (Weber, 1962:39). If behavior rests on such motives it is not necessary to resort to external deterministic forces to explain it. Instead, the social constructionist perspective suggests behavior is voluntaristic and rests on situationally based meanings rather than external constraining forces. Further, it suggests that people may construct reasons or explanations for such action that may have no connection to the actual motivating meaning that led to their decision to act in the first place.

Summary. To summarize briefly, we will analyze the phenomenon of deviance by employing the social constructionist perspective. Accordingly, it is necessary, first, to view reality as a set of human or social constructions, i.e., the meanings people create about categories of their environment, other people, and their action. Being socially constructed, we may refer to this reality as *social reality*. Second, this perspective calls for the use of *social causation* rather than causality defined in a deterministic/constraining sense. By social causation we mean the *relationships people perceive to exist* between what they take to be things and in terms of which they respond to them. Again, both these presumed relations and the "things" related are social constructions. Third, the perspective calls on us to view people as agents acting on the basis of conscious purpose rather than responding in a mechanical fashion to deterministic forces. As active, conscious agents, people create their own reality. In turn, people come to be influenced by what they create so that they may appear and even perceive that they are influenced by external forces, while forgetting their own on-going authorship of such "forces." Related to this is a fourth major element of this model, namely that reason, choice, judgments, and intention are the bases of behavior. Finally, this model proposes that society be viewed as a dynamic, on-going social construction characterized by both conflict and consensus. With these preliminaries in mind, let us turn to a more concentrated examination of the concept of "reality as a social construction" and how it applies to the study of deviance.

CONSTRUCTING SOCIAL REALITY

Viewing social reality as a human creation seems to contradict a variety of human experiences. This is because a number of actors present the vagaries of social life as prepackaged truths. For example, parents regularly introduce children to beliefs, meanings, definitions, values, rules, and understandings in ways that give these things the appearance of permanence and objectivity. Often they are presented as unarguable and "the way things are." Similarly, established meanings are presented to new students during "orientation," to military recruits by way of "indoctrination" during basic training, to new club members through "initiation," and to new prisoners as the convict code. In view of their veritable permanence, it is easy for people to regard these meanings as *given* rather than as social or human constructions, and rarely do people have a sense of themselves as creators of such meanings. How, then, shall we reconcile this consciousness with our view that reality is a human creation?

We suggest that the social construction of reality is so fundamental to people's daily lives that few are aware of being engaged in it. For example, in the course of everyday life people often confront unique situations such as encountering public nudity or being "propositioned" by a person of the same sex. Such encounters call for spontaneous definitions, evaluations, and judgments on which to establish a course of action. In these circumstances a person's initial reaction may be confusion and a tendency to rely on preexisting moral principles or "laws." But if they decide to experiment or explore the occasion further, they may readjust their views about what is acceptable sexual conduct. At such times, people are "writing the script" for subsequent relationships. It is precisely this "script writing" (defining and thereby regulating their affairs) that constitutes the social construction of reality. Moreover, the apparently routine responses to familiar or repeat situations are affirmations of earlier scripts.

A more theoretically grounded explanation of the social construction of reality calls for developing an understanding of the interrelated processes of externalization, objectivation, and internalization (Berger and Luckmann, 1967). It is these processes that *reify* meanings (i.e., make them appear objective) and lead to the perception—the consciousness—

that reality is external to people, independent of human consciousness, absolute in character, and ontologically certain and orderly. Let us briefly explore these three processes.

Externalization

The first stage in transforming humanly created meanings into seemingly objective knowledge is *externalization*, referring to the overt expression of subjective meanings, understandings, definitions, and expectations via written, oral, or gestural forms of communication. For example, when two people are interacting externalization may be quite simple and be limited to the language of gesture such as bodily movements and facial expressions, indicating acceptance or rejection, approval or disapproval, agreement or disagreement. More complex meanings expressing whole life-styles can be conveyed to greater numbers through demeanor and dress. Consider the following example of how new wave teens' nonverbal expressions through clothing and hairstyle can lead to physical altercation.

> Most of them are dressed in black with dyed jet-black hair or a bouffant, pale skin and black make-up, regardless of sex. They go to great lengths to pick and choose their clothes. They mousse and gel their hair until it stands straight on end and they stay out of the sun at all costs. They want to shock yet they want respect. Kelly was in McDonald's one night taking crap from a preppie university student. Her hair was a black straggled mop. She had shocking black eyeliner and ripped black tights with some sort of black mini T-shirt. The cross hanging from her ear didn't help. . . . The scene resulted in a fist fight outside the restaurant which brought the police and ended in arrest. How can someone's dress and appearance lead to so much trouble? (King, 1990:116)

In other cases verbalization is needed to communicate meaning as when one person tries to tell another "what" to do or how to define a situation. For example,

> I was on an unpopulated beach in North Carolina where women may go topless, legally. I took off my top and sat up. All of a sudden, a family with mom, dad, grandma, and the kids walked right past me and pretended not to notice me. The kids and dad slowly lagged behind, staring at me. The mom yelled at them saying "Don't look at that. You mustn't look at that." (Cox, 1990:124)

But whether gestural or verbal, in very small groups this communication is typically informal. In larger groups such as in workplaces, schools,

neighborhoods, or entire communities, however, communication becomes more formalized. This formalization leads to objectivation, the
second stage in the process whereby subjectively created knowledge
takes on the appearance of objectivity.

Objectivation

Objectivation refers to the way socially created meanings are reified
and made to appear independent of people (Berger and Luckmann,
1967:60). This may be understood by noting that, as the size of a group
increases and members' roles become more diverse, the variety and
complexity of the relationships between members increase. More formal
rules are then required to govern daily interaction and to exercise social
control (Simmel, 1903; Mayhew and Levinger, 1976). For example, it has
been observed (Gluckman, 1969; Black, 1976) that in face-to-face and
multistranded relationships people typically interact on many levels. As
a result they have little need for formal law since social control can be
exercised informally via any of the many channels of interaction. For
example, a group of fast food restaurant workers not only work together, but may socialize together, meet one another as students at a local
college, and so on. Because of these multistranded relationships, any
dispute arising in one setting, say the workplace, can be dealt with in
any one of the other contexts without a need for formal rules. Contrast
this situation with the more common relationships in industrial societies
that are typically single-stranded. Professors meet students only during
scheduled class periods or office hours at the university; supermarket
cashiers interact with customers only for a fleeting transaction. Under
these circumstances settlement of disputes requires formal resolution on
the basis of company rules or formal laws. Societies characterized by
such single-stranded or simplex relations also develop impersonal methods of communication and regulation such as found in schools, military
units, corporations, cities, etc. Included are standardized definitions
and rules of procedure, e.g., bylaws, to govern and coordinate members' activity. This form of communication has two noteworthy features
that are basic to objectivation.

First, objectivation involves *formalization* and *codification*. For example,
to maintain control within large impersonal groups, new members must
be quickly and efficiently assimilated and their activity integrated with
that of others. This requires they be provided information concerning
what is expected and what is disallowed, about "what" and "how"
things are to be done, and perhaps an ideology or rationale about "why"
things are done as they are. For example, new prison inmates are some-

times provided with formal rule books, the military formulates a "code of conduct," while college sororities create "standards." Each of these formalized statements is an instance of socially created, externalized, and objectivated information concerning what is and is not defined as correct action, what people have decided everyone needs to know in order to get along when engaged in routine activity in that setting (Berger and Luckmann, 1967:42). It is on the basis of such shared knowledge, called *recipe knowledge*, that social order is possible. What is most important is that, in the first instance, this formalized knowledge consists of socially (humanly) created definitions, information, and expectations and their supporting rationales.

A second feature of objectivation is *reification*, or naming parts of social life. By naming we *reify*—divide social life into categories and give these categories the appearance of having a "life of their own," independent of their human creators and actors' experience. Reification involves "elevating" a symbol to the level of that for which it stands, to become the "thing" itself. As an example, consider how episodic violent activity by adolescent groups comes to be named "gang violence" and is then attributed to particular groups such as the "bloods." In many of the cases studied by Yablonsky, the kids involved in so-called "gang fights" had no conception of themselves as "gang members." Their involvement was merely a spontaneous and chance occurrence. Nonetheless, the naming, defining, and categorization of these events as "gang war" resulted from the press, public, police, social workers, and others *projecting group conceptions* onto them (Yablonsky, 1959:110). However, it is clear that once named subsequent violent activity may be enacted in the name of the gang or because of identification with the gang. When such reification occurs, the meaning derived from experiencing life as encounters with *things* is then transferred to *the name of the things*. As a result, names and things become indistinguishable insofar as people's reactions are concerned (Kaplan, 1964:61; Berger and Luckmann, 1967:89ff). Without people being consciously aware of it, names take on an existence of their own. Names and their taken for granted or assumed meanings are what people respond to.

Reification abounds. For example, on the basis of the meaning assigned to the socially constructed categories "rape," "mugging," "drug wars," etc., people take precautions against being victimized. In many cases these symbols are cues to a defensive reaction such that the "fear of crime" is perceived to be a problem equal to victimization itself (Gordon and Heath, 1981:229). This has led to the creation of the category "the-not-yet-victimized," referring to the anticipatory nature of people's concern (Moore and Trojanowicz, 1988:1). Symbols, words, and images elicit a similar response to that invoked by the subjective experience.

Becoming sexually aroused by looking at pictures, reading "dirty" stories, watching soft or hard core pornographic films, or becoming apprehensive and fearful due to statistical reports of increasing crime (all of which are symbolic representations) illustrate how meaning is invoked. However, this is not an automatic response of a passive actor to stimuli. Rather, words and symbols serve as cues for human actors to create meanings in their mind. It is the meanings that we actively construct from the words and symbols that are the grounds for our subsequent actions.

Names may appear to take on meaning and importance independent of their objective referent in other contexts as well. For example, an Arizona man was asked to surrender his personalized license plates after having had them for four years. The plates read "JAZZ ME" and had been reported to authorities as "offensive to good taste or decency" as a result of the sexual connotation of the term (personal communication). The man taught music at the University of Arizona and was director of the school's jazz program. In such instances, those offended are responding to symbolic representations of things (i.e., words) on the basis of a publicly shared meaning. These words seem to have taken on *suprahuman* properties and their meaning or the knowledge they represent is regarded by participants as independent of their creators. The sense that this knowledge is objective is promoted, too, by the process of internalization. Let us turn to it.

Internalization

Internalization refers to the process whereby seemingly objective knowledge—recipe knowledge—is acquired by people, resulting in the fusing of self and others. This occurs when people commence playing roles in family, school, church, and the workplace and are introduced to the "commonly accepted and established ways of doing things" (Scott, 1972:18), i.e., the formal and informal institutions of society (Henry, 1981). This knowledge tends to be presented to people as a set of nonnegotiable formal rules and expectations. For example, employers do not usually discuss the propriety of workplace rules with employees or debate with them about the circumstances under which some exception to the rule will be tolerated. Such rules as "no smoking on the job," "wash your hands before returning to work," or "don't exceed the allotted break time," tend to be uttered in absolute terms often backed up by written rule books or laid out in a contract of employment that is binding on employees. They are perceived as the only way of doing things and challenges such as "Who says so?" are met with the response "That's the rule, take it or leave it!"

Such seemingly absolute, universal, and nonnegotiable recipe knowledge promotes the idea that there exists some objective foundation for these rules and expectations. So, while parents, teachers, bosses, and police officers announce and enforce rules, they are not necessarily seen as their creators. Losing the distinction between "the rule" and "the rule enforcer" tends to encourage a belief in the objective reality of the rules and the system that they sustain.

Paradoxically, after being involved in an organization for a time, this formal knowledge is itself recognized to be merely a fabrication, something used for public not private consumption. The *real* knowledge is the experiential "tricks of the trade," the "informal institutions." The following experience of a restaurant worker is illustrative.

> This was Lauren's first job waiting tables . . . 'I just thought the bad tips were because of my service. After I'd been here about three months I felt comfortable enough to complain about tips. Then someone started telling me about stereotypes'. Now Lauren works the system of stereotypes to increase both her tips and, with them, the feeling of having done a good job. She looks at customers' physical experiences and particularly at their dress in order to classify them. She feels that if someone is dressed well and presents themselves accordingly, then they will have too much pride not to tip: 'I also look at how receptive they are, their smile, their body language. Eye contact is important too. Usually that helps your tip a lot . . . It shows that you're paying attention'. (Miller, 1990:41–42)

Such informal, experiential knowledge is viewed by the workers as real in the sense that it is more meaningful and a more accurate description of what the work is about. Thus, by contrasting this knowledge with the obviously fabricated formal knowledge the appearance of a real reality of work is sustained.

Much the same sense of objectivity of recipe knowledge is generated when, as a result of their imposing rules and meanings on others, rule enforcers reinforce their own acceptance of this objectivated recipe knowledge. This is particularly so when, in the face of a challenge to a rule, a justification is called for. Thus, when "Eat your vegetables!" is met with resistance, one possible response (justification) is "They are good for you." As a result of seemingly endless repetitions (i.e., externalizations), parents (like the first umpire) come to regard "the goodness of vegetables" and the related rule as objective knowledge. They then regard themselves as impartial reporters of fact—of "things as they are." Both the rule giver/enforcer and the receiver internalize this objectivated material and the meanings become shared or common. As this occurs, actors become "fused" and at least a minimal degree of social integration or "order" is established.[3]

The integration or order created in this way goes well beyond the level of interpersonal relations in dyads or small groups. On a far grander scale, we create very abstract sets of meanings and ideas intended to unify all institutional activity into one coherent whole. These meanings or integrative ideas are referred to as the *symbolic universe*, and consist of socially constructed beliefs that provide the appearance of transcendent orderliness to our world. All things come to have a place in "the scheme of things" and a place is provided for everything. We create meanings about how an abstraction called "family" harmonizes with an equally abstract entity called "the economy," how "government," "religion," "economy," and "education" complement one another, and, ultimately, how all are unified into "one nation under God." Birth, our own as well as that of our ancestors and descendants, death, and all in between, is incorporated into one meaningful, ongoing scheme, and is assigned a place in the cosmos. We create intellectual mechanisms for interpreting history and assign these mechanisms absolute power, as when they appear as *Geist* or *Espiritu* (Weigert, 1981:152). These integrative ideas and mechanisms, constructed by people, externalized, objectified, and internalized, appear in everyday life as ideologies, mythologies, cosmologies, theologies, and similar constructions (Berger and Luckmann, 1967:92ff) to which their creators have become subordinate. In sum, just as people in small groups become "fused" as a result of acquiring shared understandings, so does an entire society experience some sense of unity by means of abstract symbolism.

To summarize briefly, we have examined the processes of externalization, objectivation, and internalization, processes by which people (1) transmit subjectively created meanings and understandings to others, (2) formalize and reify such knowledge, and (3) internalize their own objectivated knowledge. As a consequence, what was initially a human creation appears to be suprahuman, and society and self are linked (Berger and Luckmann, 1967:89).

MULTIPLE REALITIES AND PROBLEMATIC MEANINGS

We have indicated that on the level of everyday life there is no single social reality, only a variety of such meanings and understandings. Let us explore this general issue of multiple realities (Schutz, 1945) and their problematic meanings.

Everyday life in our heterogeneous postmodern society reveals that, no matter how much lip service is paid to "public morality," and no matter how much legitimacy may be claimed for a specific version of social reality, people's morality, rules, understandings, and meanings are conditional and highly variable. For most children any sense of certainty and universality of truth is short-lived, surviving only until they move beyond home (if it has survived that long) and into the morally heterogeneous neighborhood, street and school, subcultures and other progressively larger, more complex social situations. In each of these settings children are introduced to a variety of different and often contradictory social realities and subuniverses of meaning reflecting the diverse biographies of people differing in race, ethnicity, age, gender, sexual orientation, religion, social class, and occupation. If they have been taught tolerance at home, they soon learn it is an abstraction, often more spoken about than practiced. If they had been weaned on the ideas of human equality, and liberty and justice for all, they soon recognize that, apparently, some are more equal than others and some less entitled to justice. Taught to respect the nation's leaders, they find a number of them accused of high crimes and misdemeanors. In these numerous ways, people are exposed to a series of contradictory and highly variable understandings, to events and conditions reflecting markedly different meanings, many of which challenge the notion of a single, absolute or dominant morality. The result is that people often are left confused, not knowing who or what is true or who to believe.

People's sense of stability and moral unity also founders on the "rocks" of contextually based meanings. For example, in societies having a puritan heritage that to some extent still associates naked bodies with prurient sexuality, people often internalize a general condemnation of public nudity. But what if the public nudity is that of a model in a drawing, painting, or art anatomy class? Does the same general negative association of public nudity and sexuality apply in that specific situation? What of the display of "skin" in advertisements for automobiles, alcoholic beverages, clothing, scents, recreation, and any number of other items? For many people, given the situation or context in which the display of the naked or near naked body occurs, the general condemnation (i.e., the prurient meaning) of public nudity is withheld. Clearly, moral meanings are situationally based.

Another illustration of situational variation in moral meaning is found in the case of the "symptoms" associated with various psychiatric conditions. Depending on the context in which they occur and the social position of the person exhibiting them, these symptoms may or may not be defined as evidence of mental illness (Scheff, 1966:34). Daydreaming or engaging in reverie, hallucinating, and talking to "spirits" are symptoms frequently associated with mental illness. However, when these behaviors are exhibited in a religious context a favorable definition is quite likely. Thus, in our society we have "holy persons" who have been elevated to high status on the basis of their professed ability to experience revelations, have visions, or otherwise "bridge the gap" between the material and the spirit world. Joseph Smith, founder of the Church of Jesus Christ of Latter Day Saints, and Mary Baker Eddy, founder of Christian Science, are cases in point (Brodie, 1945; Powell, 1940). Such variability is not unique to American society. For example, though physical disability is a sign of moral pollution among India's Hindus, wealthy Hindus are often protected from such meanings by their high caste position. As a consequence of one's wealth, then, the moral meaning and social consequence of blindness and other disabilities can vary greatly (Mehta, 1982).

In short, people discover that absolute moral meanings are abstractions and are of little use in helping us understand how people behave and respond in specific situations. More relevant is the idea that the meanings we construct are problematic or indefinite. This is a consequence of the "script writing" and script replay that we earlier suggested all people engage in. Because those "scripts" are "written" under highly variable conditions and rewritten in different conditions the certainty (moral and otherwise) many people pursue seems always to elude them.

To summarize briefly, the absence of moral certainty precludes the idea that socially constructed reality is all of a kind. Social reality is multiple rather than singular, and the several realities both coalesce and contradict one another. *Consistent* moral definitions may be said to exist only in the abstract. As applied to concrete events, these definitions are highly variable and fluctuate from one setting or context to another even though they may be treated as though they are the same. It is out of the conflict between these different social realities and the variable moral meanings that deviance emerges. Indeed, deviance (connoting the construction of moral meaning) is part of social reality. Let us conclude with a consideration of deviance as social reality.

DEVIANCE AS SOCIAL REALITY

Based on the principles we have discussed, deviance may be defined as a concept that refers to the socially constructed negative moral meanings that are situationally generated to describe behavior and personal attributes perceived as different and disturbing to certain audiences. The unifying factor among all behaviors and attributes named and categorized as deviant is that they are perceived to be at variance with some group's definition of what is preferable or morally acceptable.

But what is meant by the term "moral meanings"? When subjected to analytical scrutiny, the term "moral" may appear terribly abstract and unrelated to our daily affairs. Yet people do have a sense of things as being moral, preferable, respectable, virtuous, and right. People best understand the everyday meaning of these terms by their opposite, with which they are linked (Douglas, 1970:3–4). We can best know our sense of morality (what is right) by pointing out what we regard as wrong. For example, some people believe abortion is wrong because they believe it is right that the life process not be interfered with and that pregnancies be allowed to come to full term. Others believe abortion is right because they believe it is wrong that women should have to forfeit control over their own bodies. Many believe stealing is wrong because they are committed to the idea that people have a right to possess and own property privately. Left-handedness is wrong only in relation to right-handedness. Creating deviance, then, is linked to people's sense of what is nondeviant, to creating normality (Durkheim, 1895). Goodness is relative to evil, morality relative to immorality, and, as polar opposites, these categories are inextricably linked in pairs. *To create one is to automatically create its opposite; we can know the one only in relation to the other.*

Moral meanings are also recognizable by the fact that their violation may result in the violator being defined as socially unacceptable and subjected to a public transformation of their moral identity whereupon they may be seen "as a special kind of person, one who cannot be trusted to live by the rules agreed upon by the group . . . [and] is regarded as an outsider" (Becker, 1973:1). At least in the abstract, then, the category "rule breaker" is designed to include persons held to be qualitatively different from others. Later we will talk at length of this difference.

That rule breakers are regarded as both different and special is seen in the way people construct and assign stereotypical character traits to different types of deviant actors. Adulterers are perceived to be insecure, lonely, self-interested, passionate, and irresponsible. Homosexuals are perceived to be effeminate, lacking self-control, secretive, sensual, and sensitive (Simmons, 1969:29). Though not always so explicit, each category of deviant has an associated set of negatively valued character traits. The construction of these labels and character traits, and the consequent classification of behavior and people, is not simply a consequence of the rule breaker's condition or behavior (alleged or otherwise). Labels also reflect the audience's moral sense and are an integral part of their social reality.

How, then, shall we define deviance and deviant when viewed from the social constructionist perspective? Basically, *deviance* refers to the behaviors and attributes that people define as problematic. The basis of such definitions rests on the definer's interests, which are felt to be jeopardized or threatened in some way by these acts or conditions. As we shall see in Chapter 4, when such concerns are linked with power and given legitimacy, the label of deviance may be assigned. *Deviant*, on the other hand, is the category used to describe persons or groups seen as violators of moral rules or other standards. The term also reflects the discreditable character usually attributed to such persons and their having been discredited. In turn, on the basis of their being discredited, such people tend to be assigned to a lower moral and social status.

Such definitions are deceptively simple. An understanding and appreciation of the dynamics of the *phenomenon of deviance* and of deviance making (i.e., how these definitions or meanings are created) call for the examination of a complex social process. That will be our concern in the chapters to follow.

SUMMARY

The present chapter has focused on a theoretical foundation for the study of deviance as a social process and the assumptions that will guide our investigation. In contrast with other models, the one used here is intended to help people understand the process by which they introduce order into their world. This process is called the social construction of reality. By this means people create, reify, and assign meanings and then apprehend their creations as if they were objectively real. Included within this socially constructed reality are the moral meanings that underlie deviance. Deviance, then, is an ongoing outcome of the complex process through which people seek to create a sense of social order; most especially it emerges from their rule-making and rule-enforcing activities.

In contrast with other models, the one used here does not seek information about supposedly inherent meanings of an alleged objective or real world. Indeed, our approach questions whether such a world exists. And, even if one does exist, it is of no consequence since people respond to the humanly created meanings rather than to the things those meanings are supposed to represent. As noted earlier, our goal is to understand the origin of these meanings and how people deal with them.

Accordingly, we will examine deviance as an interactional process by investigating how rule breakers and others shape the direction and outcome of the social reality they create. Who defines behavior as deviant? How do they do this? How do individuals labeled deviant respond to that definition? And with what consequences? These and other questions, considered in the following chapters, make it clear that deviance is a process and that understanding it calls for more than an examination of deviant actors. With these considerations in mind, let us begin to examine the deviance process in detail.

NOTES

1. Deviance is not restricted to things judged to be negative. It may also include things given a positive meaning: gifted children, extraordinary talent as in athletics, acting, etc.

2. It calls for a method rooted in participant observation that is sufficiently involving to gain access to the participants' meaning structures and sufficiently objective to allow the researcher to analyze the meaning produced (Douglas, 1972). Techniques such as covert role taking, triangulation, and a dramaturgical approach to interviews might be employed. For additional methodological direction, see Schwartz and Jacobs (1979) and Berg (1989).

3. In noting that persons internalize these meanings and rules, that understandings become shared, and that one's self and others thereby become "fused," we do not mean to imply that people are being "programmed" or otherwise rendered incapable of resisting, of exercising independent judgment, making decisions, choices, etc. and acting upon them. We are saying only that people "inherit" meanings and understandings; they are equally capable of changing them, challenging them, and acting in ways contrary to them. Likewise, as we will see in Chapter 8, the realities people construct may also be reconstructed and deconstructed. Thus, internalization does not reduce people to the level of automatons (see Piven, 1981:496).

CHAPTER

2

Counting Deviants

INTRODUCTION

In Chapter 1 we commented on people's interest in gaining knowledge of the real world and argued that such knowledge was not objective but socially constructed. One very important way the world is constructed and given the appearance of being "real" is through the faith people invest in numbers and in the implicit claim of numbers to present objective truth. Counting deviance confers a sense of concrete reality on what might otherwise be disparate instances of diverse behavior.

Various government and private agencies, as well as independent researchers, count instances of behavior, classify them into event categories, organize these into information packages, and disseminate them to other agencies and the mass media. From here they are filtered to the general public as news stories. Accompanying agency, expert, and journalistic commentary frames issues of rule breaking and norm violation to cue a vivid sense of meaning for the media consumer. "Violent crime increases 5%, FBI reports" screams the front page headline (*Ann Arbor News*, 1992b), underpinning earlier individual case reports with a sense of the reality of crime waves and crime trends. Very often such packaged statistical information impacts on people's awareness and understanding of a supposedly "real world" and influences their judgments and behavior. An underlying assumption is that numbers symbolize "facts"—the stuff of objective reality—and that they constitute a measure of "truth" and rational knowledge. People feel that even though "liars use numbers," the "numbers don't lie." Like the first umpire, numbers "tell it like it is."

The view of numbers as an objective indicator of reality is a traditional feature of western culture that reflects the trust and faith people have in using the methods of the physical sciences to investigate social life and formulate social policy. History is replete with examples. Thus, the accu-

mulation of data by nineteenth-century *moral statisticians* such as Henry
Mayhew and Charles Booth was used to "prove" the existence of the
dangerous classes and to provide evidence of their inherent immorality.
Regarded as "rational knowledge," these data and analyses became the
basis for establishing and administering social policies designed to curb
immoral behavior (Douglas, 1971b:52). After all, "what could be more
certain than ideas and findings based on the ultimate criteria of scientific
methods and knowledge" (Douglas, 1971b:53)? To be sure, in the present century people have developed a more cynical attitude toward statistics. Nonetheless, they are still awed by numbers, regard them as a way
of providing rational, objective knowledge, and believe they have near
unquestionable validity and utility.

Believing that knowledge is advanced by numbers, statistical data can
have a profound effect on people's view of crime and deviance, their
cause and their control. First, when they are viewed as symbols of objective reality, statistics on crime and deviance may have a marked impact
on people's sense of the moral character of society. If the statistical rates
of crime, drug addiction or suicide increase or decrease people regard
such fluctuation as a sign of "real" changes in the occurrence of these
behaviors. Depending on how the changes are interpreted, they may
help promote a sense of security and well-being or may increase our
apprehension, fear, and defensiveness. A major issue, then, is whether
such feelings and reactions are justified on the basis of the sense people
make of numbers. Do numbers represent objective moral conditions?
Are people victims of a "tyranny of numbers" rather than the objective
reality of deviance or crime?

Second, official statistics are typically used to support explanations of
deviant conduct. Following Guerry's essay on French "moral statistics"
in 1833, and Emile Durkheim's classical nineteenth-century study of
suicide, several generations of positivist sociologists and criminologists
have used statistics to establish and test theories of deviance and crime
(Douglas, 1971a:67–68). This effort rests on the premise that deviance is
a "real" phenomenon. This effort parallels the use of standardized (uniform) offense categories created by the FBI to report national crime data
and create crime rates to be compared between cities and states at various points in time, as well as to discern "trends in crime."

Third, the major producers and controllers of crime statistics are representatives of official state social control agencies. As Douglas notes,

> *most forms of deviance today cannot be said to exist until they are legally (officially)*
> *defined in concrete cases*. That is, crime, suicide, and so on, exist only when
> . . . legal procedures have "certified" them. . . . Basically, then, most

forms of deviance . . . are constructed by official action and by law. (Douglas, 1971a:68)

It is necessary to examine how this process of classifying instances of behavior to stand for actual cases is carried out, how it is influenced by agency interests, and, in turn, how these matters impact on the ways officials name and record information.

Finally, these data often are used as the basis for formulating and legitimating public policies, legislation, and/or the allocation of resources to "fight crime" or combat other "social ills." Logically, one might argue that the promise of these "remedies" hinges on the validity of the assumptions made about the world that statistics describe, and the ways they are used to construct particular views of social problems. With these considerations in mind, let us examine the social construction of official statistics on crime and deviance.

THE SOCIAL CONSTRUCTION OF OFFICIAL STATISTICS

Viewed from the social constructionist perspective, official statistics—especially those dealing with deviance—are part of *culture work*. Culture work is institutional activity leading to the creation and maintenance of particular conceptions of deviance (Michalowski, 1985:261). Statistics are the result of creating categories and assigning instances of behavior to the categories, which are then compared. As such, statistics represent the objectivation of meanings. The categories are rarely naturally occurring, or even based on anthropological ethnography. Rather, they are typically the product of government agency convenience. Accordingly, these official categories of data—"crimes known to the police," arrest rates, victim surveys, suicide rates, rates of child abuse, rates of mental illness, etc.—are records of the way state officials categorize information and more accurately reflect agency practices than actors' realities. On the basis of their "agreement" packages of data emerge out of the interaction of a variety of actors—victims, witnesses, police, prosecutors, coroners, social workers, mental health specialists. etc.—operating in widely differing contexts, and representing equally varied values, motives, interests, and goals. Thus, the resulting statistical data are perhaps best seen as an abstract, highly selective record of the activities of these many actors rather than a simple tally of objective events or conditions. To appreciate this, however, it is necessary to examine the "number creating process."

Producing Numbers

The process of generating statistical data, far from being objective, involves a variety of subjective interpretations and selective decision making that is influenced by structural and personal conditions. These conditions influence (1) whether people perceive situations or events as significant enough to be reported, (2) their willingness to report, (3) their knowledge of how to report, (4) whether officials record or respond to what is reported, and (5) the way officials record and process reported information. Let us examine the influence of these factors on the production of official statistics.

The Problem of Defining, Classifying, and Reporting. The official statistical records of all categories of deviance are influenced by people's personal definitions of their situation. Of critical importance in shaping the ultimate rate of any deviant activity are the definitions of those who regard themselves as having been victimized and who are able to make their experience public. However, with regard to criminal victimization, at least, it seems that only a minority of actual victims make such reports. For example, a 1990 nationwide survey reports that only 38% of *all* victimizations were reported to authorities. Of cases classified as violent victimizations 48% were reported, 29% of those defined as personal thefts were reported, and 41% of the household crimes were reported to the police. In instances of "household" and "personal theft" victimization, people are more likely *not* to report their experience (U.S. Dept. of Justice, 1992:100). A major problem also underlies victimization data itself. People who are asked if they are a victim of personal or household crimes are, by definition, not asked if they are a victim of consumer fraud, corporate price fixing, or are subject to workplace hazards stemming from criminally negligent employer practices. The biannual Department of Justice survey of crime victims does not include such questions. As a result, the very instrument used to gather victimization data excludes what would be considerable victimization and ideologically serves to further sensitize people to existing conceptions of criminal deviance (street crimes) while denying the validity of any new alternative constructions of crime (suite crimes). The result is a partial picture or people's victimization experience.

Moreover, nonreporting of officially designated crimes reflects the way people define their victimization experience. Many do not regard their experience as important enough to warrant reporting; others define it as a personal and private matter; some think the police would see the offense as trivial or that they would not deal with it in an efficient or effective way; some believe that reporting would lead to reprisals, and/or that reporting would be too inconvenient or time consuming. Together, these understandings accounted for approximately 25% of the reasons why both "personal crimes" and "household crimes" went unreported (U. S. Dept. of Justice, 1992:110–111).

The influence of victim perceptions and understandings on reporting and, ultimately, on the statistical record, is particularly apparent in the case of rape, alleged to be one of the least reported violent crimes in the United States and Canada (Williams, 1984). According to a 1992 nationwide telephone survey of 4008 women and a mail survey of 370 rape crisis centers conducted by the National Victim Center, five of six rapes are never reported to police (*Ann Arbor News*, 1992a). Sixty-one percent of victims said that they had been raped before their eighteenth birthday and most of the rapists were either spouses, ex-spouses, fathers, relatives, or family acquaintances, with only 22% being strangers. Many of the reasons women give for not reporting their assault reflect the "rape-supportive" meanings that have long existed in our society (Burt, 1980; Russell, 1982:7–9). Thus, many women avoid reporting because they fear not being believed, offender retaliation, being blamed, and being stigmatized by going public. Others do not report rape because they feel shame and want to avoid the anticipated rejection of friends, spouses, and/or other family members, and/or because they want to spare their family any embarrassment. Some women avoid reporting their rape experience because they do not define themselves as rape victims even though they may have been subjected to "strenuous encouragement." If rape involves low levels of physical force and does not result in injury, then women are less likely to view themselves as victims and less likely to report the matter to the police (Williams, 1984:464). Finally, others may refrain from reporting as a result of being in an economically dependent power relationship, either as a daughter, wife, or employee (Box, 1983:122–127). Clearly, reporting is a socially constructed activity that can be experienced differently for different people, and what is officially counted as a crime is heavily influenced by the conceptions people have of what counts as being a victim.

Because reporting reflects people's cognition, shifts in their interests and concerns will result in fluctuations in legal definitions, reporting behavior, and therefore in what becomes official data. For example, the change in the official rate of child abuse in recent years has been associated with increased public alarm, investigative journalism, innovation in public policy, and the passage of new public laws. Prior to the 1960s, few instances of child abuse were reported or recorded, and seldom were reported cases defined as deviant (Pfohl, 1977:311). Moreover, no laws existed that made child abuse a crime until 1962 when, as a result of the work of pediatric radiologists who had X-rayed broken bones and other abnormalities, all 50 states began to pass laws criminalizing child abuse (Pfohl, 1977). Shortly thereafter the number of cases of child abuse reported and recorded began to rise (Fontana, 1973:27). However, there was no evidence of a qualitative change in adult–child relationships or any increase in the frequency of child abuse consistent with that upsurge in reporting. Rather, from a social constructionist perspective, this shift in reporting and recording stemmed from a change in people's consciousness and sensitivity as a result of the *child-abuse reporting movement* (which we will discuss later) that was accompanied by a barrage of horror stories in the mass media (Pfohl, 1977). In turn, this resulted in heightened public "awareness" and "sensitivity" to already existing phenomena and a change in the public definition of parent's rights to impose physical or corporal punishment on their children. In short, changes in the statistical record reflected a "reconstruction" (redefinition) of parent–child relationships rather than a change in the "real" world incidence of child abuse.

Another category of behaviors whose statistical record is substantially affected by people's definitions and perceptions is called *crimes without victims*. These are activities involving "willing exchanges of strongly desired (though legally proscribed) goods or services" (Schur, 1979:451). Included are homosexual relations between consenting adults, drug use or chemical dependency, sale of pornographic materials, prostitution, and other forms of illegal sexual behavior. Because these goods, services, and relationships are sought by people who, insofar as they derive some satisfaction from the experience, do not define themselves as victims, one would expect few complaints and, consequently, a statistical record reflecting those understandings. In recent years, however, participants' meanings have been overridden as a result of increased police undercover work and the use of sting operations. Because police undercover work is regarded as particularly effective in the area of "consensual crimes," we can expect an atypical increase in the statistical rate of these behaviors in jurisdictions using undercover methods. As one example, it is reported that

> Between 1960 and 1980, arrests for offenses where undercover tactics are often used rose from 5.8 to 10.8 percent of the total. There was a significant increase in arrests for narcotics, prostitution and commercial vice, fraud, and possessing and receiving stolen property; only gambling arrests declined. (Marx, 1988:14)

Another category of deviant behaviors that is seldom reported or represented in official data because of people's definitions, interests, and other personal matters, is the so-called *low visibility* sexual offenses: male prostitution, male rape, sexual fetishism, sadomasochism, pederasty, and incest. There are several reasons for this. First, these behaviors are typically closely guarded secrets among participants. Second, they often involve consensual relationships, reflecting strong affection between partners who wish to avoid disclosure. Third, as sometimes happens in cases of incest, youngsters are involved who are not free to report because they are under the power of adults. Last, reporting incest may be avoided to prevent the negative consequences of losing adult members of the family through arrest and imprisonment (Hughes, 1964:325–326). Because some of these "low visibility" offenses (e.g., sexual fetishism) have received so little official attention in the past, a relatively modest change in reporting behavior may result in a sizable statistical or proportional increase (Finkelhor, 1979; Gordon, 1986) and generate disproportional public concern.

Official rates of mental illness may also be considerably influenced by people's definitions. To some, "mental and personality disorders" exist in fact (like broken bones, infected kidneys, etc.); it is assumed that people either do or do not display the signs we have learned to define as symptomatic of these "diseases" (Taber et al., 1969:351; Movahedi, 1975:313). Others suggest that the assignment of diagnostic labels (e.g., in alleged instances of "neurosis") is quite "primitive" and uncertain (Lemkau and Crocetti, 1967:228). Among those who believe mental disorder is objective fact, this uncertainty is variously explained as due to a lack of contact between patient and physician prior to diagnosis, inadequate psychiatric sensitivity to "classificatory criteria," and/or a general disinterest among psychiatrists in classifying illness (Clausen, 1976:113). When viewed from a social constructionist perspective, however, it is necessary to investigate how the "diagnosis" or labeling of conditions as mental illness is influenced. At what point in time and by what indications do people define themselves as needing help with "emotional or mental problems"? When do people come to define other's behavior as mental illness? When are people officially classified as mentally ill? In each of these, under what circumstances or situational context are these designations made? Given the subjectivity of these matters, it seems unlikely that official rates of mental illness represent conditions in a "real" world.

That identifying (defining) instances of mental illness rests on subjective and situational elements is seen in Rosenhan's (1973) study of the experiences of hospitalized pseudopatients. Employing one psychology graduate student, a pediatrician, a housewife, a psychiatrist, a painter, and three psychologists to act as pseudopatients complaining of hearing voices (using words such as "empty," "hollow," and "thud"), these people were voluntarily admitted to 12 different mental hospitals. Beyond reporting these alleged symptoms, the pseudo-patients did not falsify medical information. Indeed, following admission, none of them complained of persistent "symptoms" and most told attending psychiatrists that they "felt fine." Nonetheless, 11 of the pseudopatients were diagnosed as schizophrenic and one as manic depressive. Instances of behavior, which in other contexts would be seen as normal, here were identified as indications of illness, such as "patient engages in writing behavior." Similarly, conventional past biographies "were unintentionally distorted by the staff to achieve consistency with a popular theory of the dynamics of schizophrenic reaction" (Rosenhan, 1973:253). Finally, each was discharged with a diagnosis of schizophrenia "in remission."

The question raised by this research is why the attending psychiatrists were unable to detect "sanity" among these pseudopatients on admission or during hospitalization? The answer, Rosenhan suggests, lies in the way physicians, including psychiatrists, *define* the patient population, i.e., physicians "are more inclined to call a healthy person sick . . . than a sick person healthy" (Rosenhan, 1973:252).

To determine if psychiatrists might also be inclined to label "sick" people healthy, Rosenhan conducted a second experiment in which psychiatrists were led to believe a portion of the patients to be received in a 3-month period would be pseudopatients; the staff was asked to rate these patients as to whether they were genuine or not. In fact, none of the patients admitted in the 3-month period were pseudopatients. Nonetheless, the rate of "diagnostic error" (i.e., the rate at which "genuine" patients were labeled sane by one or more staff members) was so high that Rosenhan concluded that "any diagnostic process that lends itself so readily to massive errors cannot be a very reliable one" (1973:252). Rosenhan's investigations suggest that rates of mental illness are unlikely to represent conditions in a "real" world.

In conclusion, it is questionable that statistical data on deviance represent "objective fact." In view of the problematics of reporting and defining, they are more accurately perceived as social constructions, an index of people's definitions, awareness, understanding, interests, and judgments. But there are other matters that also influence the construction of these records.

The Influence of Organizational Interests.   In addition to being shaped by the meanings of victims and witnesses, official statistics also are influenced by the interests of the agencies that compile them. We have already mentioned how certain official conceptions of what counts as crime perpetuate the omission from crime statistics of major categories of criminally harmful behavior, specifically those resulting from corporate and government offenses. However, statistics that *are* compiled may be "adjusted" (i.e., events defined or redefined and "categories" created) to present the most favorable image of the recording agency. There are expedient reasons for this. Agencies (psychiatric hospitals, public health facilities, coroner's offices, courts, drug and alcohol rehabilitation centers, police departments, prisons, etc.) are charged with "managing" socially disruptive behaviors. Accordingly, they have the authority to assign official meaning to the behaviors/conditions coming to their attention. These designations often are influenced by the perceptions agency representatives have of organizational needs or interests. For example, police use crime data for purposes of self-justification and organizational survival, and to improve community relations (Manning, 1971:175). One statistical category, the *clearance rate*, designed to show the ratio between crimes solved by arrest and those reported to the police, has been used by many police departments to promote a positive organizational image and is regarded by some departments as the most important *index of police performance* (Skolnick, 1966:167). This "indexing" reveals an awareness among officials of the virtue of "image management." Thus when actual crimes increase, officers use a variety of methods to inflate the number of arrests, such as writing two or three tickets per traffic stop for very minor offenses, counting as separate offenses several burglaries committed by a single offender on the same night, and arresting street fighters instead of the usual practice of releasing the person at the scene with an appearance ticket.

In addition, officials can also "adjust" the data by not recording all the information coming to their attention. For example, though a "common sense" case of rape may be reported, it may be labeled *unfounded*, a technical-legal term bearing on whether or not authorities define the reported case as prosecutable. Research by LeGrand (1973) indicates that, historically, reports of rape have often been "unfounded" on the basis of elements having no discernible relationship to whether a woman was the victim of sexual assault or rape. These elements include

1. victim intoxication,
2. a delay in reporting by the victim,
3. a lack of physical condition supporting the allegation,
4. [victim's] refusal to submit to a medical examination,
5. the nature of any prior relationship, especially sexual, between the victim and the offender, and
6. the use of a weapon without accompanying battery.

Because these elements (which only officials can certify) may reduce the likelihood of obtaining a conviction (and threaten a prosecutor's image of competence) or increase the time and resources needed to secure a conviction, agencies may withhold legal recognition of the reported assault. In official terms, it "never happened." Also, unfounding "adjusts" the ratio between cases "reported" and "cleared" and thereby helps police departments maintain a satisfactory image. Of course, unfounding is not restricted to rape.

Similar to unfounding is the practice of *defounding*, in which reported acts that could satisfy the legal criteria of felonies are recorded as misdemeanors (Lundman, 1980:65). For example, acts satisfying the legal definition of burglary (a felony) sometimes are redefined through plea bargaining. As a result, a *charge* of burglary, a felony, is "plead down" (i.e., redefined) to "breaking and entering" (a misdemeanor). By artificially raising or lowering (i.e., "adjusting") statistics by underreporting or compositing a number of offenses into a single category or by over arresting, police departments and other agencies validate their requests for additional personnel, budget allocations, and/or show how well the agency is operating (Seidman and Couzens, 1974; Sanders, 1977:83; Sutherland and Cressey, 1978:30). In these ways a facet of social reality has been created. However, its creation has no discernible relationship to "crime" and "justice" viewed as objective conditions. Instead, this reality (a set of definitions) is negotiated by public officials who are differently motivated. They may save the time and expense of conducting a trial, secure a conviction in spite of "weak" evidence, or bargain for the lowest possible punishment for one's client (Rosett and Cressey, 1976:85–97; Klein, 1984:77). However, the statistical record of convictions reveals nothing of the dynamics of this effort to "manage" the case load, but it is this very manipulation that creates the reality of the statistical data.

The influence of organizational interests on the official record of deviance is broader yet. It is an almost universal principle that bureaucracies function so as to maximize their rewards and minimize their strains or trouble (Chambliss, 1969:86; Chambliss and Seidman, 1971:100–101). This is because, irrespective of its "mission," the organization's agents view its perpetuation and well-being as an interest or goal in its own right. In terms of everyday operations, this means that people will be drawn into sting operations, investigated, arrested, tried, sentenced, hospitalized, declared mentally ill, have their deaths declared suicides, and so on, in inverse ratio to the trouble or strain (vs. the rewards) such actions are expected to bring to the agency.

Regarding some behaviors such as murder, it may appear that enough (at least abstract) moral consensus exists that their suppression would receive near universal social support and that organizational action would be spontaneous and unequivocal. However, even in cases of apparent "murder," rape, fraud, and other behaviors, there are times when officials withhold the seemingly appropriate meaning.[1] Further, though people give lip service to the general idea of "law and order," the practical meaning of the term varies over time and place and not all the values endorsed by law are backed with equal zeal. Likewise, as we have noted, "crimes without victims" are subject to very different meanings and serve as the basis for significant social conflict as revealed in the current controversy over abortion, decriminalization of possession of marijuana for medical and personal use, the definition of pornography, and some forms of sexual behavior, particularly prostitution and homosexuality. Such conflicts are rooted in a condition of value pluralism.

Pluralism influences law enforcement in that no matter how rule enforcers perform their assigned tasks, they will likely be damned by some and praised by others. This is because in a pluralistic society rule enforcers will almost certainly "violate" some powerful group's interest and arouse their opposition and antagonism. To maximize rewards and minimize strain, rule enforcers exercise discretion in performing their duties. In the case of police, laws are more likely to be enforced when doing so is felt to promote positive recognition or will not generate organizational problems. When enforcement is predicted to promote problems, *discretionary nonenforcement* is most likely to result.

But how do rule enforcers know whether enforcement or nonenforcement is the most judicious course in any given situation? Certainly, they do not know this in any definitive sense, but there are situational factors and "rules of thumb" that help them arrive at answers and make decisions. Included is the knowledge that power in our society is differentially distributed. Thus, public agencies sometimes are called on to deal with persons who have sufficient political influence to have penalties imposed on them or their agency if their interests are threatened. Included as "penalties" is the ability of powerful groups to generate media criticism and, perhaps, influence budget and resource allocation. Viewed as "strains," these penalties are critical because public agencies (e.g., law enforcement and social service departments) seldom produce their own resources (Chambliss and Seidman, 1971:266). They are dependent on others—legislative assemblies, county commissions, city councils, donors, etc.—for operating funds, personnel allocations, salary and benefit increases, among other things. Being aware of this, astute administrators ordinarily try to conduct agency business so as not to "bite the hand that feeds them." Likewise, individual police officers are least likely to process those who provide the most resistance and who threaten potential "trouble" (both "within the job" and "on the job") for their careers and their agency's operation (Chatterton, 1976:118). Typically "police officers know that the higher the social class of the complainant, the greater the likelihood that he will appeal over the officer's head (Bayley and Mendelsohn, 1969:102).

Organizational pressure to make "appropriate" discretionary decisions also comes from several other sources. First, given that resources are always limited and given the fact that deviance and law breaking are universal and pervasive, there are never enough police officers to arrest everyone and so full enforcement is a practical impossibility. Instead, the field must be limited by officers selecting "appropriate" offenses. Second, even if the police had unlimited resources, other criminal justice agencies, such as courts or the correctional system, could not cope with the massive increase in case load. They exert pressure to contain the input at the enforcement end by asking that only "serious cases" be prosecuted. Third, there are "protected areas." Some of these, such as the "institution of privacy," mean that those with control over large areas of private property have their law breaking more protected than those whose only arena is the public street. The crimes of still others are protected because they are helpful to the police as in the case of "grasses," "snitches," fences, and other police informers, whose unofficial "license" to operate allows police predictable control (Henry, 1977). Yet others are protected because "police are embedded in a network of relations with bureaucracies" out of which develop *reciprocal obligations* that, in part, have the effect of constraining the police from full enforcement" (Box, 1981:162). Thus, as part of their reciprocal relationships with police, corporations, schools and universities, labor unions, and professional organizations "are frequently allowed . . . to administer their own justice to members who have violated a state legal code" (Box, 1981:162). This means that some people's crimes are of a low visibility. For others the very privacy of the organization both facilitates and conceals deviant behavior. For example, between 1 and 2% of the physicians in the United States are addicted to chemical substances—alcohol, drugs, or both, a condition largely unknown to the general population. Official recognition of this level of addiction has been minimal due to physicians' ability to obtain drugs within the context of their normal medical routine and, thereby, conceal their drug dependency. Treatment, too, serves to obscure physicians' addiction in that errant doctors are assured complete anonymity during treatment and rehabilitation, and are afforded the support of their professional colleagues (*Arizona Republic*, 1982b, 1983a; Grosswirth, 1982).

Concerns over interests and strains and the existence of protected areas impact on official records by influencing organizational action and bringing about a substitution of informal for formal goals (Etzioni, 1964:10–11; Chambliss and Seidman, 1971:266). Because these actions are to some extent discretionary, and because discretion is not exercised randomly, the resulting record (statistical and otherwise) will display a systematic, discernible pattern, reflecting an "undercount" of some deviant acts and a relative excess of others.

Organizational sensitivity to "rewards and strains" is also apparent in the way some private agencies compile statistical data. This is revealed in the statistical records created by a private child service agency concerned with the prevention and treatment of child abuse. Once a month this agency created a statistical report providing its board members, private donors, and media personnel an "at-a-glance" summary of the agency's actions. Included in the report were three sets of numbers designed to highlight the "community's intense need" for the agency's services. These included (1) the number of cases turned away by the agency, (2) the number of repeat cases coming to the agency, and (3) the number of agency beds slept in each night by children. The following comments on the meaning and operation of this data-gathering process derive from an unpublished investigative report written by a student who was employed at the agency.

> The turnaway category is designed to keep track of the number of people who were determined to be in need of the agency's services, but were not served. Why are these people counted? This category happens to be a crucial one for exemplifying organizational interests, for while it establishes need, it provides for the perpetuation of the agency as well as paving the way for future expansion. The question remains as to whether this category is a true measure of the number of people in need of the agency's services.

> As is the case with underreporting, often in the course of performing other important tasks, intake workers . . . forget to record the number of children turned away. But more often the . . . turnaway tally reflects a . . . case of over counting. For example, families calling in for the agency's services several times a day may be counted each time they call. Hence, if a family with four children calls in three times in one day, the turnaway tally would read 12, even though only one family was actually in need of the center's services. Another example of over counting happens when the intake worker neglects to ask how many children are in the family when they are turned away over the phone, and then records a randomly selected number. Also included in the turnaway tally are those families turned away for other extraneous reasons, such as those whose children are too old to be admitted, people who are perceived to have other resources available, or families who decide in the course of the conversation with the intake worker not to place their children at the present time. Such over counting exists primarily because these intake workers, just as the persons in higher positions . . . , are investing in the perpetuation of the agency.

Another category . . . is termed "repeats," . . . children who have utilized the center's services at some other time in the past. This category is used primarily to point out the need for services other than shelter which are provided by this agency . . . and serves to rationalize the existence of . . . the "Prevention Program." The function of the Prevention Program is to provide services such as parent education, counseling, and support systems for those families who utilize the shelter over and over, with the alleged goal being to decrease the number of families "repeating." What is questionable is the . . . motives of the Prevention Program, for if the repeat category no longer existed, neither would the funds for the program. With this in mind, it becomes fairly easy to explain the biasing of these data.

Again we see the over counting in the following example: if a family with four children is accepted into this agency once, it counts as four admissions. If this family is accepted into the agency on three different occasions, it will count as 12 repeats and 12 admissions. Rather than one family in need of the Prevention Program's services, it appears as though *twelve* families are in need. Also counted as repeats are . . . families transferred to another part of the agency because they are in need of more time than the originally agreed upon 72 hours. The children are "released" by one part of the agency and "admitted" to another. This transfer exists on paper only—the children remain in the same place but the result is a double admission tally and a double repeat tally!

In addition to the self-serving categories of turnaways and repeats, a category deceptively slipped into conversations with the press and fund allocators is one termed "beds slept in." This is defined as the total number .of beds slept in by the children each night. No explanation exists for this category other than that it provides an attractively large number with which to influence the public. (Anonymous, 1986)

The Problems of Law Enforcement.   As we have already seen, the statistical image of the amount and distribution of rule breaking is influenced by discretionary and differential law enforcement practices that have no discernible relation to the legal criteria of crime (Manning, 1977:162ff). No where is this more apparent than at the various stages of the criminal justice process. The decision to arrest or not to arrest often is based on inferences officers make about suspects' character and that emerge out of the police–citizen encounter (Piliavin and Briar, 1964). The bases of these inferences are officers' *perceptions* of a suspect's age, group affiliation, race, dress and grooming, and general demeanor. Authorities use these and other factors to typify and categorize people; these typifications then influence reactions to suspects, victims, etc. (Harris, 1973; Van-Maanen, 1978). According to some observers, such categorization promotes intolerance on the part of police toward members of groups who are negatively stereotyped, while providing a kind of immunity for others (Cameron, 1964; Chambliss and Nagasawa, 1969). One of the best illustrations of this process is in the use by police of suspect profiles indicating likely offenders. These profiles are used in various contexts such as airports and when stopping motorists. The following composite description was derived from a field manual for the London Metropolitan Police (Powis, 1977) and actually puts in print the practices many officers use to spot "suspicious characters." Suspected offenders are

> young people generally, but especially if in cars (and even more so if in groups in cars);
> people in badly maintained cars;
> people of untidy, dirty appearance—especially with dirty shoes (even manual workers, if honest, he says, are clean and tidy);
> people who are unduly nervous, confident or servile in police presence (unless they are doctors who are naturally confident);
> people whose appearance is anomalous in some way, e.g., their clothes are not as smart as their car;
> people in unusual family circumstances;
> political radicals and intellectuals, especially if they "spout extremist babble." . . . These people are particularly likely to make unjust accusations against the police.
> Normal, unsuspicious people are those outside the above categories, especially if they are of smart conventional appearance (which commands natural authority and respect) and even more so if they smoke a pipe. (Roshier and Teff, 1980:89–90)

The outcome is differential law enforcement and biased data. In short, a person who does not conform to the profile or one who behaves "disrespectfully" or in a "threatening" manner toward a police officer is more likely to be arrested and formally processed than one who exhibits the symbols of "respect and deference." Authorities' definitions of these same factors may also serve to influence the number and variety of charges brought against a suspect. A similar pattern of differential law enforcement based on stereotypy has been observed in the way private store detectives identify and respond to shoplifters (Cameron, 1964). This stereotypy also sustains the assumption that theft losses from stores are primarily from external shoplifters rather than from internal employee theft, when the research shows the reverse to actually be the case (*Wall Street Journal*, 1987).

The statistical record of crime is also influenced by differential law enforcement practices. We saw earlier how organizational influences prevented police visibility from being 20/20 by creating numerous protected areas. The converse of this is that some areas are subject to special scrutiny. For example, as a condition of their life-style and material circumstance, the less affluent are subjected to more observation than others. As a result, the "rule breaking" of these people is more likely to be observed, reported, and officially recorded (Bensman and Lilienfeld, 1979:31). This is the case among persons receiving welfare and others who, as part of the price of obtaining public assistance, are subject to sometimes microscopic scrutiny. Their lives are an "open book." This greater level of visibility and reporting serves to increase the statistical relationship between poverty and rule breaking behavior, and helps perpetuate the myth of the "dangerous classes" (Pepinsky and Jesilow, 1984:35–46).

Suicide is another category of deviance in which official data are likely to be influenced by people's definitions. For example, given the relatively stronger condemnation of suicide among Roman Catholics and Mormons than other religions, one would expect a greater effort by members of these religions to resist having that label used to explain the death of a member. Accordingly, Douglas hypothesizes that "attempted concealment will vary directly with the degree of negative moral judgment associated with the act of suicide and with the degree of negative sanctions believed to be imposed for violations of moral judgments" (Douglas, 1967:208). Douglas also suggests that concealment likely varies in terms of the degree to which the suicide victim is involved in supportive social relations and according to the social status of the deceased (1967:209).

Suicide also indicates how the factor of *ambiguity* influences the way events are defined or categorized and official data are shaped. For example, suicide is defined as self-imposed extinction by methods the deceased knows will result in death. Accordingly, defining a suicide is always post hoc and logically rests on authorities' understanding of (1) knowledge possessed by the deceased, and (2) the role played by the deceased in their own death. The "after-the-fact" difficulty of certifying these two elements suggests that officials may sometimes be uncertain that the person did kill him or herself. How many deaths are labeled suicide without resolving this uncertainty? The importance of these two factors is also seen in the effort to decide whether or not to bring charges of homicide against Dr. Jack Kevorkian, an admitted advocate of euthanasia and creator of devices intended to assist terminally ill persons to commit suicide. What was the role of the deceased in these cases? Resolution of that question will surely influence the ultimate legal definition of the behavior of physicians who make these machines available to terminally ill patients who request them. Shall it be defined as homicide or as compassionate medical practice (*Time*, 1991c)? Further, what is the role of the taken-for-granted assumption implied by the definition of suicide that the "self-imposed extinction" has to be conducted in a very brief time period? A person would be equally guilty of homicide if they poisoned their spouse over a 3-year period as they would if they did it all in one meal. Why is that not also true for suicide? Is a person who decides to drive recklessly, knowing the outcome can be fatal, or one who smokes cigarettes or consumes excessive amounts of alcohol or other drugs knowing that the probability of eventual death is high, not also committing suicide? Such "slow suicide" is not included in the official category of suicide, even though the social meaning that brought about the death may be identical to that of short-term "normal suicide." Such concerns indicate that designations such as "suicide," "accidental death," and others are social constructions. How authorities arrive at these designations needs consideration when assessing the "validity" of official statistics (Douglas, 1967:185–190).

Finally, even in the case of law enforcement there is the inevitable ambiguity of the law that makes the officer's actual interpretation of events difficult. As Steven Box (1981:162) so aptly says, this can privilege some suspects over others:

> In the social construction of reality the suspect may sometimes be better able to manipulate the symbolic meaning of behavior and the situational context so as to persuade the police that nothing really wrong occurred, or, even if it did, that it was accidental and reflected little about his character.

Ambiguity may also influence the official record concerning homicide. For example, based on observation of police investigative methods, Terry and Luckenbill (1976) suggest that homicide detectives tend to divide cases into one of two classes: *walkthroughs*, those in which detectives experience little or no difficulty in agreeing on how to classify a case (i.e., accidental death, death from natural causes, suicide, homicide, etc.), and *whodunits*, cases in which detectives might reasonably define the event in a number of different ways. The ambiguity of the "whodunit" is the result of an inability to (1) establish the identity of the deceased, (2) establish the identity of the assailant (if, indeed, it is decided that there is sufficient evidence to justify referring to the deceased as a victim), (3) determine the events leading to the death, and (4) secure other possibly relevant information. In such instances the classification and response to the event are a matter of social construction. For example, in one case

> Detectives entered the scene of an apparent suicide. They found a "suicide note" written in the victim's own hand; her relatives and a close friend related that she had been very depressed the previous few weeks over her

family affairs; the room was locked from the inside; she was found slumped on her bed with a pump-action shotgun wedged between her legs. The victim was dead, the top of her head splattered against the ceiling.

Closer examination of the scene gave investigators cause to consider the possibility that there had been another person who either assisted in the suicide or killed the victim. Of primary importance in this regard was the observation that the breach of the pump-action shotgun was open and the shell casing in the wastebasket on the other side of the room.

By testing the victim's shotgun as the victim would have had to use it in order to have shot herself—that is, with the gun stock on the ground and light pressure applied to the slide—it was discovered that a shell would indeed eject from the chamber. That the casing landed in the wastebasket was held to be pure happenstance. Consequently, the case's designation changed from "possible suicide" to "suicide." (Terry and Luckenbill, 1976:85)

In this case the initial classification of "possible suicide" reflected an element of uncertainty that detectives resolved only after investigation and their evaluation (judgment) of the results. The essential point is that how cases are classified is far from certain. This is because our social world consists of ambiguous events—they have no inherent meaning. Thus, when detectives deal with events

they are active agents. Their activities determine whether a set of events will be placed within the criminal homicide column or seen as instances of suicide or natural death. . . . To assume, therefore, that statistical data accurately represent the universe of criminal homicides overlooks both the ambiguous and perplexed, albeit reasonable, nature of investigations and the probable inaccuracy in the reports of homicides. In the light of these difficulties, the thought must at least be entertained that official documents reflect only those homicides that are readily visible and capable of being investigated. Thus, murders committed by urban ghetto dwellers of the lower socioeconomic and racially disadvantaged classes are heavily overrepresented in the official statistics. (Terry and Luckenbill, 1976:92–93)

Earlier, when discussing organizational interests and the unequal distribution of power, we referred to *discretionary nonenforcement* of law. In practical terms this entails a relative overemphasis by police on the activities of lower social status groups in contrast to higher status groups. As we have shown, police agencies are not as concerned with patrolling the suites as they are with patrolling the streets (Pepinsky and Jesilow, 1984:81). This pattern of law enforcement, together with the generally positive moral stature stereotypically assigned to upper status groups, affords their offenses a low level of *social-psychological visibility*, i.e., authorities are less likely to perceive and officially define these behaviors as intentional violations. It is more likely that they will be defined as "exceptions" and dealt with as informally as possible (Westley, 1970:97–98).

This reduction in "social psychological visibility" is closely related to the traditional reliance of American police on citizen complaints to initiate the law enforcement process—the so-called *reactive* style of policing (Black, 1968; Reiss, 1971). As a result, the construction of official statistical records will in some measure reflect the variable social psychological visibility of offenses among complainants and witnesses. For example, the greater awareness people have of being victimized by burglary or auto theft (as contrasted with being victimized by means of consumer fraud) suggests they will be more prone to report "street" types of crime. Selective reporting will inflate the statistical record for one pattern of offense and deflate it for the other. However, even when offenses are reported, whether they are taken seriously by police will depend on the complainant's attitude, behavior, whether the complainant was civil or antagonistic, whether prosecution was preferred, and the police officer's assessment of the complainant's social status and moral worth (Black and Reiss, 1970).

Despite this feature of American law enforcement, many people ignore its consequences for the public "image of crime" and continue to believe that the "rich and poor are equal under the law" and do not recognize that "law enforcement involves an exercise of power over a citizenry." The exercise of that power will be oriented in favor of those segments of the population perceived to have the greatest amount of influence. "Our crime statistics reflect this political reality, and so produce evidence that criminals are poor" (Pepinsky and Jesilow, 1984:80–82). Moreover, this selectivity reflects a tacit rule in labeling people criminal or deviant: "the greater the social distance between the [labeler] and the person singled out for [labeling] the . . . more quickly . . . [a label] may be applied" (Rubington and Weinberg, 1973:8). As a fundamental characteristic of rule enforcing, including labeling, such selectivity has an ultimate effect on official statistics, rendering them unreliable as measures of the "real world" of crime and deviance.

SUMMARY

In this chapter attention has focused on the matter of counting deviants and related issues. The importance of this rests on the uses of official statistics for formulating public policy, for building and testing

theories of deviance, and the way enumeration contributes to the objectivation and reification of the phenomenon of deviance. Underlying
these uses and consequences of statistical data is the public's apparent
acceptance of the data's adequacy or validity, i.e., that they measure
what they claim to measure. The fundamental question, then, is whether these data are a faithful representation of a "real" world or whether
they are an elemental aspect of the social construction of reality. To
examine this question several elements were considered in terms of their
influence on the rate-producing process and the rates themselves: variability in reporting, the definitions of deviance among witnesses, victims, and officials, the differential "visibility" of some forms of rule
breaking and rule breakers, the role of organizational interests, and the
patterns of rule enforcement. On the basis of this examination we conclude that official records of deviance are not an adequate or faithful
representation of some supposedly objective world. Because they are
social constructions they reflect the values, interests, judgments, and
understandings of their creators. Their apparent meaning cannot be
taken for granted. Overall, these data are the output of a process by
which agencies (e.g., police, public welfare, mental health, etc.) systematically and selectively identify "incidents" of crime and deviance
and thereby create and/or perpetuate a perspective (a reality) concerning them.

In consequence, we have moved beyond such objectivist questions as
whether it is true or false that middle and upper income groups engage
in unlawful or deviant behavior, or whether whites and blacks engage in
objectively similar or different patterns of rule breaking, or whether
police and other agencies manipulate official data for organizational advantage. The more crucial question is whether the materials and analysis
presented here are sufficient to challenge the orthodox explanations of
crime and deviance and/or the social policies based on these data. For
example, what is the foundation of the deeply rooted belief that the bulk
of our delinquency, crime, and deviance occurs among the lower class
and minority groups and reflects their lack of ambition, avarice, and
dependency? On what basis do we continue to believe that the "real"
danger posed by criminals is so-called "street crime" and that it is
against such miscreants that the bulk of our social control efforts must be
directed?

Based on this analysis we conclude that juvenile court records, police
arrest statistics, records of correctional institutions, mental hospitals,
coroner's offices, and other agencies—public and private—are highly
suspect when used to explain allegedly objective differences in the distribution of deviance in society. However, these official data may be
adequate for research on the operation of agencies that compile them

since they are, in the first place, indices of agency operations. They are "an artifact of enforcement procedures and routines" (Stoddard, 1982:425). In that sense they may be used to study *official* delinquency, *official* crime, *official* deviance, but not to inform the creation and implementation of public policy. The critical issue, therefore, is that what is presented as crime and deviance is shaped by interpretive processes and is validated by faith in data gathering. What it represents, however, is a partial picture of rule breaking and only one dimension of its multiple reality.

NOTES

1.   An instance of this involved the intentional shooting of a member of one of Long Island, New York's wealthiest families by his wife. All newspaper coverage of the event was immediately suppressed and within hours of the death the physical evidence was removed never to be seen again. Witnesses to events associated with the death were never permitted to be heard in public. At an inquest held 5 days after the death it was officially established that the wife was awakened when she thought she heard burglars, went to investigate, and, because she was groggy with sleep, accidentally shot her husband. The death was officially declared an accident (Chambliss, 1975:259–261). It would appear the elements of murder are not always defined as murder.

For a case displaying remarkable similarity, involving the shooting death of New York socialite William Woodward, see: "The Shooting of the Century," *Life*, November 14, 1955, pp. 34–45. This article reveals the rather mysterious, but never fully explained deaths of several other socially prominent persons.

3

Breaking Rules

INTRODUCTION

Among criminologists and sociologists the most popular explanations for rule breaking behavior assume that deviance is the result of forces or conditions that compel people to behave in particular ways. These forces are seen as part of the real world and are said to be located either within the individual or in their environment. As we noted in Chapter 1, these explanations view people as "hockey pucks" propelled by forces (e.g., genetic predispositions, "things" or events) over which they have little or no control. In contrast, we embrace a social constructionist perspective that views rule-breaking merely as one type of *social* behavior, and assumes that *all* social behavior is a matter of volition, a consequence of people's choices, decisions, judgments, reasons, and motives. Moreover, these cognitive elements are created, maintained, and changed by people acting in the context of ongoing social relations. Because they create and act on socially constructed meanings, we regard people as self-ordaining. It is these ideas, reflecting a humanistic orientation, that we believe offer the most enlightened analysis of the rule-breaking process. However, before we examine the core concepts of the social constructionist approach, we would be remiss not to briefly consider the more traditional explanations for deviance. We begin, therefore, by illustrating how biological and psychological ideas can explain some deviance but also argue that they are inadequate to explain most of it.

CAUSAL EXPLANATIONS OF DEVIANCE: THE EXCEPTION NOT THE RULE

Traditionally, deviance is seen as a consequence of either individual (microlevel explanation) or societal (macrolevel explanation) defects, with organizations, families, and peer groups as intermediary influences (mesolevel explanation). Microlevel explanations are basically of two types. One sees the cause of rule-breaking "born" into certain individuals rendering them biologically different or "defective." As a result, they are unable to learn or to conform to the norms others follow. The second type of microexplanation sees deviance as learned through primary group socialization or role-modeling in a family environment whereby it becomes integral to an individual's personality and mental processes.

Macrolevel explanations, on the other hand, locate the cause of deviance in the external "environment." Thus, neighborhood subcultures, disorganization of an area's social institutions, undercurrents or conflicts within a society's culture, or organizational and structural arrangements are all held to create a variety of stresses and strains that pressure individuals to break rules.

Each of these explanations has its sociological and criminological advocates. Elaborated versions of them under such titles as "social learning," "differential association," "control theory," "strain theory," "conflict theory," and "critical theory," can be found in any introductory criminology text as well as in many deviancy texts. Each also has its popular counterpart. These range from the "born deviant" who has "lawlessness in the blood," through such succinct common sense wisdoms as "she's crazy," "he's from a bad home," "they'd had a lot a family trouble," "he hung out with a bad crowd," "peer pressure," "the devil makes work for idle hands," "birds of a feather flock together," "they don't care how they get to the top," and "life's a war and everyone's out for themselves." To illustrate how these cause-based theories explain deviant behavior as involuntary we shall consider two cases: (1) homosexual *orientation* and the issue of why some people are gay, and (2) *tiny doping*—the use of marijuana by children under the age of 8 years who have been socialized into its use by their parents (Adler and Adler, 1978).

Homosexual Orientation—A "Nature" Explanation

Students of human sexuality currently are assigning increased significance to biological factors as the basis for people's *primary sexual orientation*. That is, one's fundamental sexual attraction or the sexual partner preference people have in their sexual fantasies is regarded as something we are born with (Green, 1987:6–7). Increasingly, cross-cultural evidence suggests that primary sexual orientation may well originate prenatally, that it appears in early childhood, substantially predates people's knowledge about sex, and emerges in remarkably similar ways despite cultural differences. These data suggest that a homosexual orientation is not a consequence of disturbed parent–child relations, as psychoanalytic theory has maintained, is not determined by aspects of the social structure such as family configurations or social class, is ahistorical, and transcends culture. In short, homosexual orientation is perceived as an "emergent" rather than a learned condition (Whitam, 1975:5, 1977a, 1977b, 1983, 1984, 1991; Whitam and Mathy, 1986; Green, 1987:384–387; Bell et al., 1981:212). According to some studies the emergence of this orientation is linked to one's male and female hormone level, with homosexual men having significantly lower levels of male hormones than heterosexuals (Dorner, 1976; West, 1977; Margolese and Janigen, 1973), while lesbians are reported to have significantly higher levels of the male hormone testosterone than heterosexual women (Gartell, Loriaux and Chase, 1977).

On the basis of such evidence it is contended that a homosexual orientation must be kept distinct from the *homosexual role*, which is a cultural element based on recognition of homosexual orientation (Whitam, 1977a:2, 1977b). The point here, however, is that biology may explain sexual orientation in some people. However, this does not mean that all homosexual *acts* are biologically determined, nor that all who adopt the gay life-style do so as a result of a biological predisposition. *Primary sexual orientation or primary sexual identity is not to be equated with sex roles, sex norms, or sex-related behavior.* Rather, the latter may be personal or cultural choices. Moreover, just because an activity is defined as deviant does not mean that all instances of it can be explained by a single analytical framework. Missing from the biological account is the *process* of how biological differences are signified and translated into meaningful social interaction. We shall return to this approach to explaining deviance shortly.

Tiny Doping—A "Nurture" Explanation

Just as some deviance is biologically based, other rule-breaking is said to be the outcome of conventional learning. The tiny-doper is introduced to marihuana smoke and accompanying patterns of "smoking behavior" while still a diapered toddler, as a result of being taken by parents to gatherings where others smoke pot. This reflects neither biology nor self-reflective decision making since prior to 1½ years of age these children simply breathe the air in a marihuana smoke-filled room. The drug's effects calm the child. Between the ages of 1½ and 3 years, youngsters become more aware of their surroundings, are "free" to watch and imitate, and "play" with marihuana, "the baggie" and "the bong." However ineffective are their efforts at this stage to inhale the smoke, retain it, and experience the high, the breathing of marihuana smoke-filled air continues, sometimes augmented by a mom or dad exhaling a lungfull of pot smoke into the youngster's mouth.

By the age of 3 or 4 inhalation is often achieved, as is a more sophisticated appreciation of smoking paraphernalia. By the age of 4 or 5, tiny-dopers acquire a vague social sense regarding pot smoking. Children of 7 or 8 differentiate between users and nonusers, and who should and should not know about their pot smoking. In short, by the age of 7 these children have become socially sophisticated and know the rudiments of legal and public moral meanings applied to marihuana smoking, as well as the private meanings shared by their immediate family, and parents' friends. Moreover, from their parents the children learn to distinguish between situations when these different meanings are operative. Overall, however, from a state of total innocence to one of active and knowledgeable participation, the tiny-doper's involvement rests on intergenerational transmission in which the children are largely passive agents.

In short, because pot smoking is normative in their families, from their earliest years these children associate with meanings supportive of marihuana use. From parents playing the roles of instructor or "orientational other" (Kuhn, 1967:181) they learn the vocabulary, basic concepts, and categories, the social, legal, and moral meanings of pot smoking, and the general recipe knowledge appropriate to marihuana use. This process leads to the conclusion that tiny-doping rests on normal socialization; for these children the use of marihuana is normative. However, this analysis tells us little about deviance at a societal level. It tells us more about rule-following than rule-breaking, and informs us of the influence of socialization on meaning structures. The account would have varied little had we had been describing the making of a professional tennis champion or young computer whiz. To know about the *deviance* of tiny-dopers we would need to know why some of these children choose to "break the rules" by *not* smoking, why some *reject* their childhood socialization, and why a few even turn their parents in to law enforcement agents. It is these latter rule-breaking activities that students of deviance must explain. Thus while learning theory concentrating on the child's "family environment" might explain these children's deviance from society as marihuana smokers, it does not explain the deviant behavior of those tiny-dopers who break from their family's marihuana convention and go straight, which from the social constructionist perspective is the more interesting phenomenon. Nor does it explain the deviance of all those marihuana smokers who did not have such "privileged" socialization and who, instead, *choose* to participate in this behavior.

In both the biological account of homosexuality and the learning environment account of tiny-doping we see what at first sight appears to be an external forces explanation. However, in both these cases what we fail to see is the *process* whereby people who know they are breaking rules go ahead and choose these behaviors anyway. It is this aspect of deviance that has to be explained and to do so we first need to revise the passive account of "environment" presented so far.

BREAKING RULES: EFFECTIVE ENVIRONMENT, BIOGRAPHY, AND BEHAVIOR

Effective Environment

One of the most basic concepts in sociology is that of environment, variously defined as "external, physical, and sociocultural elements," one's "physical surroundings" or "milieu," consisting of "things" having a fixed character that influence people's behavior in more or less similar and determinate ways. To distinguish our perspective from that usage, and to be consistent with the ontological position of our third umpire, we will use the term *effective environment*, referring to the social and physical environment *as people define it* and in terms of which it is experienced (Meltzer, 1967:16–17). For example, though its physical properties remain unchanged, when viewed from the context of the hospital emergency room, doctors regard heroin as a life-threatening substance of abuse, the cause of considerable pain to addicts and their families. However, from the perspective of the cancer ward the same drug is seen as a therapeutic aid in the relief of pain suffered by the terminally ill. Similarly, as Jeffrey (1979) has shown, in hospital emergency rooms people with similarly urgent medical conditions are treated differently depending on whether the hospital staff judge them to be morally deserving and/or define them as "good patients"—those who allow the staff to practice their competency and specialty—or "rubbish patients," defined as those who break various unwritten rules surrounding what is seen as appropriate behavior for occupying the sick role. Patients in the latter category included drug overdoses, tramps, and drunks. Thus, depending on how they are defined, drugs and people can be "experienced" (i.e., defined and responded to) in very different ways depending on their environmental context and on how they appear in that context.

Further, environmental elements may be defined in very different ways by different people. Thus, the same drug that doctor's perceive as addictive and harmful may well be defined as a "Godsend" by the weary frontline marine. What is important is that the elements of environment have no inherent meaning. They have only the fluid, ever-changing meaning people create in particular social contexts.

Finally, one's effective environment includes the actor. Just as people reflect on, define, and respond to elements in the world perceived as external to self, so do they become the subject of their own thoughts. As we will see later, by means of introspection or self-examination people judge, evaluate, and act toward themselves. This capacity to engage in self-scrutiny is critical to a social constructionist explanation of behavior.

The individualized nature of effective environment does not, however, preclude shared meanings. As our earlier comments on externalization, objectivation, and internalization indicated, through communication people come to share interpretations, definitions, and understandings. As a result, the concept of effective environment does not preclude coordinated social action on the basis of those shared meanings. Indeed, the social construction of shared meaning is often mistaken for "forces" external to the individual rather than as meaning effectively constituted by the actions of purposive human agents.

Biography

A second concept central to our analysis of behavior is *biography*. Like effective environment, biography has both an objective and subjective dimension. It consists of the highly individualized and variable circumstances, events, and their changing meanings that constitute individual social and moral careers. These might include experiencing differences and similarities in gender, neighborhoods, minority or majority status, economic wealth, subculture, the meaning of being able-bodied or disabled, being defined by others as attractive or unattractive, and so on. Biography is no one of these, but is a compound of fragmented experiences and conditions woven together into a life. As they are constructed and confronted, defined and responded to by the actor, such individually unique and endlessly varied experiences are the social fabric of meaning in a complex social structure.

Additionally, no one's biography is ever fully or finally developed. It is constantly in the making, being added to, reaffirmed, and denied as actors define ongoing experiences. Over time biographies are frequently subject to redefinition as people "look back," evaluate, and redefine prior experiences in the light of current events. Thus many of the "painful" experiences of youth may be regarded with nostalgia during later periods of life, and many of the wild and gratifying experiences of youth are recalled in middle age with dismay. As people accumulate experiences, different meanings are constructed of past events. Because people are influenced by their selective memories and current interpretation of these events, and because presently constituted meanings are subject to change, their relationship to subsequent behavior remains indefinite.

In summary, people's biography is what they perceive it to be from their present standpoint; it is a series of events without essential or fixed meaning. Applying our earlier ontological concerns to biography, these life course events are nothing until we place them in the context of our present view of the past. As a result, and despite its relevance to understanding behavior, biography lacks a *determinative* influence; it does, however, have sensitizing influence.

BIOGRAPHY, AFFINITY, AND WILLINGNESS

Two concepts relating to the sensitizing effect of biography are *affinity* and *willingness*. Though biography does not determine behavior, people's experiences do leave them with a general affinity or aversion to engaging in specific behaviors. Those who have an affinity or favorable disposition are *willing* or "free" to experiment in the unconventional (Matza 1969:116). Willingness, then, is an evaluative meaning that a person constructs regarding whether behaviors that they classify as being of a certain type are potentially pleasing/satisfying or painful/unsatisfying.

Whether people act on those meanings rests on decisions they make in an immediate context or situation. Being open to a particular behavior does not itself mean people will do it. Even though they have the opportunity, people may resist participating because of the relative importance of competing options. For example, although many students are generally willing to use alcohol, most would likely refrain from using it just prior to taking a major exam, because either their own past experience, that of others, or fear of uncertainty has shown alcohol consumption to reduce performance. The meaning of the exam, together with their sense of "conventional student behavior," their personal goals and well-being are linked with the event and constitute the context in which the use of the drug is defined as inappropriate. Generally, people do not break rules at every opportunity despite their willingness to do so under some circumstances. To repeat, then, an affinity and a willingness to engage in certain behaviors are no more than a general disposition; they are not determinants of all future actions. They are, however, linked to a variety of biographical elements. Let us consider several of these.

Everyday Life

That people's everyday experience can promote a willingness to engage in behaviors others regard as deviant may be seen in the case of how striptease dancers become attracted to lesbian activity. According to one study, homosexual behavior in the stripping occupation is supported by (1) isolation from affective (emotionally significant) social relationships, (2) unsatisfactory relationships with males, and (3) an opportunity structure allowing a variety of sexual behavior (McCaghy and Skipper, 1969:266). Lack of affective ties may result from marital problems and/or the job-related difficulties strippers have establishing relationships of trust with others. Working at odd hours and moving from city to city leads to loneliness. Further, the men with whom strippers have the most frequent contact are those in their audience, unattached men that they define as "degenerate" because of their tendency to engage in exhibitionism and masturbation during performances. Added to this is the presence of lesbians among the strippers and the warm reception strippers are likely to receive from those who frequent gay bars where they sometimes go for relaxation. Taken together, this complex of elements serves to promote a negative definition of relationships with men and a positive definition of relationships with women, meanings that are consistent with these women's willingness to enter into a lesbian relationship.

Further, consider the elements leading some young men to choose pimping as a way of making a living. Research on the biographies of black pimps has found that the early experiences of many of these men encouraged them to define sex and hustling as a normal way of life, and to define formal education as largely unrewarding and irrelevant (Milner and Milner, 1973:124). Though not compelled into pimping, these and other experiences led the men to conclude that despite its hazards, pimping pays more than the "chump change" earned at jobs such as store clerk or working for Ford or GM. Some men became willing to pimp while in high school when, by chance, they encountered a girl willing to trick for them, or perhaps because a neighbor or relative was a pimp. "Others get turned out after they have been married and had children, been in the Service, and tried working to support their wives. They are disillusioned with what society offers them because . . . they have tried living "straight" as adults and found the experience not only wanting but emasculating" (Milner and Milner, 1973:127–128).

From these examples we see that people's involvement in rule-breaking behavior rests on the decisions they made in a social context. Neither example suggests that occupation, place of residence, or other aspects of environment exert a determinant force. Indeed, there are numerous cases of people in similar circumstances who do not opt for deviant life-styles. On the other hand, to reinforce our earlier remarks, these examples do indicate that people's effective environment includes conditions that shape the meaning that they construct of the situation, and demonstrates how willingness can be a prelude to deviant action. However, whether someone actually decides to try deviant action also depends on interaction with significant others.

The Role of Others

One's willingness to break rules often is promoted by the support and encouragement received from friends and other trusted persons. This occurs directly when one person actively seeks to raise another's level of willingness by asking them or even repeatedly pressuring them to take part. It occurs indirectly when actors attribute certain attitudes and expectations to trusted or esteemed others, and then use those assigned meanings to rationalize or justify their own rule-breaking. In both forms of support, the meaningfulness and social definition of an action is coconstructed as a viable reality. However, it is the actor who ultimately makes the decision "to do" or "not to do" the act.

Goode (1972:40) has identified three ways friends may influence another's willingness to engage in rule-breaking. First, because friends often serve as behavioral models, their involvement in rule breaking may increase another's willingness. Given the idea that "good people don't do 'bad' things," it is easy to conclude that if friends are doing it, it can't be so bad. Typically, many candidates for rule-breaking perceive rule breakers as "people like themselves," people who are not different in any appreciable way. This is critical since it is what distinguishes those who are tempted but decline, from those who are tempted but willing. Identifying with respected and trusted relatives and friends and obtaining their support allows a reconciliation of seemingly contradictory positions and thereby enhances willingness.

Further, friends engaged in questioned behavior may assist the novice to deal with objections based on stereotyped definitions of "people like that." Weinberg reports that prenudist attitudes consist of such stereotypes. For example, one respondent thought that nudism was "a cult—a nut-eating, berry-chewing bunch of vegetarians, doing calisthenics all day, a gymno-physical society . . . carrying health to an extreme, being egomaniacs about their body" (Weinberg, 1981:292). Such attitudes need to be dissipated or resolved in order that one be willing to engage in morally questionable behavior.

Second, friends often provide a rationale—a reason, a foundation—

and as we shall see later, excuses and justifications for the behavior. Third, with particular relevance to behaviors that depend on the use of "facilitating substances" (such as drug use), or skills, or special equipment, friends may make such supports available. In these ways, the contribution of friends is crucial and, in some cases, quite indispensable.

Supportive others may also assist the "willing but hesitant" to deal with indecision or ambivalence, to overcome negative definitions and attitudes, or to strengthen a mild affinity. For example, Weinberg (1981:292) notes how interpersonal relations helped potential nudists overcome their ambivalence regarding participation in nudist camp activities.

> [Whether or not I would go to a nudist camp would] depend on who asked me. If a friend, I probably would have gone . . . If an acquaintance, I wouldn't have been interested . . . If it was someone you like or had confidence in, you'd go along with it. If you didn't think they were morally upright you probably wouldn't have anything to do with it. (Weinberg, 1981:293)

Weinberg also notes that the majority of his female interviewees were introduced to nudism through their husbands, parents, or inlaws. Relatively few became interested through impersonal sources such as magazines or motion pictures (Weinberg, 1981:292).[1]

The way most people get introduced to the "nude beach scene" reveals a similar pattern. "Nude beach seductions" (i.e., ways hesitant or reluctant people are encouraged to take off their clothes in public) often involve subtle pressure put on girls ("nude beach virgins") by their boyfriends, as well as friendly persuasion by others (Douglas and Rasmussen, 1977:74). Such efforts frequently result in bringing the willing but hesitant novice to the point of experimentation.

Another study found that, initially, women typically perceived spouse swapping with revulsion. This reaction was followed by the husband's efforts to alter his wife's definition of "swapping" by means of a "convincing" or "coercing" process that brought the wife to the point of being willing to experiment (Varni, 1972:511–512).

In addition, others help potential deviants grapple with public definitions of their shameful behavior. For example, in examining middle class women's entry into prostitution, Douglas (1977) suggests that these women do not "fall" into whoredom. Rather, the entry process extends over a prolonged period:

> [Women] think about it and generally talk about it with similar friends—testing out the idea and its fateful shame implications. They are all intellectually convinced that sexual freedom and so on are good ideas, but their

bodies at this stage are still saying something different—almost a dread of being shamefully ostracized from society, that is, stigmatized. (Douglas, 1977:66)

Because these women discuss their concerns with "insiders" (e.g., women who support sexual freedom, or those who are already involved), they are being shown that shame is manageable:

This connection with the insider is often crucial. The person who is already inside has . . . overcome most of the fear of shame and may feel pride by now. They provide evidence that shame can be overcome or avoided, or . . . they act as if there is no such thing. . . ." (Douglas, 1977:66–67)

The role of others in the social construction of willingness also incorporates public discussion of topical issues, which are subsequently reconstructed at an interpersonal level. For example, with the emergence of public debate and fear about the spread of HIV among multiple partner heterosexuals, gays, and IV drug users, participation in previously acceptable sexual deviances now demands additional "safe" support to overcome reluctance. With these broader constructions of meaning prevailing, potential participants now need reassurance about limited physical risks, additional safe sex techniques, and personal biographical information before they are prepared to experiment. Indeed, such public debate has led to private reconstruction of the meaning and value of monogamous marriage and the importance of the family.

Commitment

Willingness is not simply a product of direct interaction between one's self and others. Often included is an actor's need to reconcile their involvement in proscribed behavior with what they perceive as contrary *commitments*, i.e., the "pledges" or bonds they may have with other persons (e.g., family) and/or their dedication to a specific course of action (Johnson, 1973:397; Becker, 1960). Willingness may be especially influenced by one's commitment to or stake in conformity (Toby, 1957) and is often balanced against the actor's anticipation of the possible consequences of public disclosure on one's ability to maintain valued statuses and relationships with others (Briar and Piliavin, 1965:39; Hirschi, 1969).

As an example of constraint generated by commitments, some sexually inactive coeds have indicated that their decision to remain inactive rests on their parents' expectation that they avoid such involvement.

These women's sense of commitment to their parents (i.e., a wish to avoid hurting them by violating their trust and to avoid the costs of damaging a valued relationship) is a major element in preventing their participation in deviance. In another case, a 16-year-old youth who has grown up in a neighborhood that is home for Newark's most notorious car thieves (many of whom are his friends) has resisted the allure of that activity. "I couldn't do it because it would break my mother's heart" (*New York Times*, 1992c) he states, and plans to study automotive design in college. Similarly, in studying homosexual pederasts (pedophiles), Rossman (1976:180) discovered several persons who refrained from actual sexual encounters because of (1) a concern for the feelings of and a desire not to hurt family and friends, and (2) a reluctance to do things that, if discovered, would destroy one's life, especially (but not only) in a professional sense.

More generally, commitment to conformity has been examined by Travis Hirschi as part of his bonding or control theory. This argues that for most people conformity to convention is established through (1) commitment, (2) attachment, (3) involvement, and (4) belief. People who do not develop these bonds to conventional others are more likely to be willing to experiment in rule-breaking activity since they have nothing to lose, no one that they care about to hurt, few involvements in conventional activity to be displaced, nor any strong belief in the value of refraining from violation (Hirschi, 1969). More concisely we might say that conformity is not particularly attractive if there is nothing in it for those in pursuit of pleasure, and nothing to lose for those in fear of pain.

Definition of Self

Among the complex of meanings that comprise willingness, none is more important than the actor's definition of self. Just as experience leaves us with definitions of things external to self, it also leaves us with a self-identity. In turn, our self-identity influences our willingness to engage in various behaviors. Would the person we see ourselves as being engage, even experiment, in the behavior in question? Does the prospect of participation leave us utterly disgusted, mildly intrigued, pleasurable excited, or strongly attracted? By defining prospective participation positively, the meanings we have of self in relation to the activity constitute a kind of *self ordination* in which we define ourselves "as the kind of person who *might possibly* do the thing" (Matza, 1969:112, emphasis added). Thus we become candidates for participation.

As part of the dynamics of effective environment and a constantly developing biography, people construct meanings leaving them more or less attracted to particular patterns of behavior. However, these meanings are not indelible since they may change or be reconstructed anew in the course of subsequent experiences. Accordingly, affinity is a general condition in which people regard rule-breaking as "possible, permissible, rationalizable and even valued within a particular context" (Pfohl, 1985:274). At any particular point in time to "do or not to do" is a contextually structured individual choice; it rests on decisions made in the situation and that may or may not be consistent with one's prior general affinity/aversion. As we will see, affinities are resistible and aversions may be overcome. In short, whether we break rules depends on the meanings we construct of the particular situation in which we find ourselves and our sense of self-identity based on our past biography.

The social constructionist perspective clearly assumes people have considerable authority over their actions. However, this does not exclude the social conditions that people daily confront. People's definitions of these conditions help inform their actions. *Both are involved and neither may be excluded from an explanatory effort.* For example, no adequate explanation of involvement in gang violence or drug trafficking can omit the lack of formal employment opportunities available to inner city youth, the high level of unemployment prevalent in some areas and among some populations, the poor quality and overcrowded housing for low income families, and the physical dangers of living on "crack street." Likewise, these conditions alone are inadequate explanations without a microscopic analysis of the process of how people come to define themselves as "members" or "dealers," and how they perceive society and their relationship to it. Rule-breaking behavior, then, while partly a matter of individual judgment and decision, is no less a matter of people adapting to the social constructions of others and of making sense of the social contexts of their daily existence (Conrad, 1975:19). Indeed, while often diverging from their fellow human beings, rule-breakers also substantially recreate the environment of which they are a part and that appears to confront them as an external force.

WILLINGNESS AND THE NEUTRALIZATION OF MORAL CONSTRAINTS

Quite commonly, people's willingness to experiment in rule-breaking is limited by their internalized moral and ethical beliefs. However, everyday experience and systematic research reveal the ease with which people violate the norms and values to which they are committed. Serving to resolve this apparent contradiction between what people say and what they do is a series of *neutralizing techniques* or devices, i.e., words and phrases people use to preserve a moral conception of self while simultaneously engaging in proscribed behavior.

Crucial to the process through which morally committed individuals are rendered free to engage in deviant behavior is the *timing* of neutralization. It has long been established that words and phrases can be used as part of "account giving" *after* an act has been committed. As "rationalizations" such accounts protect a person from recrimination and minimize the consequences of untoward behavior (Allport, 1938). Rationalizations serve to appease the audience through what Goffman (1971:139) calls "remedial work," the function of which "is to alter the meaning that otherwise might be given to an act, transforming what could be seen as offensive into what could be seen as acceptable." We shall discuss this remedial process in Chapter 7 when examining stigma management. Here, however, we are concerned with the way words and phrases occur *before* an act is committed and how their use can actually be motivating (Mills, 1940).

There are two points at which morally neutralizing words and phrases occurring prior to rule-breaking can motivate participation. The first was identified by Cressey (1953) in his study of embezzlers. Cressey found that people could contemplate their own participation in such activity and then consider the moral implications through a mental role-play of how others might respond, and what account they would give, should their contemplated behavior be called into question. If they were able to find acceptable words and phrases (which Cressey calls "verbalizations") that would be "honored" by others, they were then morally free to participate in the activity. However, if they could not find acceptable accounts they would refrain. Thus, words and phrases may serve either to facilitate or inhibit one's involvement in the activity. As Cressey (1970:111) says, "I am convinced that the words the potential embezzler uses in his conversation with himself are actually the most important elements in the process that gets him into trouble." This process was also observed in Henry's (1978a) study of those who trade in stolen goods. For those people, the embarrassment of selling stolen goods at extremely low prices was avoided or explained away by using words and phrases that exist as part of legitimate commerce. Thus, rather than acknowledge their goods were stolen, sellers described them as "poor quality," "seconds," "rejects," "fire damaged," "bankrupt stock," "poor design," "perishables," "damaged," "off cuts," or claimed they had acquired them as "legitimate perks" or through "bulk purchase" from a warehouse or discount store and so on. In this sense words and phrases serve the Machiavellian purpose of defining their behavior as morally acceptable.

A second use of the concept of "neutralization" reflects the *unwitting* motivational role of discourse. This occurs when morally neutralizing words and phrases occur, not simply before the act is committed, but *before it is even contemplated*. Indeed, Matza (1964) argues that neutralization is not an intentional or purposive act, but something that occurs to an individual as a result of the unwitting duplication, distortion, and extension in customary beliefs under which misdeeds may be condemned and sanctioned (for a similar view see Taylor, 1972). Matza says, "neutralization of legal precepts depends partly on equivocation—the unwitting use of concepts in markedly different ways" (1964:74). Thus it may be that a deviant act is sometimes contemplated *after* its unwitting neutralization through discursive construction in specific interactive situations. In Henry's study of amateur fences the neutralization was implemented by the dealer's use of presentational skills and an accompanying discursive "gloss," which depended on the buyer "filling in" its meaning on the basis of conventional stock of knowledge. As one dealer told Henry (1976:100):

> I never tell them it's stolen. I just say I got it from somewhere. See I sell it to them at slightly dearer than what they could get it for if it was "knocked off" (stolen). This leaves it that the stuff needn't be stolen. It could be damaged goods or soiled or anything like that.

Thus, words and phrases may explain the situation in such a way that a person is freed from any moral constraint and is liberated on a "moral holiday" wherein they may begin to contemplate the act and to construct motives for participation.

Since Matza and Sykes first coined the somewhat misleading term "techniques" of neutralization, commentators have established several additional categories of neutralization. The first five categories listed below are those originally formulated by Matza and Sykes; the metaphor of the ledger stems from Klockars (1974) work on professional fencing and the other three were identified in Henry's (1990) book *Degrees of Deviance*. Let us briefly look at each of these.

Denial of Responsibility

This category of neutralization refers to excuses alleging a loss of control over action such that one is driven to the behavior by forces beyond self control. Sometimes a society's culture contains built-in excuses, such as the moral meaning of alcohol in Western cultures. As MacAndrew and Edgerton (1969) point out, we are brought up to believe that we are not ourselves when drunk. Simply using alcohol allows us moral "time out" to engage in deviance, while separating the "real" self from the behavior. This form of denial of responsibility was found by McCaghy (1968) to be the preferred "deviance disavowal" technique of child molesters who normalized themselves as being "drunk at the time." Other external forces used in accounts of deviance to excuse the behavior include "poverty," "coming from a bad area," "peer pressure," and so on. In each case a person might claim that "under the circumstances I had no choice." Accordingly, they see themselves as essentially blameless, powerless, and "more acted upon than acting" (Sykes and Matza, 1957:667).

One subtype of denial of responsibility is the technique known as "defense of necessity" proposed by W. W. Minor (1981). This form of verbal "slight of hand" involves the contention that though one's behavior is morally wrong in an ideal sense, in a practical or "real" sense it is mandatory. Thus, among others, Minor cites the example of the white-collar offender's contention that illegal business practices are "necessary in a competitive business climate" (Minor, 1981:298).

Another variant of denial of responsibility is the claim of restricted or limited responsibility. For example, in the case of B.F. Goodrich Co. engineers falsified test results and issued false qualification reports on military aircraft brakes. Company personnel neutralized their moral culpability prior to falsifying reports by convincing themselves that they were "minding their own business," that doing their part of the fraud did not constitute the fraud itself, and that if they were in control of the whole operation it would not be allowed to happen. As the chief engineer of the plant producing the defective brake reportedly said to a quality control person who was reporting the problem:

> It's none of my business and it's none of yours. I learned a long time ago not to worry about things over which I had no control. I have no control over this. . . . I just do as I'm told, and I advise you to do the same. (Vandivier, 1987:114–115)

Of another colleague Vandivier said, "He was trying to persuade himself that as long as we were concerned with only one part of the puzzle and didn't see the completed picture, we really weren't doing anything wrong" (Vandivier, 1987:113). Similar arguments are used by middle managers who often blame CEOs for "setting the ethical tone," "the standards" of a corporation, for it is they who "give the orders" to "the troops below" (Clinard, 1983). One of the middle managers Clinard studied said, "Price fixing is none of middle management's damn business. If there is a general in charge you do not blow the whistle on him." Repeatedly, the statements "none of my business," and "not my responsibility" pervade these accounts. The very same denial of responsibility led Lieutenant Calley, who gave an order to "get rid" of the Vietnamese men, women, and children of Mylai in order to secure a military position, to the claim that "personally I didn't kill any Vietnamese that day. I mean personally. I represented the United States of America" (Calley, 1970).

Denial of Injury

Denial of injury refers to neutralizing morality by denying that an action causes harm. This rests on a morality of consequences, i.e., whether one's actions may be properly referred to as deviant or immoral depends on the injury or harm resulting from those acts. Examples of the use of "denial of injury" are abundant. Employees who pilfer from their employer sometimes deny that their action causes any harm since "the company can afford it," "they are covered by insurance," or "they won't even miss it." Indeed, Hollinger found that more active rule-breakers in the retail, hospital, and manufacturing industries were significantly more likely to use guilt-neutralizing techniques such as "denial of injury" than their less deviant peers (Hollinger, 1991). People who cheat on spouses also justify their action as not hurting anyone since their spouse does not know about it and "what you don't know won't hurt you" (Frost, 1990:31). Perhaps more dramatically, following his rape conviction, former boxing champion Mike Tyson contended:

> I am not guilty of this crime. I didn't rape anyone. I didn't hurt anyone. No black eyes, no broken ribs. When I'm in the ring, I break their ribs. I break their jaws. To me that's hurting someone. (*Time*, 1992a)

By such symbolic legerdemain, actors categorize their behavior as being of harmless intent, and preclude the idea that they may have injured persons or property. By virtue of the meaning constructed through the use of words and phrases actors either believe and/or claim that they are blameless.

Denial of Victim

This is the more confusing of Matza's categories of neutralization since at first it seems little different from denial of injury. In fact it is very different, for unlike denial of injury, denial of victim admits harm. Its claim to moral appropriateness is that the offended party is not deserving of victim status since the "harm" is a retribution for previous harms or injustices the "victim" inflicted on others. The accused may question the right of the supposed victim to moral sanctuary on the grounds that "she asked for it," or "they had it coming," or it was "only retaliation for them hurting me." For example, some assaults on homosexuals by "gay bashers" are justified by the claim that because of their homosexuality, gays offend and disgust others and so deserve to be assaulted. In a more common example, employees who perceive injustices in a company, because of poor wages, denied vacations, or a lax or abusive supervisor, feel justified in stealing from the company on the grounds that "the company deserves it," or as one commentator put it:

> Pilfering and fiddling are the "honest" response of millions of people to being exploited day in, day out, by employers. We're not stealing. We are taking back what is rightfully ours . . . its a crime to steal from your brothers; it's a public service to help each other nick (steal) from millionaire companies. (Up Against the Law Collective, 1974:33)

Whether such resentment is experienced prior to the contemplation of deviance is the critical issue. Some research, for example, shows that feelings of inequity generated by company pay reductions, when not accompanied by thorough and sensitive explanations or alternative accounts, often lead to an increase in employee theft (Greenberg, 1990). In these cases the "victim" is socially constructed as a deserving and legitimate target, while the actor becomes a "moral avenger." Some studies have suggested, for example, that employee theft is socially constructed with a wholly different meaning by the participants, who see it as a form of discipline (Gouldner, 1954) or as self-help "social control," especially where the employee is marginal to the company (Tucker, 1989) and without legitimate alternative means to resolve their grievances (Sieh, 1987). In this process the rule violator quite often becomes a modern day Robin Hood dealing out deserved "justice" to "evil doers." For example, in research on the behavior of unwed fathers, one man was encountered who had, unknowingly, steadily dated a women engaged to marry someone else. On discovering this, the man quickly perceived the women as the "transgressor" deserving of punishment and himself as the "avenger." He states:

> I found out about the two of them and played the dumb routine. At the time I thought she was a virgin. . . . She was pretty religiously hung up. . . . . She was anti-abortion, anti-sex, and she was kind of a tease—letting you go just so far and then clamming up and saying she had a headache and wanting to go home. And at first I thought she was just hanging on, but then I found out about this other guy. So then I just began trying a little harder . . . so I could get to her. She misled me to think that I was the only one for her . . . it wasn't just that she didn't tell me about this. That was

what offended me so much. I didn't like being used this way. She was Miss Socialite, and I was supposed to escort her around, pay her way here and there, and all the time she was tight with this other guy.

Asked how he felt when he learned she was pregnant he replied:

I was happy about the predicament she was in and that if everyone found out it would put the damper on the angelic front she was putting up. I wouldn't have been happy had the circumstances been different. I had finally gotten to this girl after she had made a monkey out of me. (Pfuhl, 1978)

Condemnation of Condemners

Yet another use of morally neutralizing words and phrases challenges the moral superiority of those asking questions about the rule-breaker. In these instances violators reject the implied disapproval of the questioning by rejecting the persons who condemn them—"they reject the rejector" (Sykes and Matza, 1957:668). For example, religious moral leaders such as Jim Bakker and Jimmy Swaggert are cited as being self-confessedly guilty of sexual infidelity, police are pointed to as guilty of corruption and violence, prosecutors and judges are described as hypocrites, senior government officials as lying to Congress, and congressmen as writing bad checks (kiting) to get money. To have been rejected or condemned by such morally "reprehensible people" has been defined by convicts, for example, as an "honor." In a broader form, since "everybody cheats on their taxes and embezzles from their employer," no one is honest and therefore no one has the right to condemn others. The use of words and phrases in this manner, after an act, deflects negative judgment and reassigns the roles of judge and judged, condemned and condemner. However, it is also clear that the presence in a society of increasing public knowledge of immorality among those in positions of power can serve as a repository of neutralization. As such it can predispose the prospective deviant to disregard conventional morality as a sham and thereby preempt any moral inhibition *prior* to contemplating the commission of a deviant act. This is especially likely if the deviant act is perceived as violating the same general type of rule that is disregarded by significant, powerful, or public figures.

Appeal to Higher Loyalties

This use of words and phrases is often a form of role conflict. Where people are faced with incompatible expectations as a consequence of inconsistency in roles, such as loyalty to family and loyalty to a peer group, disentanglement necessarily entails violation of one set of demands or expectations. The expectations that are violated are seen as less important and as a result, in the circumstances, their constraining influence is reduced. Thus to the potential deviant, the immediate group may be so important that wider and more abstract commitments to convention or moral principle are lost to the moment as in, "I was only helping my mates." Sometimes the resolution of the conflict involves balancing conformity with general laws, ethics, or public safety against the interests of family and directives of the corporation. Thus, one company executive engaged in fraud reasoned as follows:

> At forty two, with seven children, I had decided that the Goodrich Company would probably be my "home" for the rest of my working life. The job paid well, it was pleasant and challenging, and the future looked reasonably bright. My wife and I had bought a home and we were ready to settle down into a comfortable middle-age, middle-class rut. If I refused to take part in the . . . fraud, I would have to either resign or be fired. . . . The report would be written by someone else anyway, but I would have the satisfaction of knowing that I had no part in the matter. But bills aren't paid with personal satisfaction, nor house payments with ethical principles. I made my decision. (Vandivier, 1987:115)

As well as family, peers, and organizations, social movements may also effectively convey imperatives that raise the value of personal moral decisions, as in the women's movement to legislate and defend a women's right to choose abortion. As a consequence of their effort, "women opting for abortion can appeal to . . . the highest loyalty, that of one's own conscience" (Brennan, 1974:363). Alternatively, wider loyalties than those of personal or secular humanity may supplant the wants of the situation as in the accounts of numerous right-to-life advocates who justify breaking laws protecting the privacy, property, and "right to choose" of abortion advocates and practitioners with the claim that they are obeying God's law "which is higher than man's law." Of course they also, by implication, claim the right to determine what counts as God's law, as do child murderer's and serial killers who have claimed they were on a special mission from God.

Metaphor of the Ledger

In the metaphor of the ledger the person contemplating deviant activity considers the particular instance of rule-breaking activity as one in a series of otherwise good behavior. Thus any adverse implication of immorality stemming from the act in question is offset by considering it in light of total past behavior, which on the whole is judged to be good. Thus Carl Klockars' professional fence Vincent Swaggi said:

> Sure I've done some bad things in my life. Who hasn't. Everybody's got a skeleton in his closet somewhere. But you gotta take into account all the good things I done too. You take all the things I done in my life and put 'em together, no doubt about it, I gotta come out on the good side. (Klockars, 1974:151)

In retrospective reflection the metaphor of the ledger can be seen as part of the preservation of self and avoidance of negative labeling. However, a green light to rule-breaking is signaled in advance when the personal ledger of morality holds enough credit in its coffers to allow another expense without turning a total biography into the red.

Claim of Normality

In this category are all those utterances accepting that an instance of behavior is technically against the law, rules, or moral code, but pointing out that in practice "everyone is doing it." Whether it is cheating on taxes or on relationships, pilfering from the office, or buying stolen goods, the claim of these unwitting legal realists is that the rule is a fiction. As informants engaged in fencing stolen goods told Henry:

> Every single person on this earth has received something that's fell off the back of a lorry. . . . I don't know anybody who hasn't had furniture, washing machines, kitchen things. I don't know anybody who would say, 'Oh I don't want it'. They'd all say 'Ooh can you get *me* one?' " . . . People, reformers and everything want to stop looking through their rose colored glasses because the whole world is bent. (Henry, 1978a:50)

In these cases then, the rule is not denied, but its moral significance is trivialized. A variant of this is the claim that one's own participation in the act is of little moral impact because, "if everyone is doing it" then "if I don't do it, someone else will." In other words it is going to happen anyway so *my* doing it is of no moral consequence. With such seductive reasoning prior to an act, there may be little to prevent a person choosing to take part if they desire to do so.

Denial of Negative Intent

This is the acceptance of responsibility and acknowledgment that harm resulted from an act but claiming that the harm was not intended. In other words it is an appeal to an audience to share the experience of the moment, the thrill, excitement, the prank, or the joke, for what it was at the time, an occasion of "just having fun." Fundamentally it is a request to understand that the intentions were not bad. Again, while this might be employed as a tactic of biographical defence after the fact, it is also typically a neutralizing motivation prior to the act as in the case of students terrorizing other students with bottle rocket "mortars" whose use they defined as "hysterically funny" and "just a joke" (Moss, 1990:112–114).

Claim of Relative Acceptability

Unlike the neutralizing effect of the assertion that "everyone is doing it," the claim of relative acceptability relies on the construction of discursive categories by the deviant actor. Typically these categories seek to alter the public definition of the rule-breaker's deeds by pointing out that others' behavior is worse than the action in question. In effect the perpetrator is actually asserting that they are relatively moral. This account is typically used by employee pilferers who claim that they are only taking "bits and pieces" and that others are the *real* criminals, or that they only occasionally take stuff home, unlike those who do it *regularly* or those who take large quantities. Similar to that is a justification of illegal ownership and use of an AK-47 made in Moss's account of student gun use:

> It was the better of two evils. . . . If Dave had not acquired the rifle it would have fallen into worse hands. Instead of target practice it could have been used to harm someone. So in a way we were preventing a potential crime. (Moss, 1990:113)

One of the most public cases of this type of justification was made by one of the LAPD officers in their defence arguments during the first Rodney King beating trial. It was claimed that the beating was actually helpful to King as it prevented him from being killed by nervous fellow officers! If this "kind" thought was genuinely present at the time, then it would certainly neutralize any moral inhibition against the use of excessive force.

WILLINGNESS AND VALUES

Our comments on neutralization rest on the assumption that ordinary people are committed to the established institutional system and its values. However, such an assumption is not always warranted. In many cases, "neutralizations and rationalizations are simply unnecessary" (Minor, 1980:115). They are unnecessary, for example, when potential rule-breakers define themselves as the arbiters of their personal morality and single out that aspect of western culture, which proclaims "freedom of the individual." Thus people having extramarital affairs have claimed:

> I don't care what the rest of society thinks. I'm doing what I want and that makes me happy and that is all I care about.". . . "They are living their lives and I am living mine. If they hate the idea of me seeing someone and being married then they are not considering my feelings and whether or not I'm happy. I am happy with my friend and with our relationship. I'm making my own decision about my life. I find it objectionable for other people to tell me what to do with my life. (Frost, 1990:31–32)

For others the neutralization of conventional morality is rendered unnecessary because "society or subculture has already accomplished the task" (Sheley, 1980:51). Given the pluralistic value system in societies such as ours, many rule violations reflect subcultural, countercultural, or *contracultural values* (Yinger 1965:231). Numerous studies, for example, have demonstrated that employee work groups develop their own subcultural values sustaining some types of employee theft as morally justified (Horning, 1970; Mars, 1974; Hawkins, 1984), while punishing others (Henry and Mars 1978; Hollinger and Clark, 1983; Henry, 1983).

In contrast, countercultural values are typically more dramatic, more explicitly opposed to the dominant society, and, as a result, are often held to be deviant (Glaser, 1971:15–19). At one level there are those countercultural groups that are focused on specific causes or who pursue such alternative life-styles as "new wave culture," "survivalism," "naturalist nudism," and "vegetarianism." Survivalists, for example (the paramilitary groups that organize with the aim of ensuring that their members survive in the event of a major societal breakdown), see their secret unlawful weapon-related activities as fully justified by the desire to survive after nuclear war or economic collapse. As one survivalist explained, the laws controlling firearms "don't apply to [us], because [we] are not criminals or murderers . . . we don't want to take over the world. We just want to survive" (Fisher, 1990:132–133).

Other contracultural groups such as the Baader-Meinhof group, the Aryan Nation, and the Irish Republican Army do want to take the world over, or at least a geographical part of it, and want to do so through *terrorism*, the "the deliberate and systematic use or threat of violence against . . . human targets" (Schmid and De Graff, 1982:15). The terrorist's efforts stem from religious, political, and other secular disputes and "have as their objective the destruction of the society's system of power, changes of policy by means of violence, or the forceful removal of those exercising power in the system" (Sykes, 1972:413; Rapoport and Alexander, 1982). Their actions reflect their perceptions, beliefs, ideology, and values, as well as their opposition to the values represented by the status quo (Wilkinson, 1977:93–102).

Somewhere between the extremes of alternative life-style groups and terrorist groups is rule-breaking based on promoting limited, caused-based, social change known as *civil disobedience* (Bay, 1967:166). Embracing this principle, and the practical goals on which it rests, means one is unlikely to be constrained by rules that derive their legitimacy from the very system or subsystem one wishes to change. Members of the "right to life" movement who bomb or picket abortion clinics represent one example. Such behavior is more widespread in our society than most recognize. There are numerous groups who openly violate public law as an expression of opposition to dominant public policy. Issues and disputes leading to such behavior include use of nuclear energy, disposal of hazardous waste and defiling the environment, transportation and use of nuclear weapons, and providing sanctuary to illegal immigrants. Yet others have organized their own inner city neighborhoods to "take back the night" from the drug dealers and crack addicts, and, through groups such as "the Guardian Angels," have engaged in violent vigilantism and the illegal burning of abandoned houses.

A final condition in which people may deviate without a need to secure "release" from moral rules are situations involving behavior they define as *amoral*, i.e., behavior about which some people feel no sense of wrongfulness since they define it as outside the realm of morality. Largely as a matter of social change and the dynamics of moral meanings, behaviors having strong negative moral meaning sometimes undergo a change in public definition (Sykes, 1972:415). As a result, behaviors once regarded as immoral and taboo become normalized and generally tolerated. One example is divorce, which was once regarded as a shameful event but is currently accepted with few if any moral connotations. Another is cohabitation, which used to be grounds for condemnation and derision. Another recent instance involves informing or "snitching." Despite its long-standing moral condemnation, informing has recently been redefined in the United States, Canada, and other countries having Crimestoppers programs, which make it moral and proper (and sometimes profitable) for people to inform on others to the police (Pfuhl, 1992). This has received added momentum as a result of the recent availability of video camcorders (Einstadter and Henry, 1991).

A Cautionary Note

At this point a cautionary word on the general issue of willingness and commitment is in order. First, a person's willingness to break rules should not be perceived as a commitment to deviate. As with Matza's (1964) delinquents, most people are neither fully committed to conformity nor deviancy but flirt, now with one, now with the other, postponing commitment and evading decision. Their biographies demonstrate that (1) rule-breaking is most often an episodic thing, a "momentary digression," and (2) people are not committed exclusively either to legitimate or to illegitimate values. Categorizing people in such ways lacks validity. Few persons, including the most dedicated criminal, engage in rule violating behavior all of the time. Even professional "hit men" acknowledge their love for children and the pleasure they get "playing with their mutt" (Levi, 1989:456). "Severely disturbed" mental patients conform to most of society's rules, most of the time. And those who violate some rules are violently opposed to other forms of rule-breaking, as many child molesters have discovered during their imprisonment.

Second, for most people a willingness to deviate, like a willingness to conform, must be renewed. This is because release from moral constraints is often "episodic," limited to the specific situation and short lived. As a result, a person's willingness to engage in one form of rule-breaking at one time is not necessarily generalizable to other forms, or to that form at other times. For example, evidence suggests that as people age and their responsibilities and opportunities change, so do their options, commitments, self-conception, and, hence, their behavior (Brown et al., 1974). Likewise, many people simultaneously live a public life of normality and a secret life of rule-breaking (Bensman and Lilienfeld, 1979:60–61). Thus, numerous news media interviews with neighbors of murderers and rapists typically report: "He was a friendly guy who always said hello and would help friends when asked. I am shocked by this!"

Finally, while some persist as deviants, others abandon rule-breaking, undergoing what Matza (1964) calls "maturational reform." Thus, it is no surprise that "radical hippies" of the 1960s become published authors and elected officials in the 1970s and the 1980s and that yesterday's marihuana smokers have become today's mominee for the U.S. Supreme Court and candidate for the Office of President. As we noted earlier, biography is constantly in the making.

In summary, being willing refers to no more or less than that one is available for participation in some form of rule-breaking. One who is willing is merely a *potential* rule-breaker. Whether or not one does in fact break a rule is yet highly problematic, dependent on opportunity, one's commitments, the encouragement of others, whether contrary values and beliefs are neutralized, and the extent to which one subscribes to countercultural values. Moreover, following their initial participation in rule-breaking, people continue to retain control and are able to make decisions about whether to avoid further involvement or persist. Let us examine these decisions and how they are made.

TURNING ON—TURNING OFF

Having once engaged in rule-breaking, whether to persist is a matter for the actor to decide. The decision rests on whether one's experience with rule-breaking (part of an everchanging biography) results in their being "turned on" or "turned off" (Matza, 1969:177ff). One definition of "turned on" involves being familiar with a thing as a consequence of experience rather than on the basis of abstract knowledge (Partridge, 1970:1484). In this sense, being "turned on" is not synonymous with "being hooked" or being indelibly committed to the behavior. Simply, experience renders one at least minimally knowledgeable. For example, through experience one may come to associate with others engaged in the same behavior and, presumably, become familiar with and adept at using justifications or excuses for it. On the basis of this knowledge one decides that continuing in the behavior either is or is not appropriate and may either abandon the behavior, engage in it on a casual or transitory basis, or escalate their involvement. Those who persist may be said to be "turned on" or "hardened" (Minor, 1981:301) while those who abandon the behavior are "turned off." Let us first consider the matter of turning off.

Turning Off

As a result of experience people often have second thoughts and decide to abandon a line of action. For example, the initial experience some people have with mood-altering drugs precludes further use; abstinence becomes mandatory. Consider the following results of snorting heroin for the first time. After the initial "rush,"

> My guts felt like they were going to come out. Everything was bursting out all at once, and there was nothing I could do. It was my stomach and my brain.
> My stomach was pulling my brain down into it, and my brain was going to pull my guts out and into my head. . . . And then it seemed like every-

thing in me all of a sudden just came out, and I vomited. . . . I was dying, . . . I threw up and I threw up. It seemed like I threw up a million times. I felt that if I threw up one more time, my stomach was just going to break all open; and still I threw up. I prayed and I prayed. . . . After a while I was too sick to care. . . . I was sick about two days after that. I didn't even want a reefer. I didn't want anything, anything that was like a high. I started drinking some of Dad's liquor after that, but I was scared of those dry highs. Anyway, that was the big letdown with horse. . . . The horse had turned out to be a real drag. (Brown, 1966:111–112)

Becker also indicates that novice marihuana smokers who do not smoke "properly" do not get high. "If nothing happens, it is manifestly impossible for the user to develop a conception of the drug as an object which can be used for pleasure, and *use will therefore not continue* (Becker, 1973:47, emphasis added). In other instances of rule-breaking actors are overcome with remorse and some have even been known to return stolen property with apologetic notes (*Arizona Republic*, 1982a).

Experience may also refresh or renew the actor's commitment to a prior set of meanings, a prior reality (Matza, 1969:112). For example, Douglas and Rasmussen (1977:77–78) relate the case of Kay, a Kansas school teacher, whose introduction to the nude beach was with an experienced fiend, Diana. When going to the beach was first suggested, Kay "thought it sounded great and decided to go nude publicly for the first time in her adult life." On arrival at the beach Diana immediately stripped and encouraged Kay to join her. Despite every gentle encouragement from her friend and other acquaintances, Kay ended the day fully clothed, crying "I can't."

These examples indicate that people sometimes change their definition of the priority of engaging in deviance and become "turned off" or unwilling. On the basis of *their evaluation of their involvement* actors can experience feelings of remorse, guilt, and shame. An enticing novelty or a moderately tolerable possibility comes to be rejected. This suggests that though people are attracted to the proscribed behavior by one set of elements, they are also aware of the public definition of the behavior, their sense of self, and that they may risk loss of esteem. As a result, they may experience strong sensations of moral ambivalence. However, the decision to reject may not be permanent. Concerns may dissipate; one may not be turned off forever. But transitory or not, such consequences *are* sufficient to dissuade many.

Turning On

Unlike those who are turned off, others' rule-breaking experience leaves them satisfied and promotes a decision to persist. In contrast to the first experience with heroin use reported earlier, the following initial experience of the drug is positive:

> I adapted to it very well, probably because I was having a hard time trying to establish relationships with people—I couldn't get to know people very well . . . but I discovered that if you were a junkie in my neighborhood people really didn't expect too much from you. That was an easy way out: if I became a heroin addict, I wouldn't have to try to meet people and people would leave me alone. . . . Well, anyway, heroin sort of satisfied my feelings of frustration, and I really became quite involved in it—as a user mostly. (Rodriguez, 1974:84)

On the basis of positive or utilitarian experiences, then, people may be "turned on" or "converted" to the behavior. From experience they have at least limited knowledge of the positive (and negative) features of the behavior. The experience helps them revise or supplement former meanings so that behaviors once defined as taboo come to be redefined as having "good purposes" or, at least, lacking the negative properties attributed to them.

This "conversion" or redefinition was noted by Varni in his study of spouse "swapping." Though they characteristically approached swapping with anxiety, apprehension, and misgiving, many wives reported that,

> the main effect of the first swinging experience was to greatly reduce the level of anxiety . . . and thus provide a climate in which the experience could be evaluated in a more "objective light." If anything, the experience was anti-climactic in relation to the woman's expectations. The typical response was that it was not such a big deal after all. Many women made guardedly positive remarks such as "Well, it wasn't as bad as I thought it would be," or "I might try it again." (Varni, 1972:512)

Varni also reports that if the initial swinging experience is not traumatic a couple will likely try it again. On the basis of the knowledge provided by the first experience, and its tendency to reduce anxiety and apprehension, people usually report the second experience to be more enjoyable. Such a reaction, of course, assumes that no unmanageable or threatening conditions arise to alter the definition of the experience. "This second experience, if it proves to be nonthreatening—and especially if it is enjoyable—is usually the clincher in that it validates the nonuniqueness of the first experience" (Varni, 1972:513). On that basis (and that of subsequent nontroubling experiences) the actor is proceeding toward constructing a new set of moral meanings—a "new" social reality.

Experiences of this sort are the stuff of everyday life. Some things we experience positively, others negatively, and still others lack appreciable consequences of either sort. On the basis of their socially constructed meaning, we validate and reinforce, or question, revise, and reject our conceptions of events and experiences in our environment. It is these experiences that enable people to make decisions regarding the appropriateness of their behavior in light of self-attitudes, their position in society, and the perceived emotional value of the behavior. It is out of this experience that the once willing but reticent, now turned on, actor builds a revised social reality. This is a learning experience in which one social reality supersedes another (Varni, 1972:510).

Consistent with our social constructionist perspective, during this learning process actors are in a position of authority over their actions (Matza, 1969:123). People perceive themselves as a sometime rule-breaker in the context of their various social positions. They contemplate the possibility of social rejection should their rule-breaking be made a public issue, and they mediate and resolve any conflict between their rule-breaking and other commitments. In short, people perceive themselves in a relational sense, i.e., in relation to other people and positions. On the basis of such perceptions, people make the decision whether to pursue rule-breaking behavior (Matza, 1969:122). As noted earlier, rule-breaking (like conformity) is self-ordained.

THE QUESTION OF MOTIVES

Earlier we argued that rule-violating behavior is volitional and based on reasons. Among these reasons are *motives or motivation*, the "complex of meaning which appears to the individual involved . . . to be sufficient reason for his conduct" (Weber, 1962:39). Once any moral inhibition has been neutralized, and once the influence of biography and experience has rendered a person available to experiment, the decision to engage in the proscribed behavior is a matter of motivation, taken here to be intentional meaningful reasons that make doing the act desirable. Many different kinds of deviant behavior have similar motives and these motives are often no different than those for conforming behavior. The following classification, adapted from one developed by Henry (1990:145–146), is neither exhaustive nor mutually exclusive but includes many of the motives most commonly constructed by participants to deviant activity:

1. *Pecuniary, material, or tangible motives*: to make money; to obtain goods or services; to obtain sex;

2. *Recreational motives*: to enjoy fun and excitement; to obtain thrills, to play; to get high; to beat the system (seen as a game);
3. *Interpersonal or social motives*: to achieve status; to earn honor and prestige; to repay favors; to gain acceptance, fit in or feel normal; to stand out; to express friendship, loyalty, or resentment; to fulfill role expectations; to compete or meet a challenge;
4. *Problem-solving motives*: to relieve pain, stress, tension, or boredom; to establish identity; to compensate for missing expectations; to cope; to avoid or escape responsibility; to preserve self (self-defence); to restore control over one's life;
5. *Political motives*: to correct injustices; to gain domination over others; to gain freedom from others; to beat an oppressive system; to change society or parts of the social system; to express allegiance to alternative religious, moral or ethical beliefs.

Space does not allow us to illustrate each of these motives here, although many of them underlie cases of rule-breaking cited elsewhere in the book. However, in what follows we shall try to highlight those that go deeper than the obvious material rewards.

Political Motives

We have already seen how beliefs in countercultural values and in the need for social change can lead people to perceive deviance as instrumental to achieving those ends. A classic expression of political motivation is the more than 250 revolts by blacks during the period of American slavery that were designed to obtain personal freedom (Aptheker, 1943:162; Franklin, 1956:208). Other examples of political motivation for deviance include feminists whose action has been held to violate traditional gender norms (Bell, 1976; Schur, 1984), student protests of the 1960s and 1970s, the gay liberation movement, both sides of the abortion issue, and more recently ACT UP, the proponents of rights and support services for AIDS victims. Less organized are the motives of some individuals who engage in industrial sabotage, vandalism, and looting. A classic example of such protest is the activity of Michigan physician Dr. Jack Kevorkian who has vigorously worked—illegally, some claim—to legalize doctor-assisted suicides for the terminally ill.

Problem-Solving Motives

Perhaps the most dramatic examples of the problem-solving motive is the shooting deaths by several postal employees of their former supervisors and co-workers on being dismissed, or the murder of doctors by patients or of professors by disgruntled students. Rejecting traditional materialist accounts of crime as inadequate, Katz argues that

> Central to all these experiences in deviance is a member of the family of moral emotions: humiliation, righteousness, arrogance, ridicule, cynicism, defilement, and vengeance. In each, the attraction that proves to be most fundamentally compelling is that of overcoming a personal challenge to moral—not material—existence. For the impassioned killer, the challenge is to escape a situation that has come to seem otherwise inexorably humiliating. Unable to sense how he or she can move with self-respect from the current situation, now, to any mundane-time relationship that might be reengaged, then, the would-be killer leaps at the possibility of embodying, through the practice of "righteous" slaughter, some eternal, universal form of the Good. (Katz, 1988:9)

Perhaps a less obvious problem solving example is the use of drugs by medical students:

> It was never a conscious thing on my part. I never said, 'OK enough, I'm going to get snowed'. It was gradual. See there's no recourse to follow. You can't confront the attending [physician]. If you do, they think you're not a team player. That's what its all about—being a team player. Talk back and you're out of the program. So you learn to swallow your anger. When I'm loaded it doesn't bother me. But when I'm not, I look for someone to dump on. Usually that's a patient.
>
> The use of drugs provides a way of getting through the day. It also allows one to cover up and appear normal. . . . "I felt like I was going to explode, like I was going to go in one day and lose it. I started taking Xanax, at first just to calm down, just to go out there and face it. I mean I knew I couldn't walk around like that any more. I was afraid everybody would notice and think I couldn't take it. I started off with just .25 BID, just enough to robotize myself. And it helped. I felt numb." (Hart, 1990:93)

Similarly, some college students drink alcohol to help them fit in or become more relaxed talking with girls, and to "break the ice" at parties. Yet others break gun laws in order to compensate for a fear of being a victim of street crime or because of a general need to feel more powerful in today's society (Gaines 1990: 123–125).

Theft, especially occupational pilfering, can also be based on more complex meaning structures that are part of the context in which it occurs. The following case of a student who, as a route salesman for a wholesale bakery, found it necessary to cover "short" receipts through stealing, illustrates the general case found by Ditton (1977) in his study of the bread industry:

Being a novice, . . . I came up short all too often. The amounts were usually small, but they added up. A dollar or two a day devastated my budget. Even more inconvenient was an occasional major (to me) shortage—$5–$10. I would have to settle all the shortages on the weekly payday. When I would go home with the remains of my check and tell my wife how much I had left, she gave me the practical advice "Either stop coming up short or get another job." She wasn't recommending stealing. She was recommending that I change jobs. . . . There was no real wrestling with conscience. It was more the feeling of agony, of being substantially short again with my stomach knotting up and muttering a vow. "Shit, this is going to happen to me again." There were no trips to the Garden of Gethsemane in making the decision to steal; they came later. There was just an awareness of what to do then doing it. (unpublished paper)

As Ditton (1977:34–35) showed, the novice bread salesperson is typically guided into the revelation that, by various means "extra" bread (either "refurbished" stale bread or pilfered bread) can be sold, or that by adding a few cents on to the bills of those customers who are unlikely to check, he can eliminate the inevitable mistakes and shortages for which he is accountable.

Interpersonal and Social Motives

Many deviant activities are the outcome of social motives. In studying the amateur trade in stolen goods, Henry (1978a) found that in spite of claims to the contrary, dealers rarely made money and, more importantly, they did not define their activity in monetary terms to themselves. Rather, the trade was understood as an activity providing the opportunity to experience the rewards of social network relationships, to accumulate prestige from being "the person who can get stuff cheap," and for doing friends favors. As one of Henry's informants told him:

It's not important in money terms. I believe money's not the thing. They might say it is in order to justify the risks in terms that everyone can understand, but that's not it. When it comes right down to it nobody *really* makes any money. The rewards are more social than monetary. (Henry, 1978a:93)

And another said, "It may sound odd but its sort of like a community action group. . . . They'll say, 'I'll do this for you' or 'My brother will get that for you'." For these people, trading in stolen goods, while "technically illegal" was experienced as "very, very moral—a good thing"; people were "not getting anything out of it personally" but felt "satisfaction out of knowing what they were doing" (Henry, 1978a:101). Similar social satisfactions have been noted among those who participate in the "irregular economy" and who avoid taxes by working off the books (Ferman and Berndt, 1981), among restaurant waiters engaged in "social theft" (Hawkins, 1984), and youngsters who steal "dream" cars and demonstrate their deft driving ability in order to establish an identity and gain the respect of their peers (*New York Times*, 1992d).

Recreational Motives

Finally we might consider those forms of rule-breaking motivated by the pursuit of "fun, excitement, thrills, sport or play" (Sykes, 1972:411; Richards, Berk and Forster, 1979). The idea of rule-breaking as fun was noted in the 1920s by Thrasher (1963:269) who identified "going robbing" as a "common diversion" among gang members, and in the 1930s by Tannenbaum (1938:17) who recognized that delinquency could bring play, adventure, excitement, mischief, and fun. Sexual deviance is pleasurable for the participants, as is the use of mood-altering drugs, if only for the euphoria and pleasure during the "honeymoon phase" of heroin use (Goode, 1972:172), or the "A-side" of crack house cocaine smoking, which is typically combined with oral sex or "buffing" (Williams, 1992). Marihuana is used primarily as a social relaxant and is believed to heighten the enjoyment of music, art, films, and food (Geller and Boas, 1969:65; National Commission on Marihuana and Drug Abuse, 1972:37).

The nonmaterial pleasures and emotions of much crime have been documented by Katz who describes the sensual attractions and feelings of moral restoration and the "genuine experiential creativity" that constitute the essence of much rule-breaking. For example,

> For many adolescents, shoplifting and vandalism offer the attractions of a thrilling melodrama about the self as seen from within and from without. Quite apart from what is taken, they may regard "getting away with it" as a thrilling demonstration of personal competence, especially if it is accomplished under the eyes of adults. (Katz, 1988:9)

Similar expressions of recreationally motivated rule-breaking include the construction and operation of complex gadgetry in order to "beat" the telephone company out of the cost of long distance calls, computer "hacking" or intruding on and disrupting computer files and operations (Pfuhl, 1987; Michalowski and Pfuhl, 1991), interfering with national poll samples, rerouting mail and tampering with radio and television broadcasts. Twenty years ago Toffler predicted such diversionary forms of deviance as an outcome of antisocial leisure cults, "organized groups of people who will disrupt the organization of society not for material gain, but for the sheer sport of 'beating the system'" (Toffler, 1970:289).

RULE-BREAKING AS NEGOTIATED EVENTS

Motives do not always arise well in advance of the behavior in question. Rather, some motives emerge in the course of the action itself, largely as a consequence of the perceived nature of the interaction between one's self and others. Viewed as the outcome or "settlement" arrived at by the actors through interaction, these instances of proscribed behavior may properly be said to be cases of *"negotiated deviance."* Here our focus is on how people's motivations arise sequentially in the context of an ongoing relationship. We shall illustrate this process with the case of homicide, although evidence is also available supporting this interpretation of burglary (Thrasher, 1936:300–303) and robbery (Luckenbill, 1981).

As a result of an intensive study of 70 murder cases, Luckenbill concluded that in every situation the death was the culmination of situated transactions, i.e., "a chain of interactions between two or more individuals that lasts the time they find themselves in one another's physical presence" (Luckenbill, 1977:177). These transactions are carried out in a wide variety of settings (bars, automobiles, parties, people's homes, dances, etc.), and between persons representing a wide array of relationships (spouses, friends, co-workers, acquaintances, and strangers). The critical element is the dynamics of these situated transactions. Luckenbill contends that these murders are the result of an intense period of interaction between persons, one of whom eventually becomes the victim, while the other becomes the offender, the ultimate determination of these positions being entirely problematic. Each of the parties is a contributor to the final outcome of the event.

Quite often these negotiated events are "character contests" in which (1) one person says or does something to another that (2) is perceived by the other to be a disparagement, insult, or other affront to their self-image. This is accompanied by (3) a retaliatory move by the offended person consisting either of a verbal or physical challenge, or a direct physical retaliation resulting in the death of the original offender. If the third step is limited to a challenge by the offended person, the initial offender is now in a position to effect a possible fourth stage of the transaction: he or she must now "either stand up to the challenge and demonstrate strength of character, or apologize, discontinue the inappropriate conduct, or flee the situation" (Luckenbill, 1977:182). They must "put up or shut up." Any response other than the first (i.e., a demonstration of character) constitutes a loss of face and an abandonment of the self-image the person has claimed in that situation. To avoid a loss of face and a demonstration of weakness, many people at this point tacitly define the use of violence as a suitable means of resolving the problem. At that point the probability that violence will occur is enhanced.

This analysis suggests that both parties are contributors to the emerging "working agreement" that results in homicide. The outcome of their interaction is a shared understanding that the situation is one calling for a violent solution. This conclusion need never be verbalized. Yet it is clearly understood and agreed on via the "cues" and signals exhibited by both parties (Cohen, 1955:60; Matza, 1964:51–59, 62–64) that each is motivated to save face, demonstrate character, and/or develop or preserve a reputation. The regularities and development of homicide result from an interaction rather than being the consequence of an aggressive offender imposing his or her will on a passive victim (Luckenbill, 1977:185–186). Homicide, then, often is a joint enterprise, situationally based, problematic, and reflective of people's existential condition.

SUMMARY

In this chapter we have employed a social constructionist explanation to account for people's involvement in rule-breaking behavior. On the basis of available evidence we conclude that involvement in proscribed behavior has no cognitive foundation that is unique or different from that of social behavior in general. Like other forms of social behavior, rule-breaking is volitional and rests on the meanings people create and develop about experiences and events in their effective environment. Based on experience (biography), people acquire understandings and definitions that leave them with a generally positive (an affinity) or a generally negative (an aversion) orientation toward select forms of rule-breaking behavior. However, people do not always act on their affinities; nor are they contained by their aversions. Whether or not people experiment in deviance is influenced by their definition of the immediate situations in which they find themselves, the direct or indirect influence others may have on their decision making, and their commitment to a course of action. Further, involvement in rule-breaking often hinges on people's ability to neutralize the moral or ethical constraints that may inhibit their participation. In other cases it is precisely their moral and ethical beliefs that lead people to violate institutional rules.

Once moral barriers are cleared away, people are free to construct motives. Among these are a wish to escape—either from boredom, a "bad" home situation, or poverty, a wish to express hostility and contempt, striving for political or social change, seeking recreation, seeking to make a living or just trying to "keep one's head above water," seeking to establish an identity or preserve a threatened self-image, or "keeping faith" with one's peers. Not the least important consequence of recognizing these varied grounds for rule-breaking behavior is that (1) they are equally suited to explain deviant as well as nondeviant behavior, and (2) they preclude the need to resort to deterministic explanations. What needs to be acknowledged is that "deviant" behavior is but a variant on human behavior. Accordingly, explanations of it need be no more than a special case of more general explanatory systems (Polsky, 1967:101).

NOTES

1.   Interestingly, in Weinberg's sample, more men had their interest in nudism aroused by the media (59%) than by other persons (33%). This is consistent with what is known about males being more exposed and responsive to external stimuli than women, as part of their general biographical experience in our society.

CHAPTER

4

Banning

INTRODUCTION

In the previous chapter we examined the social construction of deviance from the rule breaker's perspective. Here we explore a complementary aspect of the deviance process by focusing on the *audience* who make the rules that deviants break.

Deviance is what those with the power to influence the rule-making process say it is. Deviance is constructed to reflect the definitions of immorality held by such persons and groups. It is their private definitions of morality that are transformed into public rules of behavior, violations of which are punishable by the state. The creation of deviance, then, is part of a political process in which people's behavior (and/or condition) is publicly signified as different, negatively evaluated, and interpreted as violations deserving of condemnation and control. Rule-making also involves the process of defining rule violators as deviants liable to various actions allegedly designed to control them. These two features of rule-making are referred to as *banning*, i.e., signifying activity as evil, bad, wrong, or immoral and imbuing rule-breakers with guilt (Matza, 1969:146). Our analysis of rule-making or banning will be guided by a version of the pluralist view of law creation (Rose, 1987; Gusfield, 1963, 1981; Edelman, 1964; Carson, 1974; Turk, 1976; Dickson, 1968; Becker, 1963).[1]

THE SOCIAL CREATION OF MORAL MEANINGS

A standard feature of heterogeneous societies is the coexistence of a plurality of groups that are differentiated by their distinctive, often antagonistic belief systems and behaviors. Such societies are characterized by multiple realities, i.e., competing claims to truth and value that lead persons, groups, or objective conditions to be defined as problematic, "posing a danger or containing the seeds of some future difficulties" (Becker, 1966:12). The consciousness and strain accompanying this clash of realities predate rule-creating and is a necessary prelude to the emergence of what is referred to as "moral entrepreneurial activity."

Moral Entrepreneurs

Creating moral meanings is an entrepreneurial enterprise (Becker, 1973:162) in two senses. First, *rule-making* is the activity of rule creators who selectively ban some behaviors. Second, *rule-enforcing* is the application of rules/sanctions against some specific group and/or behavior by social control agents.[2] Here we focus exclusively on the activity of rule creators.

Rule creators operate like manufacturers in that they invest things with new form. In manufacturing raw materials are converted into consumable goods. Similarly, in banning rule creators alter the meaning that behavior or events have in their "natural" context (as constructed by the participants), assigning them new moral meanings. Moreover, just as a manufacturer transforms the image of a product from its functional utility, imbuing it with a desirable image (e.g., Nestle's chocolate is not just food, but represents "sweet dreams you can't resist"), so it is with moral entrepreneurs who may transform the meaning of a behavior from "a pleasurable accompaniment to leisure events" (e.g., the social use of marihuana) into a "moral panic" (e.g., drug use as the font of moral decay in modern society). Further, whereas manufacturers sell their packaged product via the image-producing efforts of advertising agencies, moral entrepreneurs enter the moral marketplace by having their meanings officially legitimated as public policy. Rather than employing advertising agencies, moral entrepreneurs rely on *pressure groups* who organize to convert their members' shared interests into public law or to influence public policy. What motivates this moral entrepreneurial effort is the belief that rules do not exist or that existing rules are inadequate to correct the conditions that distress them. Alternatively, they may believe that agencies such as the police, welfare, or medical fail to implement existing rules. Like distress over the condition itself, a lack of available means for its resolution may also provoke moral entrepreneurship.

Moral entrepreneurship may be engaged in by individuals or groups, but usually it is a combination of both. Some individual moral entrepreneurs are renowned for single issue campaigns such as Flora Scala, who campaigned against having her neighborhood razed to allow for the expansion of the University of Illinois (*Chicago Tribune*, 1984), or Sherri

Pitman, who campaigned in Arizona against pornography as an "utterly despicable, child destroying menace" (*Arizona Republic*, 1979). More prominent, however, are religious or political figures such as the Reverend Jerry Falwell or the Reverend Pat Robertson, who both claim to lead an amorphous "moral majority" in various crusades against moral evil. Others are affiliated through their ties to political office such as former First Lady Nancy Reagan who developed a "just say no" campaign as a keystone to her "war on drugs, or Tipper Gore, wife of Vice President Al Gore, who founded a campaigning organization. Based on the belief that children need to be protected from popular music's harmful content, Tipper started Parents Music Resource Center (PMRC) in 1985 with Susan Baker, wife of then Secretary of State James Baker, to campaign against depravity and vulgarity in rock music lyrics. (DeCurtis, 1992:17)

While individuals like Gore may front a campaign, in complex heterogeneous societies rule-creating is most frequently engaged in by organized groups. As an example of collective moral entrepreneurship, the *Encyclopedia of American Associations* lists almost 200 organizations concerned with issues of gay and lesbian rights, 220 private groups in the United States and elsewhere concerned with AIDS related issues, e.g., ACT UP (Aids Coalition to Unleash Power), and about two dozen private interest groups opposed to cigarette smoking. Included are ASH (Action on Smoking and Health), GASP (Group Against Smokers Pollution), the American Cancer Society, the American Heart Association, and the American Lung Association. However, moral entrepreneurial groups are not concerned only with banning behavior. Some, as we will see in later chapters, are groups of deviants attempting to decriminalize certain activity. Included is COYOTE (Cast Off Your Old Tired Ethics), a group of prostitutes seeking to legalize prostitution (St. James, 1987), and PIE (Pedophile Information Exchange), which lobbies to reduce the age for lawful sexual relations (Robinson and Henry, 1977). Also in this category is the American Puffer Alliance, an interest group seeking to end the antismoking crusade and restore the rights and freedoms of smokers (Markle and Troyer, 1979; Troyer and Markle, 1983).

In summary, then, banning is based on rule creator's dissatisfaction with existing conditions and represents an effort to prevent or correct them. Something the rule creators define as important, e.g., their homes, their health, or the innocence of their children, is perceived to be threatened. Moral entrepreneurs seek to have their dissatisfactions and interests (often moral concerns) officially recognized in public law and ideally to have the rules be universally applied. Accordingly, making deviance is an aspect of making public policy; it is a political act resulting in the legitimation of some people's views of reality over others.

RESOLVING DISTRESS: INSTRUMENTAL AND SYMBOLIC GOALS

In order to resolve their problems, moral entrepreneurs may pursue (1) instrumental and/or (2) symbolic goals (Gusfield, 1967). We will look at each in turn.

Instrumental Goals

There are many ways that instrumental goals may be pursued. Moral crusaders may seek some tangible authority over people or activities seen as a threat by creating laws where none exist. An example of this is "computer abuse." Thus, between 1975 and 1985, 46 states passed computer crime statutes and/or amended existing criminal codes in order to deal with computer hackers' intrusion into the computer files in "manufacturing companies, wholesalers, utilities, chemical processors, railroads, mail order houses, department stores, hospitals, and government agencies" (Allen, 1975:88; also see Parker, 1980:216). Of concern was the protection of computerized data banks, preventing the theft of trade secrets and computer programs, and preventing foreign agents and terrorists from penetrating government computer systems simply by manipulating electronic impulses (*U.S. News and World Report*, 1980:69; Pfuhl, 1987).

In other instances, moral entrepreneurs are concerned about"deficient" enforcement of existing law. As an example, a group of southern California women founded a movement to put an initiative on the ballot to tighten sex crime laws. These women, parents of young male murder victims, sought to make it more difficult for convicted sex offenders to be released from prison (*Arizona Republic*, 1980a). They call their movement the Voting Initiative Concerning Tougher Imprisonment of Molesters and Sex Offenders (VICTIMS).

Some rule creators seek to alter the content of existing rules for nonmaterial goals such as to satisfy religious or ideological beliefs about life. For example, pro-life (antiabortion) groups seek repeal of what they define as "liberal" abortion laws and policy (*Time*, 1992b). These groups want to restrict and, preferably, ban abortions. Simultaneously, other moral entrepreneurs are working to prevent such change. Similarly, antigay forces in the United States have worked vigorously to resist normalization of homosexuality. They feel that continued proscription of homosexuality is necessary to avoid an anticipated "collapse of the American family," if not the destruction of civilization itself (Mohr, 1988:42ff). Instrumental use of law, then, whether or not materially based, reflects variation in rule creators' perceptions of their needs and interests.

Symbolic Goals

In addition to their instrumental goals, moral entrepreneurs often seek to "capture" the law simply for its *symbolic effect*, i.e., its ability to give legitimacy to some interests or values, while denying it to others (Gusfield, 1967:178). Even though it may not be enforced, merely having a law on the books reflecting one's values and interests may be taken as a measure of the group's moral stature or social status. This symbolic concern was seen to be behind the prohibition laws of the 1920s and in the middle class resistance to liberalization of Boston's gambling laws. Gusfield (1967:181–182) notes, "The maintenance of a norm which defines gambling as deviant behavior . . . symbolizes the maintenance of Yankee social and political superiority. Its disappearance as a public commitment would symbolize the loss of that superiority" (1967:182).

This same symbolic or legitimating function of the law may also be seen in two other instances—the Catholic Church's position regarding homosexuality and the criminalization of computer trespassing. According to some observers, the Catholic Church resists the legitimation of homosexuality not only on abstract philosophical or theological grounds, but also to "maintain its status as a "moral leader." It must fight any change in attitude toward the laws on homosexuality . . . or it will lose its 'moral' credibility" (Simpson, 1977:60–61). Even though they are unenforced, the mere existence of laws consistent with its position ensures the church of its public and official moral superiority.

Sometimes the instrumental and symbolic uses of law are sought simultaneously, as is revealed in the criminalization of unauthorized access to computer-based information. Instrumentally, these laws extend the same legal status and protection to electronic information as already exists for material goods. On the symbolic level, however, the technology of computerization posed problems for capitalist interests similar to those raised earlier in history by the development of printing, the telegraph, the telephone, radio and television, and other technologies. Specifically, each technology was perceived as a potential threat to "existing economic relations" and to "established patterns of authority and dominance." As a consequence, by means of legislation each of these technologies became "firmly lodged within the established patterns of productive relationships and social authority in a way that diffuse[d] or minimize[d] the possibility for their disruption" (Michalowski and Pfuhl, 1991:266). In each instance, then, the hegemony of prevailing interests and established power relations were given symbolic support by law.

Bureaucratic Goals

Rule creators' pursuit of both instrumental and symbolic goals is also seen in Dickson's (1968) study of bureaucratic interests. This involved the efforts of administrators of the Narcotics Division of the Internal Revenue Bureau to deal with what they perceived as threats to the organization's continued operation in the years immediately following passage of the Harrison (anti-narcotics) Act in 1914. Division administrators strove for agency growth and expansion (normal tendencies among most bureaucracies) but were hampered by an apathetic public and an unresponsive Congress. To bring about change

> the Division launched a two-pronged campaign: (1) a barrage of reports and newspaper articles which generated a substantial outcry against narcotics use, and (2) a series of Division-sponsored test cases in the courts which resulted in a reinterpretation of the Harrison Act and substantially broadened powers for the Narcotics Division. Thus the Division attained its goals by altering a weakly held public value regarding narcotics use from neutrality or slight opposition to strong opposition, and by persuading the courts that it should have increased powers. (Dickson, 1968:149)

Other commentators maintain that a similar campaign was waged by the Bureau of Narcotics in an effort to win passage of the Marihuana Tax Act in 1937 (Galliher and Walker, 1977; Becker, 1973; Reasons, 1974). In this case the Bureau is alleged to have tried to rescue itself from the organizational perils of a decreasing budget and reduced power by means of heightening public awareness of the "dangers" of marihuana use. Lastly, it has been argued that the involvement and zeal of some federal agencies in the antismoking crusade are linked with the organizational need for "survival, role definition and power" (Nuehring and Markle, 1974:522).

Holy Crusades

In their pursuit of instrumental or symbolic goals, moral entrepreneurs often are moved by a sincere and unwavering belief that their views and interests are ethically correct, and that they represent goodness and truth. Some moral entrepreneurs are so convinced of their objective rightness that their effort approximates a *holy crusade*, i.e., one supported by scriptural and/or divine command, and is in keeping with the "natural moral order." For example, John Brown, of antislavery fame, felt he had a divine mission to take vengeance against proslavery forces and effect the freedom of all enslaved blacks. In the 1970s Anita Bryant led a moral crusade against the passage of equal rights laws for homosexuals. Like Carry Nation, the noted prohibitioner, Bryant saw America standing at a moral crossroads, one road leading to a Sodom and Gomorrah, the other to a life of biblically defined moral virtue. She and her crusade were in the vanguard of those taking the latter course (*Playboy*, 1978). Similarly, an organization calling itself In God We Trust, Inc. was established in 1981 to conduct a campaign against homosexuality through the mass media. Taking their authority from scripture, spokespersons for this group referred to San Francisco as "the Sodom and Gomorrah of the United States and the armpit of this perverted [homophile] movement" (*Arizona Republic*, 1981a). Their ultimate goal was to minister to homosexuals to stop their sinning. A similar religious tone prevails among those segments of the current antiabortion movement who regard themselves as engaged in a "spiritual battle" against "satanic strongholds" (*Time*, 1992b:30).

Our earlier discussion on the nature of social reality (Chapter 1) noted that people act partly in relation to what they perceive as an external reality, even though this reality is no more than shared, socially constructed meanings. Consistent with that position, the perceived "threats" leading to moral crusades are also social constructions, humanly created elements of social reality. The significance of these threatening conditions requires no objective external validation; there need be no "spilling of blood" for people to believe their interests are in jeopardy. Viewed as elements of social reality and a reflection of people's consciousness, the concerns of moral entrepreneurs are unlimited.

MORAL CONVERSION

The moral entrepreneur's success often rests on the degree to which their concerns are shared by a significant segment of the larger community. Achieving this shared understanding may require *moral conversion*, i.e., the alteration of people's perceptual and cognitive structures. This is necessary since, in morally heterogeneous societies, it is likely that most people are unaware of what some find to be a "troubling condition" or have little or no interest in it. And, likely, most of those who are aware of the matter perceive it differently. Some may regard the matter as a passing event; these people may be said to have *optimized* the condition. Others may have *neutralized* it, i.e., they may have accommodated to it, so do not define it troubling. Others may have *normalized* the matter to the point that it is perceived as "normal though unusual."[3] In contrast, the would-be rule creator *pessimizes* the situation, i.e., regards the matter as so troublesome as to be intolerable (Rubington and Weinberg,

1981:29). As a consequence, successful moral crusades bring others' definitions into line with the pessimistic views of the moral entrepreneur
and define them as *legitimate*, i.e., meanings that are perceived to be
consistent with prevailing public morality and, therefore granted public,
legal, and authorized status.

To achieve this legitimacy, rule makers must appeal to people's sense
of propriety. When rules are approved by the public they are more likely
to be followed and violators more likely to be sanctioned. This means
people tend to follow rules they think are proper, and rule makers they
think have a right to rule, i.e., rules and rule makers they think have
legitimacy. This tendency has been referred to as the *"rule of law"* which

> expresses the idea that people recognize the legitimacy of the law as a
> means of ordering and controlling the behavior of all people in a society,
> the governors and the governed, the rich and the poor, the contented and
> the discontented (National Commission on the Causes and Prevention of
> Violence, 1970:8–9).

Achieving this legitimacy also calls for the moral crusader to transform
personal *troubles* into public *issues*.

> Troubles occur within the character of the individual and within the range
> of his immediate relations with others; they have to do with his self and
> with those limited areas of social life of which he is directly and personally
> aware. . . . A trouble is a private matter; values cherished by an individual
> are felt by him to be threatened. . . . Issues have to do with matters that
> transcend these local environments of the individual and the range of his
> inner life. They have to do with the institutions of an historical society as a
> whole, with the ways various milieus overlap and interpenetrate to form
> the larger structure of social and historical life. An issue is a public matter:
> some value cherished by publics is felt to be threatened. (Mills, 1959:8–9)

In the hands of moral crusaders such "troubles" are, at most, nascent
or "unconstructed" social problems (Best and Horiuchi, 1985:489; Best,
1990:144–148). Their transformation into "public issues" is problematic
and depends, in part, on the crusaders' success in altering people's
consciousness and winning adherents to their perspective. Let us examine the specifics of this conversion process.

Mass Media, Visibility, and Moral Conversion

Achieving moral conversion requires that the moral entrepreneur's
views be given a high degree of public visibility. Before the advent of
electronic media and other modern mass communications this was ac-

complished through poems, ballads, plays, and broadsheets. For example, poetry and song were used in the nineteenth century crusade to convert the historically esteemed, centuries old erotic custom of binding the feet of young Chinese girls into a disdainful practice and having it banned. These poems were designed to appeal to people's emotions. One, written by a natural-footed poetess, was as follows:

> Three-inch bowed shoes were non-existent in ages before,
> And Great Kuanyin has two bare feet for one to adore.
> I don't know when this custom began;
> It must have been started by a despicable man. (Levy, 1966:68)

Essays and tracts extolling the virtues of the unbound foot were widely circulated among the masses. Posters, placards, slogans, and critical catchwords were also used. Being easily recalled and repeatable, these poems and slogans became highly popular. Some examples:

> One pair of bound feet, but two cisterns of tears.

or,

> Once feet are bound so small,
> Such effort to do any work at all!

and

> Once feet to a sharp point are bound,
> The woman's cries to Heaven resound. (Levy, 1966:86)

The impact of this effort was centered largely in urban places and their immediate surroundings, places where the masses could be reached by existing means of communication.

Like their forebears, today's moral crusaders also need to get their message before mass audiences. In an effort to highlight their experience of the anguish, pain, and despondency of inner city life, urban youth who feel they are without a voice in the conventional political and criminal justice system use today's rap songs in a strikingly similar, though more aggressive, way to the Chinese natural-footed poetess. For example, Public Enemy's "Fight the Power" calls for black pride and unity against the white majority, while their "911 Is a Joke" highlights the slow response of police to inner city areas. Another from LL Cool J called "Illegal Search" chronicles police harassment. Perhaps most famous are rappers Sister Souljah and Ice-T. The latter's "Cop Killer" was accused of inciting police deaths:

COP KILLER, it's better you than me.
COP KILLER, f--- police brutality!
COP KILLER, I know your family's grievin' (F--- 'EM!)
COP KILLER but tonight we get even.

I got my brain on hype.
Tonight'll be your night.
I got this long-assed knife,
    and your neck looks just right.
My adrenaline's pumpin'.
I got my stereo bumpin'.
A pig stopped me for nuthin!

DIE, DIE, DIE, PIG, DIE!
F--- THE POLICE. (Ice-T, 1992)

Rap music containing this type of message is less directed at changing the law than at highlighting the existence of injustice. In this sense it represents a mobilization of protest designed more for channeling emotion than promoting self-help justice. However, in the context of social upheavals such as the 1992 riots in Los Angeles, it is as much reflective of the process of moral conversion (of wavering minorities) as are the attempts by organized interest groups such as CLEAT (the Combined Law Enforcement Association of Texas) who succeeded in having Ice-T voluntarily withdraw the song from his album, but not before their much publicized media pressure to ban the album resulted in a tripling of its sales!

This illustrates the further point that in their effort to get their message before today's mass audiences moral entrepreneurs are often aided by the media industry.[4] However, securing the desired media coverage can be quite problematic and rests on a number of conditions.

First, the media industry is an interest group in its own right, part of a web of mutually supportive organizational relations. In deference to their own interests and those of the groups with whom they identify, media officials authoritatively control and protect access to publicity. As a consequence, information supportive of some group's interests may be excluded because it is perceived to be incompatible with the interests of media officials and other significant interest groups. For example, until the early 1970s it was believed that the relative absence of stories on white-collar crime in the media reflected the interests of media ownership who earned a considerable portion of its revenue from corporate advertising. Further, for practical reasons associated with the management of the news business, information vital to the goals and interests of crusaders may be seen in opposite terms by newsworkers (Altheide, 1976:112ff). Effectively, then, some social realities are "promoted" at the expense of others. As a consequence, it is a virtual certainty that not all crusaders will have equal access to the media. Indeed, some interest groups (e.g., those supporting smoker's rights and the tobacco industry) may be systematically and purposely excluded and have almost no access.

Exclusion, of course, does not mean groups are without recourse. Because "news" is as important to the newsworker as it is to the news-maker (crusader) it is possible for moral entrepreneurs to use various strategies to gain access to the media. Let us turn to some of these.

Managing Media Content

In addition to effecting some quantity of media exposure, moral crusaders must also carefully manage its quality. Of particular importance is how information is presented, e.g., the sequencing of contradictory positions, the amount of coverage each is given, and the orientations of those reporting the "facts." By altering these elements, the image and the desired definition (meaning) of an issue may be affected. Further, by varying visual and auditory stimuli it is possible to increase or decrease the likelihood that an audience will perceive a situation to be consistent with or contrary to recognized standards or principles. For example,

> Among . . . ways in which the media influence legitimacy is the pointed inclusion or exclusion of certain ostensibly critical pieces of factual information. Thus, if a news article reports that a study has shown deafening noise levels in a residential area near an airport, a reporter, or an editor, may make a point of interviewing a resident who does not mind the noise. Or if the community group has asked an expert to represent them at a hearing, a delegitimizing point may be made merely by giving the information that the expert does not live in the affected area. Legitimacy may be created, in similar manner, by following up a press conference, e.g., about rising unemployment, with man-on-the-street interviews at the lines in front of a state unemployment compensation office. (Ross and Staines, 1972:22)

Legitimacy may also be generated by careful use of emotionally loaded words or images, and selectively linking a cause with (or disassociating it from) existing positive social values. This may also be accomplished by use of cartoons, especially polemical cartoons dealing with moral issues such as crime, since these are simple, short, pungent, and easily remembered like the slogans, catchwords, and posters of an earlier time (Hess and Mariner, 1975).

Douglas and Rasmussen observed such image-managing techniques

when they studied nude bathers' resistance to beachfront property owners' effort to have their behavior banned. The nude bathers' were substantially aided by television news coverage. "The nude bathers got a
great press, especially great TV coverage, partly because they carefully
controlled what was presented . . . and partly because almost all of the
newsmen and women who covered the beach were favorable to its existence before and after coverage" (Douglas and Rasmussen, 1977:199).

The politically astute nude bathers also made use of prior information
concerning the ideological predispositions of media personnel:

> Most of the feature news coverage of the nude beach can be seen in the
> major filming and airing done by one of the network affiliates. The . . . re-
> porter in charge of this programming had done a small program on Cliff
> Beach earlier, so it was known by the beach organizers that he was ba-
> sically sympathetic or, at least, libertarian about the whole thing. They [the
> nude bathers] had decided at one of their meetings that they should try to
> get some more favorable coverage on the beach and that the reporter was
> the man to approach. They got hold of him and arranged to let him have
> an exclusive on their side of the story if he'd do it. (Douglas and
> Rasmussen, 1977:200)

To further enhance their legitimacy, members of the nude bathing
group collected trash that lay on the beach and arranged it neatly in
sacks. When the sacks were filmed, the general scene of cleanliness
provided an image indicating the nude bathers' ecological awareness
and sensitivity to "nature." Though nude bathing is hardly an ecological
issue, the two interests were shown to be compatible, thereby forestall-
ing opposition from ecology groups.

Skillful manipulation of camera persons also helped avoid display of
nude males with erections, the sexual parts of voluptuous females, or
any of the casual or heavy sex (heterosexual or homosexual) that occasionally occurs on the beaches. On the other hand, film of "a lovely
young nude mother with long, flowing blonde hair, bending over her
toddler in the shallow water, with the sun a little behind her to produce
a sparkling halo effect on film . . . and . . . no pubis shot to get it
banned by the censor" (Douglas and Rasmussen, 1977:201) greatly enhanced the image desired by nude bathers; no direct link was made between nude bathing and (negatively defined) orgiastic sex. Instead, nudity
and (positively defined) motherhood were shown to be compatible.

In addition to aligning their own aims with positive values, moral
entrepreneurs try to denigrate the opposition by linking it with negative
values. Success ensures at least a *relative* increase in one's own moral
legitimacy. So, for example, binding Chinese girls' feet was defined as
contrary to laws of nature, and a symbol of the oppression and punish-

ment undeservedly heaped on women. It was proclaimed to be an evil crippler of women, a condition that intensified the misery of the poor, raised the infanticide rate, made women dependent, and reduced their intellectual activities and their effectiveness as mothers and homemakers (Levy, 1966:77–78). It was also defined as a barrier to China's entry into the mainstream of world commerce and the modern age. As that economic goal increased in favor, footbinding, symbolic of cultural stagnation, lost favor (Levy, 1966:76–77). In short, association of the moral entrepreneur's position with publicly attractive values—motherhood, economic growth, national prestige, and opposition to infanticide and poverty—proved critical in the effort to win support and preclude effective opposition.

In the case of nude bathers vs. beachfront property owners, efforts were made to have the owners defined as selfish, i.e., wanting to control public beaches for their private use. Among people living in densely populated urban areas, such an image can have a negative effect, as it did in this case. So, too, did the image of property owners as reactionaries seeking to repress the enthusiasm and freedom of youth. Skillful use of these themes, together with upstaging the property owners by presenting the nude bathers' views earlier and more extensively, so damaged the position of the property owners that they abandoned their own efforts to use the media, choosing instead to work privately through local governmental functionaries and the courts (Douglas and Rasmussen, 1977:204–205).

As a final word, we must caution against overstating the role of the mass media in this process. Realistically, the media do not convert "puritans" into "hedonists" or vice versa; audiences are not transformed in any substantial ideological way. Nor does the media by itself construct social reality. Nonetheless, the way information is presented and manipulated may give credibility to one set of meanings at the expense of alternatives. As Shaw (1969:126) notes, in a heterogeneous society public expressions of morality reflect a range of attitudes that have a modality. By careful engineering, media officials may structure and present an issue so as to locate it within or beyond the limits of that modality. The media "molds public events" (Altheide, 1976:27). Molding the event (rather than the audience) means that conditions are assigned a definition/meaning consistent with or contrary to the moral entrepreneur's sense of prevailing public morality (we will explore this matter in detail in the next section). Similarly, while selectively presenting "facts," the media may support or discredit perspectives, ideologies and behaviors. Further, the simple act of withholding contrary perspectives or information may affect the legitimacy or credibility of publicized meanings. This is important because "not only is a symbolic environment created within the society, but personal actions take their referent from that environment. Indeed, the construction of a conceptual reality is also the creation of a social reality of actions and events" (Quinney, 1975:262). Taken together, these matters are all part of what makes deviance an "enterprise."

FOLKLORE: MYTHS, LEGENDS, AND TRUTH

Public acceptance of the crusader's view also rests on its being seen as consistent with the values, interests, and fears of the population. The crusader's message must harmonize with the dominant, publicly legitimate social reality and the consciousness of the audience. One way to effect this link is to create a moral panic that relies on the use of myths and legends, i.e., folklore.

As used here, the concepts of *myth* and *legend* refer to the usually apocryphal, but believable tales, stories, and accounts that help people make sense of (i.e., explain, interpret, justify) the stuff of everyday life (Kasen, 1980:132). Myths offer explanations for the problematic events that concern moral entrepreneurs. They also deal with "evildoers" whom they portray as opposed to the legitimate values embraced by the community, and as persons who intentionally or otherwise undermine the vitality of fundamental moral precepts and institutions. Sometimes such persons are portrayed as demonic (Best and Horiuchi, 1985; Best, 1990). As urban legends, this lore often appears as "tales" that help people make sense of aspects of everyday life (Fine, 1980). Seen in this way, myths and legends are *objectivations*, part of what we earlier (Chapter 1) referred to as the *symbolic universe* (Berger and Luckmann, 1967:92–104).

Moral Panics

Perhaps the most celebrated way of using myth and legend in the process of banning behavior is through what Stanley Cohen calls the creation of "moral panics" (Cohen, 1980). Here a feeling is promoted among the population that a particular problem exists in society because of a specific group of people who are heralded as "folk devils," or who are "deviantized" (Schur, 1980). As Goode (1989:26) says, "public concern and moral panic surrounding a given condition are only remotely related to the objective consequences or harm of that issue or condition" and he points out that "extremely damaging conditions or issues often generate little public concern or panic." He argues that the criminalization of cocaine possession and sale in 46 states and by the Harrison Act of 1914 was spurred by the fear that blacks were especially heavy cocaine users and became uncontrollable under the drug's influence (Goode, 1989:28). Similarly, he says that one of the most powerful factors in the passage of antimarihuana legislation in the 1930s, especially in the western states, was "hostility and fear toward Mexican immigrants": "Mexican-Americans were thought to be major consumers of the drug and, it was suspected, acted in a dangerous fashion under its influence" (Goode, 1989:29). Indeed, this process of constructing a demonized image in order to gain popular support for moral legislation has been common in the history of criminalizing drug use and is captured in the myth of the dope fiend.

The "Dope Fiend" Mythology

Folklore has been used in the effort to criminalize the nonmedical use of addictive drugs. Termed the "dope fiend" mythology (Lindesmith, 1940), this lore portrays drug users as defective, totally discreditable persons through labels such as "dope crazed killer," "dope fiend rapist," "moral degenerate," "thief," and "liar" (Brunvand, 1984:162–169). Lore also suggests addicts have a "positive mania" to convert others to drug addiction and proclaims the insidiousness of drugs, i.e., even using mild drugs allegedly results in an inevitable progression to the use of stronger drugs and that over time there is a need to gradually enlarge the dose. Finally, drug use is hailed as a certain path to moral degeneracy, debauchery, and the like. This supposedly irreversible process has been referred to as "the path to demoralization and despair" (Horton and Leslie, 1965:565; also see Inciardi, 1974).

Many of these themes, supplemented by visual imagery, appeared in motion pictures of the 1930s and 1940s such as "Tell Your Children" (also known as "Reefer Madness"), "Marihuana," and "Assassin of Youth." In "Tell Your Children," sweethearts Bill and Mary, a "model young couple" symbolizing youthful innocence, are victimized by two unscrupulous drug peddlers and the evil effects of marihuana. Under the drug's effects, the unsuspecting Bill becomes a "moral weakling" and is seduced by the "evil addict," Blanche. Mary and her younger brother Jimmy are also caught up in the debauchery; Mary is accidentally shot and killed. As befits peddlers of the "insidious weed," one is killed and the other is judged insane. Blanche commits suicide while the once innocent Bill survives, but his life is wrecked. Thus it is graphically demonstrated that marihuana destroys the life of all who have contact with it; debauchery, crime, murder, and suicide await the unsuspecting (*Look*, 1938).[5]

During the period in which these films were circulating, the Federal Bureau of Narcotics emphasized these same values and themes in its campaign to secure passage of the Marihuana Tax Act of 1937.

> In its publicity campaign, the bureau could appeal to a number of tradi-tional societal values . . . it could emphasize humanitarian values as well as those stressing the importance of self control, by portraying the bu-reau's efforts as preventing persons from becoming "enslaved" to drugs and protecting them from their own weakness. It could further appeal to the values of the "Protestant ethic," which disdains "ecstasy" and pleasure when deliberately sought as ends in themselves rather than as by-products of achievement and work. (Hills, 1971:70)

Given such values and the stereotypical portrait of drug users and the consequences of addiction, it is hardly surprising that the Marihuana Tax Act was passed in Congress with little opposition and almost no debate (Hills, 1971:70).

Similar tactics have been employed in other areas. Let us consider the example of white slavery.

White Slavery

The term white slave or white slavery derives from passage of the Mann Act (also known as the White Slave Act) by Congress in 1910 to halt the interstate and foreign transportation of women for purposes of prostitution. The Act itself was passed after a period of marked public concern over the immorality of prostitution, the development of a highly negative stereotype of prostitution and the prostitute, and a crusade to eradicate both. The myth of white slavery evolved out of the literature generated by this effort (Reasons, 1970:5).

In the myth of white slavery, prostitution is defined as the conse-quence of the efforts of foreigners (in lore, no native American would do such things) who were "merchants of flesh" (white slavers) allegedly recruiting "innocent, unsophisticated girls of foreign extraction, often underage, by false pretense, drugs and coercion" (Reasons, 1970:5; Feld-man, 1967). In this myth prostitutes, white slavers, and prostitution are cast in opposition to such values as premarital chastity, the purity of womanhood, and the sanctity of home and hearth. Viewed from the perspective of the public morality dominant during the late 1890s and early 1900s (a period in U.S. history noted for efforts to expunge "evil" and achieve secular salvation), persons believed to systematically threat-en these values, especially for profit, could expect only the most severe condemnation.

This lore, generated and spread by countless muckrakers and other moralists who published antiprostitution books and tracts, rested on weak evidence, at best. During the time of the myth's popularity,

> there [was] only the most fragmentary evidence . . . that any considerable number of girls [had] been forced into prostitution against their wills. A small number of instances of something like white slavery have been recorded; but, on the whole, force and deceit . . . probably never have been important in obtaining a supply of prostitutes. Men and women engaged in so-called "white-slave" traffic are rarely organized, and gangs of panderers and clearinghouses for prostitutes have been uncovered very infrequently. The average case concerns one man and one woman or two men and two women. (Lemert, 1951:255)

Despite a lack of validation, the myth of white slavery played an important part in linking new and old moralities and incorporating the aims of moral reformers into public policy. It was, then, a vital element in the crusade to eliminate prostitution.

Folklore vs. Truth

The content of these and other legends has often led objectivist-oriented social scientists and others to focus on the validity of this ideological stuff and investigate whether it is "true" that people become fanatically out of control after becoming addicted to drugs or that women are drawn into prostitution by deception. From a social constructionist perspective, however, such efforts serve to obscure the point that legends and myths do not rely on objective truth for their utility. Thus, the importance of the dope fiend example is not that media construct pure myths about drug use but that *they capture and exaggerate a part of the social reality of the drug experience*. The importance of the stereotype is that it is shared both by the deviants and by the public as one among many social categories. For example, Mieczkowski's (1992) recent research on crack cocaine dealing shows that most buyers were controlled users who preferred to make their drug purchases in the relative stability of the crack house, rather than relying on street purchases. One reason for this was that the controlled users

> stigmatized street transactions as being associated with 'fiending': acute, high-rate, compulsive crack use. Buying from the street was defined as a sign that the user was growing imprudent and wasteful. In effect, 'only a fool or a fiend' would buy from a street vendor. (Mieczkowski, 1992:157)

The myth of the dope fiend is that it is extended to include all drug users, or is claimed to be the ultimate destination of all who try drugs. However, the distortion need not only exaggerate the negative to create fear. For example, in the 1986 media portrayal of the "cocaine epidemic" news articles written about cocaine-related deaths portrayed images of healthy, well-integrated people who died from their recreational drug use. Research by Wong and Alexander (1991), however, showed that these same people were long-time drug users who died from "accumu-lated ill-health." The media here were generating a moral panic through showing how anyone could be a victim to produce support for a ban on the drug. In turn, this fed into Democratic and Republican congressional member's desire to instigate the "War on Drugs" as a safe and moral issue for the 1988 election campaign (Jensen et al., 1991). The point here, however, is not that there is a "real" truth. To regard such myths, lore, or panics as "invalid" or a "distortion of reality" merely pits one social reality against another in a battle over truth claims. Doing this ignores what is the real basis for rule making: the meaning of the rules for the rule creators and their ability to engender support for their creative enterprise. Without an understanding of the meaning of banning to the observers we cannot appreciate whether their rules are necessary, useful or even harmful in themselves. Thus, rather than evaluate the validity of competing realities, it is incumbent on students of society to take an *appreciational* view, one sensitive to the experiences and values of those involved in the situation, the moral crusader as well as others. This calls for a faithful rendering of the phenomenon, i.e., for the student of society "to comprehend and to illuminate the subject's view and to interpret the world as it appears to him [or her]" (Matza, 1969:25).

An appreciational perspective helps us to see that notions of "validi-ty" and "distortion" have little to do with the social utility of lore. It is helpful to recall that the aim of the deviance process is to incriminate, to discredit, to control, and to stigmatize, perhaps for symbolic reasons or perhaps to legitimize "treatment" of the alleged deviant. Accordingly, efforts to validate the characterization of the deviant actor and his or her behavior seem irrelevant. If any justification for the incrimination of persons is needed it is derived from the perceived immorality of their behavior, the same immorality that leads actors to be defined as deviant (Matza, 1969:157). In turn, that characterization serves to justify existing (read: appropriate) treatment of rule breakers. In other words, such lore serves to justify the crusader's position by linking it with (1) existing values, (2) the prevailing distribution of authority, and (3) the presumed moral superiority of the crusader and the audience. In this regard, lore serves the same symbolic purpose that is served by rules in general.

The symbolic use of lore is found in the media where images are arranged and presented to conform to an "acceptable" world view and an existing set of meanings (social reality). For example, decades ago Berelson and Salter (1946) noted the consistent way in which heroes and villains were characterized in fiction. Almost invariably, white, Anglo-Saxon, Protestant types were cast as heroes, while villains, fools, and other denigrative roles were played by minority group persons and foreigners. Such imagery corresponded to a world view in which virtue was regarded as the exclusive property of the politically dominant group, while all others were defined as subordinate (morally and otherwise); humankind is neatly divided into "good guys" and "bad guys."[6] Such stereotypical images and simplistic categorization help support the claim that "what is, is right" and/or to support the claims of moral entrepreneurs. To the degree that lore is accepted as valid (taken-for-granted) and acted on, our public life is shaped by them. Myths may therefore be self-validating. They serve to legitimate the institutional activities called for by the moral entrepreneur. They are another important part of the symbolic universe.

Finally, it should be noted that these images and meanings are not born full-blown but are emergent. They evolve as they are spread (Best and Horiuchi, 1985:492). They are the consequence of the accumulation of countless unconnected utterances, definitions, and meanings, each of which is originally private and subjective and some of which may have involved purposive misrepresentations and distortions (Inciardi, 1978:14). Rather than being consciously contrived, however, the larger myths and legends are constructed of specific meanings reflecting the perceptions and interpretations of people who are strategically located (such as those having access to the media) and thereby able to influence "official" reality. This accumulation results in a kind of "semantic amalgamation" whereby situations, occurrences, and utterances that bear reasonable similarity are lumped together.[7] By stages, people create subuniverses of meaning (Berger and Luckmann, 1967:85ff). As elements within these subuniverses of meaning, myths and legends assume an autonomous character. That is, the "knowledge" involved—that whoring is never voluntary, that addiction to drugs precludes legitimate role play, or that the Mafia survives on the basis of a code of silence called "omerta" (Bell, 1962:138–141; Anderson 1968:269ff)—becomes separated from the social context from which it develops. This knowledge takes on a "life of its own" and often is regarded as an accurate reflection of "what's out there." It is reified. As noted in Chapter 1, the meanings and definitions we construct tend to move from a subjective to an objective status. Myths and legends reflect this tendency. Above all, they help people make sense of and deal with what they regard as social tension and strain in everyday life.

ALLIANCES, TESTIMONIALS, AND ENDORSEMENTS

In pursuing their aims, moral crusaders must be concerned with how they are perceived by their audience. The desired image is one of respectability for themselves and legitimacy for their goals. Attention to this matter serves to (1) reduce the likelihood that questions will arise concerning the crusader's legitimacy while (2) promoting the moral stature of the proposed goal. Overall, respectability promotes moral conversion. In this section we will focus on how these images are established.

Alliances

Based on the idea that "good generates good," one method of achieving prestige and respectability is for crusaders to "borrow" it from publicly acknowledged moral leaders by establishing alliances or other affiliations. Establishing respectability by listing notables' names on the letterhead stationery used by special interest groups, or listing the names of supporters in newspaper ads favoring one or another sociopolitical position. Images may be created by groups establishing coalitions such as the Religious Coalition for Abortion Rights (RCAR), representing 35 Protestant and Jewish religious bodies. Established in 1976, the RCAR is a response to the antiabortion rights campaign of the National Conference of Catholic Bishops. The RCAR views the abortion controversy as fueled by religious beliefs, whereas the right of abortion is a matter of privacy and personal freedom guaranteed by the U.S. Constitution. Operating as a unit, these 35 groups, with support from their respective memberships, achieve a level of respectability and influence on lawmaking bodies unavailable to them as single entities, and that collectively may aid in countering the influence and authoritative position of the National Conference of Catholic Bishops (*Unitarian Universalist World*, 1976:1–2).

Similarly, the antifootbinding crusade in nineteenth-century China was substantially aided by the authority and respectability of Christian missionaries who sternly discouraged the practice among their followers, even to the point of accepting only persons with unbound feet as members of the church (Levy, 1966:75). The establishment of sex psychopath laws was promoted by the support that movement derived from psychiatrists and their acknowledged expertise on the subject (Sutherland, 1950:142ff). The benefits of affiliation may also be seen in the case of the antismoking crusade where the very existence of some groups (e.g., Action on Smoking and Health) is alleged to be dependent on the antismoking activity of several other groups, including the American Cancer Society, the American Heart Association, and insurance companies, all of whom maintain respectable and legitimate images (Nuehring and Markle, 1974:522). Each of these cases reminds us that creating deviance (like constructing reality in general) is an interactional process, the behavior of the principals being influenced to a large extent by their self-interest.

Testimonials and Endorsements

Moral entrepreneurs also try to elevate their own and their cause's image by obtaining testimonial support and endorsements from politically and socially influential persons and groups. This image management effort often proves effective because many people define endorsements by officials and other notables as prima facie evidence of the acceptability of the cause. Because officials are regarded as defenders of their constituent's views, and because other "influentials" are assumed to be aware of and sensitive to the limits of public morality, their endorsements often go largely unchallenged. In turn, attributing legitimacy to competing perspectives is precluded and the goal of moral conversion is promoted.

Endorsement by officials can also promote dissemination of the crusader's perspective via the media and, simultaneously, to limit the opposition's access to it. According to William Wilde's analysis of news organizations, "News is what officials say and do. The more sensational the more newsworthy. Even . . . outrageous charges go unanalyzed. Unsubstantiated statements go unquestioned. They are given the status of news as the media prints them without further comment or analysis" (Wilde, 1969:186). Preempting the opposition is achieved by public officials controlling and engineering the flow of information to the media and by making their comments appear to be official pronouncements. Thereby they overwhelm and delegitimize alternative perspectives. News is what officials say and do, regardless of the lack of essential meaning of those words and actions. Accordingly, public figures are among the "officially accredited definers of reality" (Berger and Luckmann, 1967:97).

Officials' ability to influence the content and the interpretation of information carried by the media, and to use the media to their advantage rests on several conditions. First, officials are able to control the flow of information and direct it to journalists who will likely provide "favorable" coverage. Second, simply being officials enables them to preempt and, thereby, overwhelm opposing points of view. Third, officials may use media to their advantage by controlling forums such as press conferences where criticism of their actions and policy may be raised. Careful selection of questioners and refusing follow-up questions are simple expedients. Fourth, the media may be controlled by its own willingness to be uncritical, to play the role of "cheer leader" rather than that of inquiring critic. This may also be promoted by the media's occasional tendency to engage in *advocacy journalism* wherein the roles of "critical questioner" and "investigative journalist" are exchanged for that of "advocate." As a result, the media tends to boost "good causes" without a comparable tendency to attack "bad causes" (Ross and Staines, 1972:23–24). By definition, it seems, this tactic promotes the conclusion that whatever is presented as a cause by the media is "good."

In some instances moral entrepreneurs have less need of outside endorsement, as when the crusader already has a credible and legitimate public image that can be used to heighten the visibility of their effort. This appears to have been the case when Anita Bryant launched her campaign against Florida laws forbidding discrimination against homosexuals in jobs and housing. Bryant's public image, a result of her roles as a former Miss Oklahoma, a Miss America contestant, a nationally known TV personality promoting Florida orange juice, and her status as a "born again Christian," undoubtedly gave added impetus to her effort and likely increased her ability to amplify a local issue and attract national media attention (Hacker, 1977; *National Observer*, 1977).

Transfer of Authority

Finally, the support of respected and prestigious figures may enhance the image of the moral entrepreneur's goals by reason of *transfer of authority* (Lowry and Rankin, 1969:254). Ideas and proposals are more likely to be awarded legitimacy when their authors are (or are associated with) admired or respected groups such as esteemed professionals, public figures, and the like. Social psychological experiments reveal that attitude change (which may be required if banning is to be achieved) is likely to increase if the communicator of a new idea is identified as a member of a prestigious group; as a consequence, the entire membership of that prestigious group may be perceived to be in support of the idea (Secord and Backman, 1964:128). Studies also reveal that even when the substance of two proposals are the same, negatively labeled proposals have less chance of acceptance than those to which prestigious labels are attached (Newcomb, 1950:235–239).

POWER

Earlier we noted that moral entrepreneurs seek to have their values and interests declared official and represented in laws that apply to the population at large. However, this does not occur unless one has the power to directly or indirectly influence the rule-making process. Consequently, an analysis of banning requires consideration of the role of power and the authority of the state in the rule-making enterprise.[8]

Attempts to control others' behavior are widespread in any society (Roberts, 1979). In terms of everyday life, this is principally limited to informal techniques such as gossip, ridicule, ostracism, and various corporal punishments. These techniques have proven highly effective under specific circumstances such as those of a small, homogeneous community, neighborhood, or family setting where primary group relationships prevail. This is because of the multistranded relationships between members of small groups, which mean that numerous contexts and occasions exist through which informal social controls can be exercised. However, in a pluralistic, highly impersonal urban society, where people's contacts are limited in time and lack social psychological depth, these informal techniques are less effective. To be effective, moral crusaders believe that a more formalized control is required, which involves having recourse to the state, where the "signification of deviance becomes a specialized and protected function . . . . The main substance of that state function is the authorized ordaining of activities and persons as deviant and thus making them suitable objects of surveillance and control" (Matza, 1969:145). Access to this state apparatus may be achieved (1) by direct exercise of power by the moral entrepreneur, or (2) by influencing those who do have power to act in accord with the crusader's goals. Power, then, requires careful attention.

Power, Law, and Deviance

The transformation of values and interests into public law, and its enforcement and administration, is the responsibility of public officials including police, prosecuting attorneys, court judges, and legislators, along with various standing and ad hoc administrative agencies of government, e.g., the Environmental Protection Agency, Department of Health and Human Services, Federal Communications Commission, the Securities Exchange Commission, and the Federal Aeronautics Administration, to name a few. These agencies create deviance when they make rules proscribing select forms of behavior or conditions, when they decide how zealously rules will be enforced, and when they decide to whom the rules will apply. Variation in these activities—the formulation, enforcement, and administration of law—has led to law being defined as "an instrument for furthering the interests of certain groups within society" (Shaskolsky, 1973:295). That is, law is an expression of the values and interests of groups able to influence peoples' actions. In a politically dynamic, pluralistic society, the special interest groups that "win the day" in the political arena are those with the greater power. Accordingly, successful banning efforts result from the interaction between legal functionaries and the representatives of interests, with power being the critical variable (Piven, 1981:501).

Based on these considerations, Richard Quinney (1969) formulated an "interest theory of law" consisting of four propositions. First, Quinney defines law as the "creation and interpretation of specialized rules in a politically organized society [the state]" (1969:26). In this sense, *law is a process* involving interest groups competing with one another for public and official favor. Thus,

> law is one of the methods in which public policy is formulated and administered for governing the lives and activities of the inhabitants of the state. As an act of politics, law does not represent the norms and values of all persons in the society. Legal decisions, rather, incorporate the interests of only some persons. Whenever a law is created or interpreted, the values of some are necessarily assured and the values of others are either ignored or negated. (Quinney, 1969:27)

Once created, law provides at least the rough boundaries of legitimate group interaction. This is the politicality of law.

Second, Quinney, notes that "politically organized society is based on an interest structure" (1969:27), i.e., the state (a politically organized society) is influenced by the interests of select groups, viz., those who are equipped to command. This leads to his third proposition: "the interest structure of politically organized society is characterized by unequal distribution of power and by conflict" (Quinney, 1969:28). This means that segments of society have unequal amounts of power or unequal access to power, and are not equally able to have their interests incorporated into public policy. Since interest groups have differing amounts of power and conflict with one another, power and conflict become critical factors in the politics of deviance. It is out of the interplay of such differently situated and equipped groups that public policy emerges.

Quinney's fourth proposition is that "law is formulated and administered within the interest structure of a politically organized society" (1969:29). This follows from the fact that it is the groups with the greatest power that influence policy makers. We thus come full circle: law is a way of doing something—it is a way of controlling segments of the society who threaten dominant interest groups. In response to the question "Which groups have the ability to create deviance?" one answer is "Those with the clout!"

The idea that law is a means of control deserves further comment. As used here, "control" is not limited to the direct influence of some groups by others, for example, by means of coercive force or the exercise of violence. "Law as control" also includes the legitimizing capacity of established law. As part of its symbolic consequence, once law is created it serves to shape people's consciousness, i.e., how people define things. "Those definitions of the real, the true, and the worthy given legal expression or approval are thereby given the support of what is not only one of the most prestigious cultural structures, but also that structure most directly supported by the apparatus of political control" (Turk, 1976:281). In short, by having power, groups are better able to use the "dignity of law" to legitimize their interests at the expense of others.

Defining Power

Given these considerations, how may we define power? Basically, *power* is "the production of intended effects by some men on other men" (Wrong, 1968:676). Transcending "force," "prestige," "influence," etc., power refers to a variety of means people use to control the behavior of others. However, the ability of one segment of society to control others is variable and ever changing. Power does not rest exclusively in the hands of some and not at all in others; power is bilateral or multilateral and power relations are asymmetrical (Wrong, 1968:673, 1979:Chap. 1). This means that those who wield power in one situated activity or at one time period (the power holders) may be quite subordinate in others (be power subjects). In short, the model employed here is one of *intercursive power*, in which "the power of each party in a relationship is countervailed by that of the other, with procedures for bargaining or joint decision making governing their relations when matters affecting the goals and interests of both are involved" (Wrong, 1968:674). Let us now examine an instance of protracted group interaction in which intercursive power relations loomed large.

Pornography and Politics: A Case in Point

In the 1970s and 1980s a number of interest groups focusing on the issue of pornography emerged in the city of Minneapolis. The interaction of these groups reflects the bilateral/multilateral and asymmetric distribution of power (Downs, 1989: Chapter 3). In Minneapolis the real source of political power is said to be more a result of a shifting series of coalitions and personal ties than a matter of political party affiliation. As antipornography politics evolved in that city four coalitions emerged: neighborhood groups, conservatives, feminists, and civil libertarians.

Beginning in the 1970s, a conservatively based effort was made to "crack down" on the sale of pornographic material in Minneapolis. This effort rested largely on moralistic opposition to such material and was largely symbolic in that it was more concerned with securing a politicolegal endorsement of the antipornography position than with the actual removal of such stuff. As a result, vice raids were staged only to have the pornography ordinance declared "vague," obscenity cases thrown out of court, and prosecutions suspended. While this did not necessarily disturb civil libertarian groups such as the Minnesota Civil Liberties Union (MCLU), it did distress neighborhood groups and feminists who were seeking more instrumental goals.

In the view of neighborhood groups (e.g., the Neighborhood Pornography Task Force), pornography shops and the activity in proximity to them was a principal contributor to a decline in property values, a rise in criminality, and a general downgrading of the quality of life in their area. In their view, porn shops were a "blight." In opposing them, neighborhood groups initially worked by picketing and demonstrating outside such places, and photographing patrons leaving the shops. However, they never took any moral or political position specifically related to the content of such material. If anything, their initial focus was on the "quality of the environment."

Soon the neighborhood interest group (actually, a coalition of several formal neighborhood associations) split into two camps, one favoring the environmental approach and the other stressing the idea that pornography degrades women (a "content" issue). However, given its greater influence at that time (1977), the environmental faction succeeded in getting an ordinance passed to eliminate porn shops from their neighborhoods by means of zoning. Supporters were soon frustrated, however, as the federal district court declared the ordinance unconstitutional.

One year later a new focus developed in the crusade; it took a feminist tack. Rather than define porn as an "environmental blight" or simply "morally repugnant," the feminists suggested it be defined as an expression of "violence against women." Within a short time, and with expert guidance from staunchly pro-feminist University of Minnesota Law School professors, an ordinance was fashioned that (1) identified pornography as a form of discrimination on the basis of sex, and (2) called for its control on the grounds that it violates women's civil rights. Proponents argued that zoning, while restricting the places porn could be sold, still *permitted porn to exist*. In contrast, they wanted it to be *eradicated*, a goal that required the stuff be redefined. Hence, they pursued a civil rights approach that, to them, promised to make its eradication possible via censorship. Not the least of the effects of this changed approach was that it established a coalition between feminists and conservatives (who earlier had pushed for censorship on symbolic grounds), as well as some former "environmentalists" who saw the feminist approach as promising. However, it also generated opposition from the city's Civil Rights Office, the Library Board, the City Attorney's office, and the MCLU. Despite this opposition, the City Council passed the feminist-oriented ordinance by a slim 7–6 vote.

That ordinance was immediately vetoed by the Mayor who claimed it was too vague and too broad, and that it needed to be more sensitive to First Amendment rights regarding freedom of speech. Efforts in the City Council to override the veto failed. To avoid its complete nullification, however, the Mayor created a Task Force to study the matter; the Task Force membership included persons representing a variety of perspectives on the issue. After repeated meetings, the Task Force issued a report identifying the harms of pornography as (1) "location-related" and (2) "content-related." Thereby, the Task Force was seeking consensus between the environmental, the feminist, and the conservative interests.

To that end the Task Force recommended a much revised ordinance to the one passed and vetoed earlier. Finding that unsatisfactory, the feminist faction submitted a revised ordinance that retained some of the provisions of the original, but altered some of its wording in deference to the political reality of the situation. That is, they had to acknowledge the power other factions could wield. Despite protest from the Civil Rights Commission and the Task Force recommendations, this revised ordinance was ultimately passed, again with a 7–6 vote. As before, it was immediately vetoed by the Mayor and an effort to override failed. However, all was not lost for the antipornography forces. "When it enacted the amended ordinance, the council also passed a resolution declaring that it would reenact the vetoed ordinance if the federal courts upheld the Indianapolis version [of a feminist oriented antipornography statute] which was then pending" (Downs, 1989:65). This resolution was not vetoed by the Mayor.

Regardless of the ultimate statutory outcome, examination of the Minneapolis experience suggests that power is, indeed, multilateral and asymmetrical. Thus, no one interest group was able to dictate terms to all others. The dynamism of "deviance as politics" is reflected in the shifting definitions of the pornography issue (content vs. location) as well as the impact those changes had on the formation of coalitions. Accordingly, several discrete interest groups joined forces and exercised variable influence on the rule-making process. That variable influence is consistent with the power model we have adopted, viz., one in which groups exert limited rather than comprehensive influence. The impact of any single interest was negotiated via an ongoing series of interactions. Taken together, these several features are consistent with an intercursive power model.

In summary, then, in terms of "deviance as politics," power is a vital element in a struggle (conflict) between interest groups. It is a struggle that involves simultaneous movements to impose restraints, on the one hand, and to limit, resist, or escape them, on the other. Further, the Minneapolis experience also indicates that shifts in the distribution of power may result from people's changing understandings and the consequent shifts in interest group alliances. But these remarks prompt additional questions concerning how power is wielded and the tactics employed in the politics of deviance. As a final item, let us turn to these issues.

The Tactics of Exercising Power

Among the factors that give moral entrepreneurs the "power edge" over their opposition is the public moral legitimacy of their aims. Given this legitimacy, many people are reluctant to publicly oppose them; to do so could result in their being discredited. As every politician knows, it pays to stand foursquare for "motherhood and apple pie," more recently expressed as the case for "family values." The reverse of this principle is that public figures do not ordinarily take a stand in support of morally questionable behaviors—even when they are convinced of the "victimless" nature of these behaviors and the pointlessness of legal proscription. And public figures are prone to lend at least minimal support to most efforts to eradicate publicly discreditable behaviors.

Reflecting this "power edge" is the case of a city council member's effort to bring about more vigorous enforcement of antiprostitution ordinances in a small city in Washington state. Publicly the council member had received little support, largely, one suspects, because the buildings housing the brothels were owned by and provided significant income for their influential owners. Privately, she was criticized for stirring up an issue that had lain dormant for years and about which the public seemed unconcerned. Frustrated beyond endurance, the council member finally confronted her foot dragging colleagues telling them she was establishing a committee to legalize prostitution and that she intended to nominate them for membership. Needless to say, their private criticism diminished and public support for the original proposal increased. Similarly, members of the "smut detail" of a southwestern city's police department publicly invited all state legislators to spend one full day viewing pornographic movies and magazines. Said one officer, "Without the legislators having firsthand knowledge of the type of filth being peddled in our communities, it is difficult to convince many of them of the need for stronger laws and penalties in this area" (*Arizona Republic*, 1976). Though the legislators declined the invitation, this was wise strategy by police. Given the public moral definition of so-called "hard-core" porn and the publicity accompanying their exposure to it, most legislators would then have been pressured to support restrictive legislation. As in these examples, the goals of moral crusaders are presented so as to appear consistent with the *public* morality to which all "right minded" people are expected to subscribe. As a consequence, support is promoted while public opposition is forestalled.

Some moral entrepreneurs may enjoy a "power edge" as a result of the public esteem and superior socioeconomic position enjoyed by many of them and their supporters. For example, historically a number of humanitarian reform movements were conducted by middle and upper-class persons ostensibly for the benefit of the defenseless or the poorer classes as well as society at large. Such instances include the temperance movement (Gusfield, 1955), the House of Refuge Movement (Pfohl, 1977), and abolition (Becker, 1973:148). Supplementing their humanitarian appeal is the support such movements sometimes receive from respectables who are recruited to lend their name to the crusade. For example, Handgun Control, Inc. attracted many prominent people who endorsed its efforts to impose restrictions on the purchase of hand guns. Included were notables such as Steve Allen, Hal Holbrook, Ann Landers, Margaret Mead, Neil Simon, Will Rogers, Jr., Rod Steiger, and Peter Lawford (Gottleib, 1986). This often results in a "halo effect" and heightened idealization of the proposal. The use of testimonials, mentioned earlier, is often necessary to offset the disadvantage of having one's position endorsed only by obscure or unknown persons. In circular fashion, then, the moral appeal of the crusader's perspective promotes its support by significant public figures, and support of significant public figures contributes to its appeal.

Moral entrepreneurial groups may also secure a power advantage by organizing and operating as pressure groups that may impact directly on public policy formation (Turner, 1958). These entities have been found to use a wide variety of means to maximize their aims and minimize the costs. One means used is securing endorsement from persons across the political spectrum in order to place the issue outside the bounds of partisan controversy. This may be promoted by expanding the group's membership in order to increase the political breadth (and strength) of its support base. Expansion also increases the probability of members engaging in direct political activity: letter writing, soliciting funds (to pay for costly advertising or an expensive media blitz), putting direct pressure on public figures, seeking to influence the media, phone campaigns, and so on. For example, the National Rifle Association (NRA) has a separate lobbying branch called The Institute for Legislative Action, which produces press releases, publishes articles and pamphlets, and writes TV scripts on the dangers of gun control. It even tracks the voting record of politicians. However, it relies on a grass roots, one-to-one approach to mobilize its NRA membership to lobby legislators. If a bill needs support or opposition the NRA sends out a "Legislative Alert" in the form of a mailgram to each member who is then requested to send personal letters to legislators because these have more impact than stylized preprinted ones. Such groups find it easier to enlist members in these labor-intensive activities if the legitimacy and integrity of the group's leadership and goals have been secured and especially if the membership, as in the NRA, are largely single issue voters (Gergen and Gest, 1989).

Another tactic used by interest groups to effect power involves establishing *coalitions*, i.e., formal or informal, cooperative relations with other groups for limited periods of time and for the pursuit of limited goals. By means of coalition, obscure and/or politically ineffective groups may become more massive and better able to exert influence. To the degree that they do not compromise the discrete interests of the groups involved, these affiliations may be mutually beneficial either in securing desired goals or frustrating others.

Examples of the establishment of coalitions among interest groups seeking change in the "moral climate" are abundant. For example, the "gun lobby" includes not only the NRA but the Second Amendment Foundation, The Citizens Committee for the Right to Keep and Bear Arms, the Gun Owners of America Political Action Committee, as well as numerous local gun clubs and survivalist groups. Among black civil rights groups coalitions have been established between militants and moderates, as well as between representatives of religious, labor, and libertarian groups (Bennett, 1965:162). Another example is the National Coalition Against Censorship, consisting of 42 formal organizations representing a variety of interests, but all seeking to frustrate government efforts to impose limits on pornography via censorship. Lastly, we may note a coalition of 25 Protestant denominations and over 250 Roman Catholic orders, called the Interfaith Center on Corporate Responsibility, that would "use church stockholdings to pressure utility companies to stop funding a $20 million nuclear energy industry advertising campaign" (*Arizona Republic*, 1984). Not all lobbying groups form coalitions, however, and the relative lack of success of some, such as gun control groups, has been attributed to their various intergroup conflicts, lack of agreement on common goals or issues, and duplication of efforts.

In addition, well-financed interest groups often hire the services of highly trained professional lobbyists, some of whom are former officials serving on the staff of the same government agencies to which moral entrepreneurs must appeal in order to achieve their aims (Choate, 1990). Equipped with secretarial services, research personnel, press agents, as well as access to government functionaries and the media, lobbyists are readily available in every capital city in the nation for testifying before legislative committees or otherwise representing their client's interests. Not the least of their effort is to impress on legislators their client's ability to reward or punish the legislator and so help or hinder their career (Turner, 1958:66).

An appreciation of the extent of the pressure placed on legislators by lobbyists and others representing special interests may be seen in the report by Common Cause that the 80 freshmen congressmen elected to the U.S. House of Representatives in 1982 received a total of 7.4 million dollars during the 1982 campaign, an average contribution of $92,500. Added to that were monies made available to these officials by political action groups and others following their election. Inclusion of these funds raised the average amount received by each congressman to $111,250 for the campaign period and the first 6 months they were in office (*Arizona Republic*, 1983b).

Lobbyists also seek to influence the executive and judicial branches of government, i.e., the President, governors, and heads of agencies and cabinet officers who regulate and rule on the basis of executive authority. For example, in 1982, then President Ronald Reagan was urged by the National Federation for Decency (a federation of religious, political, business, and educational interests now known as the American Family Association) to press for enforcement of obscenity laws and to establish a Pornography Awareness Week (*Arizona Republic*, 1982c). Similarly, environmentalist groups (e.g., Sierra Club, Friends of the Earth) and representatives of extractive industries (mining and forestry industries) pursue their respective interests when they seek to influence the nomination of cabinet members such as the Secretary of the Interior.

Efforts to pressure and influence the judiciary tend to be less blatant, or perhaps more discrete, than in the case of the legislative and executive branches. Yet no astute moral entrepreneur would ignore the fact that policy formulation involves all branches and levels of government.

In the case of courts, then, the cause of the moral entrepreneur often calls for initiating litigation. The importance of this effort is reflected in the fact that several national organizations maintain permanent legal staffs whose function includes becoming directly or indirectly (by filing *amicus* briefs) involved in court cases whose outcome is likely to shape or influence the decision of future cases—and public policy—resting on similar points of law (Vose, 1958:20ff). As Jacob (1984:151) says, the main techniques used to influence the courts are "to bring conflicts to a court's attention by initiating test cases, to bring added information to the court through *amicus curiae* (friend of the court) briefs, and to communicate with judges directly by placing information favorable to the group's cause in legal and general periodicals." The National Association for the Advancement of Colored People, the Liberty Lobby, the National Rifle Association, the National Consumers League, and the American Civil Liberties Union are just a few of the groups involved in such efforts.

Beyond these socially approved methods, powerful interest groups in our society frequently seek to compromise the integrity of governmental decision makers. Thus, our judges are said to include "the finest that money can buy" (Ashman, 1973), a claim that seems well supported by the outcome of the Greylord prosecutions in Chicago in which 11 judges, 38 lawyers, 7 police officers, 10 deputy sheriffs, 3 deputy clerks, and a court appointed receiver were convicted of federal crimes (Lockwood, 1989:ix). One Chicago lawyer, Joseph McDermott, testified he bribed at least two dozen judges (*Arizona Republic*, 1987). On the legislative level, seven members of the Arizona legislature (along with four lobbyists, and eight other persons associated with state government) were indicted in 1991 for their alleged involvement in a bribery scheme (*Time*, 1991b; *Arizona Republic*, 1991a). Lastly, there is the case of the "Keating 5," U.S. Senators DeConcini and McCain of Arizona, Cranston of California, Riegle of Michigan, and Glenn of Ohio, who were investigated for interceding in 1987 with federal regulators examining the operation of Charles H. Keating, Jr.'s Lincoln Savings and Loan. Keating was a major campaign contributor to each. In 1989 Lincoln Savings and Loan was seized by the federal government; its bailout is expected to cost taxpayers well in excess of 2 billion dollars (*Time*, 1991a).[9]

To the extent that deviance involves moral and legal issues frequently resolved in the courts and legislative assemblies, it should be no surprise that these role players historically have been targets for those wishing to control public policy-making and the outcome of criminal and civil law cases (Krisberg, 1975:35ff; Ashman, 1973:195ff). The tactics mentioned are widely employed and are a standard feature of the American political scene. In utilizing these tactics, those who have access to wealth, property, status, and the like have an obvious advantage (Gable, 1958).

SUMMARY

In this chapter attention has focused on the banning process whereby behavior is officially defined as evil, bad, immoral, and wrong, and is proscribed. This process is part of the larger deviance making enterprise and involves the work of rule creators. The interests pursued by these moral entrepreneurs may be narrow or broad, humanitarian or self-serving, and may have sacred or secular inspiration. Their goals may be symbolic or instrumental, and may be a response to real or to anticipated threats to the group's interests. In either case, the effort to ban reflects the intention to impose meaning on conditions in the world.

We have examined the banning process in terms of its several elements. Among these is the perception that imagined or objective conditions pose a problem. A second element is moral conversion, during which an effort is made to transform personal troubles into public issues. This reconstruction entails the dissemination of meanings and their acceptance by others as plausible and legitimate. Achieving widespread visibility necessitates use of the mass media. Access to the media, however, is far from universal and the visibility it affords must be engineered by a variety of techniques.

Moral conversion and legitimacy are influenced by other factors as well. Included is the prestige and respectability that may be acquired when the moral entrepreneur selectively identifies with publicly important persons or groups. Testimonials and endorsements, to say nothing of organizational alliances, are seen to promote the cause of the moral crusader.

Out of these efforts there may emerge an image or set of meanings regarding the problematic event that can promote fear and panic among the public. Called myths, legends, or folklore, these meanings seek to harmonize the claims of the moral crusader with the legitimate dominant values of the community. Simultaneously, the troubling behavior is portrayed as the acts of a feared and despised minority that runs counter to dominant norms, values, and interests.

In modern society, the conversion of any given set of beliefs into public law—thereby to control people against their will—calls for the exercise of power. Because the impersonal and pluralistic nature of our society limits the effective use of informal social control techniques, the moral entrepreneur must rely on the state, whose function it is to designate activities and persons as deviant. Access to state functionaries varies, as do the principles and tactics used by moral entrepreneurs to influence them. The successful outcome of such effort is that public policy is shaped by interest groups. The law is shown to be a means whereby the interests of some groups may be secured while other's interests are ignored. In the final analysis "the chance that a group will get community support for its definition of . . . deviance depends on its relative power position. The greater the group's size, resources, efficiency, unity, articulateness, prestige, coordination with other groups, and access to the mass media and to decision makers, the more likely it is to get its preferred norms legitimated" (Davis, 1975:54). Lastly, the public meanings of allegedly deviant behaviors may be seen to be those shared by select segments of society.

NOTES

1.   Two alternative sociological views on the creation of law are the consensus and the conflict perspectives. In the former, law is said to reflect an amalgam of the views and interests of the public and is created when custom no longer operates as an effective social control mechanism (Bohannon, 1973; Friedman, 1972). The conflict perspective, on the other hand, asserts that law is created, shaped, and enforced to maintain class interests (Chambliss, 1964; Quinney, 1973a, 1977) or, alternatively, that law emerges out of and is influenced by the structural divisions in society (Chambliss, 1979; Chambliss and Seidman, 1982; Greenberg, 1981).

2.   The distinction between rule creators and rule enforcers is analytic. In the actual process of deviance the same individuals and groups that are instrumental in the creation of rules may be equally active in their enforcement. For example, police departments may propose laws to legislative bodies as well as enforce the ensuing codes.

3.   This is not to say that people are not harmed during such action. Some parent's accommodation to their own child's abuse by another or a partner's accommodation to the violence of another are examples. However, the point here is that these accommodations prevent the activity from becoming the subject of legal intervention.

4.   U.S. morning and evening daily newspaper circulation now exceeds 62 million (*Information Please Almanac, Atlas and Yearbook*, 1992:296). Paid subscriptions to the three leading weekly news magazines—where claims of crusaders often appear as "news"—exceeded 10 million in 1988 (*World Almanac and Book of Facts*, 1990:363). It is also estimated that as of January 1991, 98% of U.S. households (93,100,000) owned at least one television set and that 63% had multiple sets, thus making this medium accessible to approximately 250 million persons with an average daily listening time of 6 hours, 55 minutes (*World Almanac and Book of Facts*, 1990:368; *Information Please Almanac, Atlas and Yearbook*, 1992:732).

5.   Though the "message" of these films is presently perceived by the general public as *camp art*, it was regarded as objective truth by an earlier generation. Such are the dynamics of moral meanings and social reality.

6.   American's categorization of people as "good guys" and "bad guys" that Berelson and Salter wrote about in 1946 persists in the 1990s. For example, in 1991 Saddam Hussein of Iraq was popularly characterized as a demonic dictator,

a reincarnation of Adolph Hitler or the incarnation of evil. A few years before, Hussein had been "courted" by the U.S. government in its effort to secure support among middle-east people for its disagreement with Iran.

7.   As a case in point, some people contend that the events now known (labeled) as Watergate were not unique in American political life. What led to the public event known as Watergate, including the meanings assigned to its components, was the work of the media. Thus, in the hands of media personalities, several discrete events were linked and given the name "Watergate." As Altheide has noted, "Nixon fell from power because the news perspective transformed the series of events known as Watergate into a whole, which was then used as evidence of corruption and immorality" (Altheide, 1976:159).

8.   Power and authority must be distinguished, the latter being a publicly acknowledged right to assert control over others. Authority is what distinguishes legislation prohibiting abortion or limiting the conditions under which it may be performed, on one hand, from the disruptive demonstrations of anti-abortionists at clinics that make the performance of abortion impossible, on the other.

9.   In April 1992, Charles H. Keating, Jr. was sentenced to 10 years in prison and fined $250,000 for his involvement in savings and loan association bond fraud (*NY Times*, 1992a).

5

Creating Deviants

INTRODUCTION

In this chapter we turn our attention to how control agents "populate" socially created categories of deviance. This is achieved by stripping the legitimate identity from selected actors through classifying and dealing with them as deviant types. We shall examine the several stages of this identity conferring process. Called a *deviant career*, these stages include (1) being publicly identified as a rule breaker, (2) being excluded from participation in nondeviant activities, (3) coming to define oneself as deviant, and (4) managing one's deviant identity. The outcome of this process is that a person is changed characterologically and comes to be regarded as "essentially" deviant, immoral, or "defective." One's being becomes deviant (Lemert, 1967:44–46). We begin by examining a number of related concepts pertaining to this process.

THE STATUS OF DEVIANT

There are two bases on which people may be assigned to the socially constructed status of deviant, set apart from others, and regarded as different from those defined as morally acceptable. One is a person's objectionable behavior, and the other is the display of objectionable traits. The first case refers to being *deviant by achievement*, and the second to being *deviant by ascription* (Mankoff, 1971). Each calls for brief examination.

Deviant as Achieved and Ascribed Statuses

An *achieved status* is one based on the official meaning of the actor's behavior; it has been banned. Examples include (1) destroying other's property or injuring them (e.g., murder and assault), (2) using and/or providing others with unlawful goods and services (e.g., vice, prostitution, drug dealing), (3) disturbing other's sense of propriety (e.g., public nudity or drunkenness), and (4) advocating ideologies or doctrines (e.g., political or religious) seen as threatening to those supporting legitimated ideologies (Glaser, 1971: Chapter 1). In each case an actor performs behavior that could have been avoided and this serves as the foundation of their being assigned by others to a deviant status.

In contrast, deviance as an *ascribed status* rests on the negative meaning assigned by an audience to unavoidable personal traits people appear to possess. These "offensive" traits contrast with what are promoted as shared values or attributes. They include left-handedness where right-handedness is preeminent (Hertz, 1960; *Time*, 1974:85), shortness where height is valued (Sagarin, 1969:196ff), obesity where weight watching is akin to a religious exercise (Millman, 1980; Chernin, 1981), being an amputee, spastic, or otherwise physically disabled where athletic and physical prowess is esteemed (Clark, 1978; Cleland, 1982), and blindness or deafness in a society dominated by sighted and hearing people (Scott, 1969; Higgins, 1980). Such conditions, even when partially present, often arouse marked feelings of antipathy or fear while the persons who display them come to be regarded as inferior—physically, psychologically, emotionally, or morally (Scott, 1969:24). Consequently, these physical conditions become *stigma*, signs or attributes that are deeply discrediting, and those who display them are stigmatized, i.e., they are "disqualified from full social acceptance" (Goffman, 1963:3). In contrast with those whose deviance rests on the definition of their performance, the status of these people rests on the definition of their being.[1]

Primary and Secondary Deviants

The concepts of primary and secondary deviance acknowledge that one's involvement in rule-breaking may have variable social and psychological causes and consequences. *Primary deviants* are those persons whose rule-breaking is regarded as incidental or subordinate to the balance of their life and to the socially approved statuses they occupy. For example, someone who uses the office telephone for personal calls or who overclaims their expense entitlement is unlikely to be defined by others as an employee thief. Among primary deviants, then, rule-breaking does not serve as the basis of an identifiable role or status position (Lemert, 1951:75). It is merely one of many things they do. Similar to this is Becker's (1973:20) *secret deviant*, referring to those whose rule violations are neither publicly recognized nor responded to as such.

It is the "privacy" of one's rule-breaking that the concepts of primary and secret deviant have in common.[2]

In contrast, some deviations—mental retardation, paralysis, blindness, and obesity—can neither be hidden nor subordinated to one's legitimate roles. As a result, these behaviors or conditions often become the central aspect of the rule-breaker's public identity (in contrast with being incidental among primary deviants), while the socially approved statuses people occupy (being a student, a spouse, a worker, etc.) become obscured because the audience's attention is focused almost exclusively on the alleged deviation. It is *the attention of others and the actor's response to that attention* that are central to the concept of secondary deviance (Lemert, 1951:75–76, 1967:17–18, Chapter 3). Similar is the concept of *pure deviant*, one who has broken the rules and is perceived by others to have done so (Becker, 1973:20). A core element in secondary deviance, then, is the rule-breaker's adjustment to others' definitions; the secondary deviant "is a person whose life and identity are organized around the facts of deviance" (Lemert, 1967:41). In sum, the principal distinction between primary and secondary deviation lies in the centrality of their deviation in *both* their public and private identities vis-à-vis other roles and statuses.[3]

Master Statuses and Auxiliary Traits

The centrality of rule-breaking for the secondary deviant has continuity with the concept of master and auxiliary status traits. A *master status* is one that "tend[s] to overpower, in most crucial situations, any other characteristics which might run counter to it" (Hughes, 1945:357). Deviance tends to be a master status. "One receives the status [of deviant] as a result of breaking a rule, and the identification proves to be more important than most others. One will be identified as a deviant first, before other identifications are made" (Becker, 1973:33). For example, being gay or lesbian typically transcends other statuses.

Closely linked to master statuses are "a complex of auxiliary characteristics [or traits] which come to be expected of its incumbents" (Hughes, 1945:353). Thus, abusive spouses (master status) are expected to be men (auxiliary trait), drug pushers (master status) are expected to be male, black, poor, high school dropouts (auxiliary traits), and prostitutes (master status) are expected to be women (auxiliary trait). It is important to note that the typical expectations of auxiliary traits are one of the reasons why others, similarly deviant, can remain "secret deviants," such as women who abuse their husbands, white business executives who push drugs, and male prostitutes.

Similarly, several behavioral auxiliary traits may be linked to specific deviant master statuses. Homosexuals (master status), for example, have been stereotypically described as effeminate, insecure, and sensitive (auxiliary traits), while drug addicts (master status) have been expected to be escapist, hedonistic, insecure, frustrated, weak minded, and dangerous (Simmons, 1969:29). Almost invariably, deviant master statuses and their accompanying auxiliary traits tend to carry negative moral valuation, while morally positive and morally negative master statuses tend to be mutually exclusive. For example, many people regard the statuses of "professional athlete" and "homosexual" as contradictory and incompatible (Garner and Smith, 1977). Other pairs of this sort include physician drug addicts, child molesting school teachers, and philandering priests. Because these pairs include moral opposites, they produce a sense of "cognitive discomfort." As the social world is currently constructed, these traits seem incompatible. However, by creating moral consistency between master statuses, and between master statuses and their auxiliary traits, the public image of a rule breaker is constructed as one who is *generally* deviant (irrespective of the statistical truth of that perception); deviance becomes the dominant element of one's public self. Such persons are regarded as essentially deviant and are dealt with accordingly (Becker, 1973:34).

To be categorized as a secondary deviant means that one's deviation is of central importance both in terms of how a person relates to others and how they see themselves. This involves problems associated with being stigmatized, punished, segregated from society, or otherwise being made the object of social control. Given the centrality of such concerns, becoming a secondary deviant is qualitatively different from engaging in primary deviation. For the primary deviant, rule-breaking is incidental to their legitimate roles and statuses, and is experienced as having relatively few personal or social consequences. In contrast, the secondary deviant's life tends to revolve around the experience of rule-breaking or others' attempts to control it.

Habitual involvement in rule-breaking is not, however, mutually exclusive of legitimate role playing. For example, research indicates that affective relationships between pimps, their parents, and family persist, often with only minimal difficulty (Milner and Milner, 1973:137ff). Similarly, the role of professional fence is quite compatible with that of straight businessmen (Klockars, 1974:77–78) and vice versa (Henry, 1977). Many families in which fathers engage in incestuous relationships with their daughters simultaneously display a host of publicly esteemed attributes (Justice and Justice, 1979:60–64). Hired killers can also be solid family members (Joey, 1973:74). Finally, many men who visit "tearooms" (public places where impersonal homosexual acts occur) are married, live with their spouses, and work in a wide variety of legitimate occupations (Humphreys, 1970). These examples demonstrate that deviant and nondeviant roles are far from incompatible and it is only the public imagination that is shocked when such dual lives are revealed. Indeed, as the case of the professional fence suggests, legitimate and deviant roles may even be interdependent (Henry, 1977). However, people can also experience profound difficulties related to their deviant status. In Chapter 6 we will consider such problems and we will refine some of the distinctions between primary and secondary deviance. At this point, however, we need to examine the informal and formal processes by which people become deviant.

STEREOTYPY

We noted earlier that through the banning process people create new categories of deviance, allocate certain others to these categories, and assign morally negative characterizations to them. These characterizations may lead to an informal transformation or redefinition of the character of rule-breakers prior to their contact with deviance processing (control) agencies. Contributing to this transformation are *stereotypes*: collectively shared ideas about the nature of people who are classified as the same based on their participation in deviance. Given the importance of this transformation, the use of stereotypes deserves careful examination.

In impersonal urban industrial society, daily interaction is based on several taken-for-granted assumptions that encourage people to make instant, summary classifications of one another, based on limited information. As Higgins and Butler (1982:129) say, "we all classify people when we interact with them. Except for intimate associates, rarely do we take into account very much of the information that we already know or could learn about other people. It would be difficult to process so much information." Thus, lacking contrary information, people define and deal with strangers as if they satisfied the stereotypical criteria of persons defined by their public social status—shopkeeper, police officer, bus driver, office worker, teacher, student. For most encounters this allows relatively trouble-free interaction. It does not mean there is total disregard of situational considerations. For example, people's speech, general demeanor, style of dress, and the like are also used as cues or symbols, i.e., stimuli that have meanings and values associated with them (Rose, 1965:44f). For example, smiles are generally invested with positive nonthreatening meaning and smiling persons tend to be defined differently than those who either frown or are unsmiling unless they are salespersons or politicians who are suspected of using the smile deceptively or for diversion. However, those who wear uniforms—whether they smile or not—are approached with great reserve. Much of our social interaction rests on the definitions we hold about these symbols.

Though people often deny that they classify others, stereotyping is a widespread means for establishing a sense of order in an impersonal, heterogeneous society (Simmons, 1969:26; Vander Zanden, 1983:19–21). Just as people have stereotyped ideas about members of various occupational, racial, religious, and ethnic groups, they also have stereotyped conceptions of various types of deviants. For example, when college students were asked to characterize homosexuals, marihuana smokers, and adulterers, among others, over two-thirds of them "wrote a highly stereotyped portrait of every deviant type, and the responses . . . all [echoed] the same package of images" (Simmons, 1969:27; cf. Vander Zanden, 1983:19–23). Such evidence suggests that we are socialized to construct stereotypical images of deviants.

This is consistent with the prevalence of stereotypical constructions in everyday speech and the mass media. These images are part of our popular culture. For example, we know that "children learn a considerable amount of [stereotypical] imagery concerning deviance very early, and . . . much of the imagery come[s] from their peers rather than adults" (Scheff, 1966:64ff). The prevalence of stereotypes of the "mentally ill" (itself a medicalized stereotype) may be noted in words that, over time, have been used to refer to such persons: "whacko," "crazy," "nuts," "cracked," "loony," "flipped," "bughouse," etc. This language is reinforced by media imagery where, in television, for example, the "mentally ill" person

> often enters the scene staring glassy-eyed, with his mouth widely agape, mumbling incoherent phrases or laughing uncontrollably. Even in what would be considered the milder disorders, neurotic phobias and obsessions, the afflicted person is presented as having bizarre facial expression and actions. (Nunnally, 1961:74)

These visual images and their associated meanings have become part of the "conventional wisdom" possessed by many Americans concerning what the mentally ill look like, how they behave, and how "normal" people ought to behave toward them.

A socially constructed stereotype of criminals is also reflected in the content of our language and the media (Klapp, 1962; Quinney, 1973a, 1975; Winick, 1978). For example, several studies report that television drama programs focusing on crime include extensive character stereotyping. Historically, villains have typically been nonwhite or Italian, older, and less physically attractive than heroes, and have been portrayed as being in a state of sexual and physical decline (Smythe, 1954). Dominick (1978:115) reports that during the 1950s nonwhites were seldom cast as police officers. More recent analysis of TV program content reveals that "law enforcers . . . were predominantly white males in the prime of life. Eighty-nine percent were male and nearly as many (85%) were white" (Lichter and Lichter, 1983:36).

In another recent study comparing the verbal or auditory portion of TV crime news with the visual images or pictures accompanying them, it was found that their respective "messages" are often quite different (National Public Radio, 1991). For example, auditory information regarding criminality, drug use, or police drug busts and related matters is often shown to be descriptively valid. However, the visual accompaniment to these stories often conveys a different message. Thus, while verbal information may indicate criminality and drug use is largely *pandemic*, the accompanying visual images will be largely *endemic* and focus only on blacks, Hispanics, or lower classes. The significance of this auditory/visual disparity is that visual stimuli seem to be primary and takes precedence over the auditory (Altheide and Snow, 1991). Accordingly, these visual images can be expected to be more readily reproduced by individual actors and to have the greater impact on people's consciousness. If it is true that "seeing is believing," there can be little wonder about the source of information concerning what "kinds of people" do crime. Of course, these images are not without consequences. Let us give some attention to that matter.

Consequences of Stereotyping

Stereotyping has numerous consequences. First, the content of stereotypes often is regarded as a valid description of the groups to which they refer. By taking the validity of stereotypes for granted, people think they "know" enough relevant information about a deviant and that they are able to recognize one when and if they see one. For example, many people have demanding jobs despite being addicted to drugs. Yet people persist in believing that drug addicts are either entertainers or unemployed. Persons who violate the stereotype, such as cocaine-consuming physicians or marihuana-smoking judges, are regarded as "exceptions that prove the rule" and validate the stereotype. The stereotype of the physician (whose auxiliary traits include being knowledgeable, gentle, understanding, ever alert and ready to do their duty for humanity) precludes them being perceived as drug addicts.

Second, stereotypical definitions become institutionalized. Stereotypes reveal what we imagine various deviants to be and tell us where to look for deviation. It is not so much that the stereotype is wrong for some of those who engage in rule-breaking behavior. Rather, the stereotype distorts both *who* engages in the behavior and *how often* they do so. Crucially, it also disregards everything else they may also do. So, if we think of "criminals" as being mainly poor and from select ethnic or minority groups, and that crime is largely a matter of individual wrong doing in urban public places, those ideas will inform our social control policies. Accordingly, we will look for crime in the streets rather than the suites. If we think of property crime largely as "street crime" motivated by a desire for money to buy drugs, that idea will influence police crime control policy. However, while control efforts are overwhelmingly focused on the streets, what decisions are being made in the suites that will impact negatively on the environment, will harm consumers through faulty product manufacture, will injure employees through deliberate avoidance of health and safety regulations, will produce advertising designed to misinform the public and induce them to part with their money by lies or misrepresentation, or fix prices at artificially high levels so as to maximize profits (Simon and Eitzen, 1990)? In short, to what degree does stereotyped images of deviants limit public awareness of and sensitivity to *elite deviance*, (i.e., the illegal and immoral acts of corporations, government agencies and their representatives) and at what social, economic and physical cost?[4]

Third, because stereotypes contain implicit expectations, people are led to anticipate special behavior by deviants. For example, homophobic persons often support antihomosexual allegations, not with evidence of what gays have done, but with what is expected of them such as the prediction that gay teachers will seduce, molest, or otherwise lead students into a homosexual life style (*Arizona Gay News*, 1978:4). Similarly, presidential hopeful Ross Perot denied gays a place on his staff because he predicted they would be a disruptive force (*New York Times*, 1992b). By accepting stereotypical characterizations as valid, one may readily make such predictions. Simply, the actor "becomes" an instance of the caricature described by the stereotype and is expected to behave accordingly. This is well illustrated by the case of the disabled who are falsely assumed to be victims of biology, to be disinterested in sex, to experience most of their problems as a result of their disability, and to need help with the most basic of tasks (Fine and Asch, 1988; Makas, 1988; Hahn, 1988).

However, stereotypes may also attribute positively defined traits to deviants. Thus, it has been found that the disabled are expected to be more sensitive, trustworthy, reliable, and virtuous than nondisabled and that this assumption places unrealistic expectations on them (Bogdan and Taylor, 1987; Schwartz, 1988).

Fourth, stereotypes may serve as a barrier between deviants and others that leads to the rejection of those defined as deviant. This happens when the validity of the stereotype is taken for granted and results in people being "put off" by and shunning the rule-breaker. Thus, it is not uncommon to find people believing that homosexuals really are effeminate, "limp-wristed," and poor athletes (Garner and Smith, 1977) or that blind people really are helpless, dependent, and melancholy (Scott, 1969:21). These negative auxiliary traits serve to justify or excuse one's behaving toward the subject in extraordinary ways. It appears, then, that when people are stereotyped as barbarians one is entitled to treat them in barbaric ways (Gerbner, 1978:14). This has led to the claim that many ascribed deviants, such as the disabled, experience more problems from the social reaction to their deviant status, than from their physical disability (McNeill, 1988; Hahn, 1985).

In addition, stereotypes may serve as the basis for selecting who will be officially designated as deviant. People are sometimes singled out and labeled because of what stereotypes lead others to think of them. For example, it is not uncommon for school teachers to stereotype and judge youngsters on the basis of the reputation for "unruly" behavior earned by an older brother or sister.

Fifth, stereotypes shape and justify the policies agencies adopt to deal with deviant clientele. One example is the way stereotyped perceptions of blind people influence the work of some agencies providing services to the blind. Some agencies for the blind prefer not to deal with all unsighted people, but only with those who conform to the agency's conception of persons who have the greatest chance for rehabilitation, i.e., the employable blind and the young. Among the agency's reasons for this limitation is that young employables conform to a stereotype that can be used effectively in fund raising campaigns in which themes of "youth, work, and hope" are used to elicit support (Scott, 1969:100). Scott also notes that "the problems of the blind" often are stereotypically defined by agency personnel while the blind person's own definition of their problems is ignored. Blind persons whose behavior fails to conform to agency definitions are regarded as "marginal" to the agency's "real work," i.e., educational and vocational training. Those not conforming to the stereotype are often defined as insoluble cases, expelled from the program and their files are closed. Therefore, to be accepted and retained in the program, blind persons must sometimes sacrifice their individuality and conform to the prevailing stereotype (a kind of "shaping") constructed by the organization's members.

Reflecting this kind of depersonalization, homosexuals committed to Atascadero State Hospital under California's Mentally Disordered Sex Offender law, risked being stripped of all legal rights, perhaps detained for life, and used as "guinea pigs" in medical/surgical experiments (including experimental use of the drugs prolixin and anectine, electroconvulsive shock, and behavioral conditioning by aversive stimuli to extinguish penile responses, i.e., erections, among the patients). Employing stereotypes as justification for treatment and control, a doctor at Atascadero is quoted as saying "These men have no rights. If we can learn something by using them, then that is small compensation for the trouble they have caused society" (Jackson,1973:43; cf. Chambliss, 1971). More recently, it has been argued that the medicalization of deviance based on the medical construction of "unhealthy behavior," "syndromes," or alleged conditions such as "hyperactivity," not only enables unwanted rule-breaking to be controlled, but justifies therapeutic intervention and the denial of due process rights to those classified (Box, 1977; Conrad, 1979).

A sixth consequence of stereotypes is that they lead to *omittive acts*, i.e., to the systematic avoidance of certain acts, words, or conversational topics when in the presence of persons allocated to select stereotypical categories. While stereotypes prescribe some responses, as we saw earlier, they proscribe or prohibit others resulting in what Lynch (1983) calls "minimizing contact." This can be achieved by ignoring or avoiding the person in an attempt to limit problematic or uncomfortable interaction. The following examples involving physically disabled people are typical:

> My girlfriend and I went to a restaurant. The waiter wouldn't even take my order. Even after my girlfriend told him I could order for myself, he still kept asking her what I would like to eat. (Kern, 1991:21)

> Once I went to a restaurant with a friend of mine and I ordered soup. When I started drinking soup directly from my cup without a spoon, my friend told me that it would be better if I used a spoon. Since then I prefer not to drink soup in public places. (Aytemiz, 1992:18)

Reflecting the stereotypical idea that disabled people are asexual, able bodied persons often avoid or are embarrassed by discussions of sexual behavior, dating, marriage, and childbearing with persons suffering extensive paralysis due to spinal cord injury. Sighted persons rarely discuss art (e.g., painting and sculpture) with the blind, and hearing persons tend to avoid conversations with people who have speech and/or hearing defects, a condition interpreted by deaf persons as a sign of other's rejection of them (Higgins, 1980:140). Finally, we have such instances as the store clerk who shuns the shopper who has neurofibromatosis (Elephant Man's disease), especially if that person wishes to try on clothing (in some instances such avoidance reflects an aversion born of fear; see Montagu, 1979:26), or the therapist who systematically counsels disabled clients away from pursuing select occupations thought by the counselor to be "inappropriate" (Scott, 1969:85). The extreme form of omittive behavior involves ignoring and refusing to acknowledge the presence of the deviant, thereby precluding all interaction. As Davis (1961:163) says:

> Whether the handicap is overtly and tactlessly responded to as such or, as is more often the case, no explicit reference is made to it, the underlying condition of heightened, narrowed awareness causes the interaction to be articulated too exclusively in terms of it. This . . . is accompanied by one or more of the familiar signs of discomfort and stickiness: the guarded references, the common everyday words suddenly made taboo, the fixed stare elsewhere, the artificial levity, the compulsive loquaciousness, the awkward solemnity.

Though it is possible to overemphasize the importance of the influence of stereotypes on people's responses to persons regarded as deviant, the role of stereotypical conceptions is critical. This is because most people have limited contact with persons characterized as secondary deviants. Their knowledge is largely derived from accounts carried in the mass media, religious writings, comments from friends and neighbors, and from public pronouncements by professional control agents such as police, psychiatrists, and social workers. Lacking direct contact and independent verifiable information, people have difficulty knowing how to relate and how to interact with persons who behave strangely, appear intoxicated or high, have attempted suicide, have committed crimes, are homosexual, or quadriplegic. In many cases, reliance on a "script" derived from stereotypical definitions may appear to be the best "recipe" to reduce the immediate interactional problems. However, the "price" of such comfort may well be not only the brutalization/ dehumanization of the stereotyped persons, but also the creation of unnecessary fear and an ultimate limit on their own freedom. We will return to these matters in Chapter 6.

INSTITUTIONALIZING DEVIANCE

We have seen that reliance on stereotypes contributes to the process of "stripping" persons of elements of their nondeviant identity. Identity "stripping" also results from the efforts of social control agencies to manage people classified as deviant. This is part of the larger process of institutionalizing deviance and requires careful consideration.

Earlier we noted that banning involves converting some people's private meanings into public laws that generally apply to all persons under the jurisdiction of the state or other regulatory body.[5] Accordingly, processing deviants is the responsibility of agencies such as police, mental health agencies, homes for abused children, drug treatment and counseling centers, prisons, and, increasingly, privately operated "community homes" under grant or contract to the state and funded by insurance agencies. Institutionalizing deviance in these settings calls for creating rules and procedures governing how different categories of rule-breakers are to be managed. These rules and procedures are largely shaped and limited by the resources of the agency. Specific roles (e.g., a new job classification) may be created to administer cases if existing roles are not sufficient for the task. Ultimately, the responsibilities become stabilized. By assigning the task of control to an agency, the roles, procedures, and meanings generated for administrative convenience come to be the "property" of organizations who then have a vested interest in perpetuating (i.e., stabilizing) the deviant condition on which the agency's existence depends.

In a specific organization these elements of institutionalization reflect bureaucratized methods of handling deviants. Within an agency one finds characteristic bureaucratic practices: specialized information, specific rules, specialization and routinization of tasks, a hierarchy of authority, and impersonal interpersonal relations. Ostensibly, these practices are intended to promote achievement of an agency's goal— correction, amelioration, containment, and rehabilitation. These elements and their associated meanings and techniques become part of the social reality of deviance embraced by the agency workers and which have been defined as the "theory of office" (Rubington and Weinberg, 1973).[6]

Theory of Office

Agencies charged with controlling deviants face a problem of what to do with persons brought to their attention. The *theory of office* is a statement of how an agency admits, processes, and manages its clients. These "theories" formalize the processes of defining, classifying, and labeling (i.e., *registry*) their client population. Theories of office provide a sense of order and meaning to controllers. However, the order created is not intended to enhance treatment or rehabilitation, but is designed to solve organizational problems, promote a smooth and efficient operation, and protect the agency from criticism (Rubington and Weinberg, 1973:118; Newman, 1975; Shover, 1984:71). Let us briefly explore these matters.

Bureaucracies are organizations designed to handle tasks in routine or standardized ways. Individual cases are managed according to rules and with minimal regard for idiosyncrasies of the case or the client's preferences. Agency personnel are discouraged from acting on the basis of their various different personal definitions of client needs. The theory of office provides "recipes for action" that serve to routinize tasks. Included are *typifications* or standardized categories based on selected characteristics by which clients are classified (Hawkins and Tiedeman, 1975:82) for routine handling and ease of processing. Agency personnel who fail to conform to these practices may well be expelled.[7]

To discourage a disparity of private meanings and to encourage the use of methods consistent with organizational interests, workers are informally socialized, tutored, and trained in the preferred routines. For example, novice correctional officers begin to acquire knowledge of working with offenders by observing older officers interact with inmates. They are expected to learn how to handle client–management problems in organizationally satisfactory ways. Novices are coached on report writing and efficient information gathering, and are encouraged to review old files "to see how it is done." In these ways recruits are introduced to the agency specific *recipe knowledge* (Shover, 1984:68–69) that promotes routinization of tasks.

One example of task routinization involves police use of *typifications*. Typifications (standard categories overlaid with stereotypical meaning) are part of the common sense understanding that officers construct about the public that serve to routinize or "normalize" their daily contacts. "If an encounter [with a citizen] can be normalized, the officer can be relatively confident of the general nature of the interaction and ultimate resolution of the problem" (Lundman, 1980:20). Two types officers use to classify citizens are "the asshole" (also identified as "creep," "bigmouth," "clown," "scumbag," "shithead," and "fool," among others), and the "suspicious person." People typed as "asshole" are likely to be dealt with harshly, while those classified as "suspicious" are inclined to be treated very professionally, swiftly, and in a "no nonsense" fashion. In either case, such typing helps "normalize" and routinize the way officers deal with people (Van Maanen, 1978).

Public defenders also typify criminal cases for routine handling. For example, to reduce costs and speed up processing public defenders and prosecuting attorneys have constructed a number of categories called *normal crimes* whose "typical features, e.g., the ways they usually occur and the characteristics of the people who commit them, . . . are known and attended to by the [public defender]" (Sudnow, 1965:179). Frequently constructed normal crimes are those for petty theft, drunkenness, rape, and drug use. The criteria of a "typical" petty theft is defined as "unplanned . . . , generally committed on lower class persons and don't get much money, don't often employ weapons, don't make living from thievery, usually younger defendants with long juvenile assaultive records, etc." (Sudnow, 1965:179). A case that substantially satisfies these criteria will likely be categorized as "normal" (i.e., ordinary) and dealt with routinely, thereby facilitating the operation of the agency. By classifying a case as an instance of the normal crime a defense attorney, for example, may claim that the crime deserves the typically associated punishment. Occasionally this can confuse the public who become outraged, as with the case of the Ann Arbor defense lawyer who sought to have the sentence for his client's rape reduced on the grounds that it was a "typical rape." This brought angry letters from women and others complaining that no rape is "typical."

Categorization is also experienced by disabled persons seeking rehabilitation services. For example, disabled persons have been denied the opportunity to shape their own rehabilitation when their wishes and goals conflict with ideas and routines of the agency staff who claim to know their "real" capacities. "When the disabled formulate innovative plans, solutions, and alternatives, such plans are . . . labeled "unrealistic," . . . especially when the plans and alternatives do not conform to the stereotyped role of the disabled and the stereotyped sex-appropriate roles" (Safilios-Rothschild, 1976:40). Thus, as Scott (1969:76) points out for the blind, by manipulation of the reward and punishment system that they monopolize, agency workers "pressure the client into rejecting personal conceptions of problems in favor of the worker's own definition of them . . . and accept the agency's conception of the problems of blindness." This same depersonalization and routinization occurs in schools (Schostak, 1983), in probation departments, in hospitals, in welfare agencies, and other client managing organizations.

The value of typifications is that they maximize rewards and minimize costs, thereby helping agencies deal with their clients within the limits of their finite resources. These resources shape how categorization is used. For example, legally and ordinarily, maximum security inmates are not allowed outside the walls of maximum security prisons. However, when an insufficient number of minimum and medium security inmates are available for harvest on the prison farm (work requiring inmates to go outside prison walls), or because there is a lack of bed space, a change in classification may conveniently be arranged (Sykes 1958:25–31; Shover, 1984:71; Michigan Judicial Institute, 1991). Thus, prison inmates may have their custody level changed not to facilitate "rehabilitation" or because of any character change among them, but to satisfy administrative needs. Similarly, using typifications assists agencies to keep their clients (e.g., the disabled) in a dependent and inferior role so as to promote control (Safilios-Rothschild, 1976:40). In both cases, then, official classifications serve organizational goals. Conversely, when clients' characteristics do not allow them to "fit" the organizational apparatus, they may well be expelled.

Lastly, these categorizations render the treatment or other disposition of specific cases authoritatively appropriate. Categorization legitimates client processing. For example, a judgment of "incompetency" by a duly convened board of psychiatrists paves the way for the hospitalization or outpatient treatment of a mental patient. Declaring a person "criminal" legitimates their incarceration and makes it appear proper and defensible (Shover, 1984:71). A teacher's designation of a student as "hyperactive" medicalizes and thereby legitimates subsequent treatment for what otherwise might have been merely boisterous behavior. It is in terms of these designations and their meanings that bureaucratic social control agencies manage the client population. This defining process, along with other aspects of the theory of office, serves to "shape" persons to the needs of the bureaucratic machinery. Such shaping, however, is only one step in the "career" of the deviant.

RETROSPECTIVE INTERPRETATION

In attempting to cast rule breakers as deviant, many social control agencies seek to "discover" evidence of an actor's prior rule-breaking. This effort stems from at least two sources. First is the need to legitimate the agency's activities and justify casting specific offenders in the status of secondary deviant. Stereotypical labels are only partially self-substantiating because they refer to categories rather than specific persons. Control agencies also need information that will integrate (1) the moral definition of the banned act, (2) the presumed character of particular rule breakers, and (3) the treatment to be accorded. Second, except with heinous offenses, actors are rarely cast in the status of deviant because of one or a few instances of rule-breaking behavior. One who is to be cast as deviant must be shown to be devious in character (Matza, 1969:157). This link between behavior and character is created by *retrospective interpretation* (Lofland, 1969; Schur, 1971). In this process, observers look backward over a person's biography and select information consistent with what is now known about actor's behavior and so build the case that these were "indications" that the person was different all along. As a result, "deviants" can be characterologically differentiated from "respectable" rule breakers. With this finding of difference audiences establish the essential meaning of the deviant as an "outsider," as a "special kind of person."

Examples of recasting or transforming people as "special" and essentially different regularly appear in newspapers and other media wherein alleged rule breakers are subjected to extensive, selective biographical scrutiny and to "character reconstruction" (Lofland, 1969:149ff). The everyday features of this reconstructive process are noted in the comments of journalist and commentator Andy Rooney concerning Jean Harris, who murdered Dr. Herman Tarnower, a Scarsdale, N.Y. cardiologist. When Harris' role in Tarnower's death became public, Rooney (who knew Harris personally) commented:

> Most of us were surprised . . . stunned. While it is easy *in retrospect* to interpret things she did in ways that suggest evil, she did not seem evil. . . . Now, of course, *you search your memory for clues* that might have made you aware that she may have been a woman capable of buying a gun in Virginia and driving with it in a car to shoot a man in his house 400 miles away. . . . Was the impression I had of Jean Harris as an attractive, intelligent woman wrong, or were those characteristics only a small part of what she was? *What other quirks of personality manifested themselves in what actions over the years*? (*Arizona Republic*, 1980b, emphasis added)

Another example of character reconstruction involves John W. Hinckley, Jr. who, in 1981, attempted to assassinate President Reagan. Soon after the shooting, Hinckley's life was selectively scrutinized by media persons who concluded that he did not play football, excel in school, or have girlfriends, he worked in fits and starts, his life was marked by alienation, a gun fetish, and failure, he failed to graduate from college, he failed to measure up to his brother and sister, he failed to connect with his father, he failed in his efforts to win the heart of a teenage movie star, he was never a part of this world, he passed from freshman to senior year without leaving a trace, he had a sporadic college career, dropping out at least three times, he lived in one nondescript or seedy apartment after another, he was a wanderer, and he spent time in squalid motels rather than his parent's luxurious home. Consistent with that characterization, reporters concluded that "the person firing [at President Reagan] is just a bit of tan coat, a swatch of sandy hair and a half seen face in a crowd" (*Arizona Republic*, 1981b).

It is questionable whether the totality of anyone's biography can be validly summarized in such terms. Yet by means of the selective nature of retrospective interpretation, such one-sided biographies are constructed and enter the cultural repository of knowledge. A balanced account is not their purpose. Rather, it is to discover features of the rule breaker's life that are consistent with their known present deviation and that allow them to be defined as a "special kind of person." Information is acknowledged only if it is perceived to be consistent with the definition of the deviant episode. Like astrological charting and personality assessment, contradictory information is discounted or, if it cannot be ignored, is explained away.

Though not always successful, retrospective interpretation helps to establish consistency between the actor's behavior and alleged character and thereby legitimates labeling the offender (Lofland, 1969:150ff). Questionable conduct becomes understandable when engaged in by a "special kind of person," and if the actor can be shown to be an "outsider," the legitimacy of defining and responding to the person as a deviant is more readily assured.

Imputational Specialists and Case Records

In their effort to retrospectively reconstruct rule breakers' identities, people rely heavily on the work of a subcategory of control agents called *imputational specialists* (Lofland, 1969:136ff) whose ordinary occupational routine involves imputing character traits to others. Such persons include school teachers who record "suspicions" about a child's learning ability, social workers who inject moral evaluations into client's files, probation officers who identify offenders as "habitually troublesome," or prison psychologists who convert the "negative" results of paper and pencil tests into categories of personality type. For example, "correct" answers to questions asked of prospective mental patients may well be ignored, while "incorrect" answers are dutifully recorded and taken as evidence of mental inadequacy (Scheff, 1964; Rosenhan, 1973). Such entries reflect the perceptions of a vast number of persons in our society (imputational specialists) who are trained to "find" the very conditions referred to.[8]

These records are not compiled only for the purpose of validating a deviant label, nor are they typically the product of malevolence. In many cases they reflect an organization's need to protect its members from prosecution by the client or their agents. Whatever their ostensible purpose, these files often constitute the only record of events. Should an incident arise these otherwise "innocent" files will be examined selectively by control agents who are seeking information that will make sense of the offender's behavior and legitimate the label. Information that flatters the client or is contrary to control agent's interests is often left open to doubt or ignored. On the other hand, data supportive of the label are likely to be accepted unequivocally (Goffman, 1961:155ff).

Given the authority vested in the agencies engaged in retrospective interpretation, little of one's biography is beyond scrutiny. From the vast array of materials available are selected the misadventures, examples of poor judgment, regrettable incidents, cases of impetuousness, records of intemperance, and other things (which all people have accumulated in quantity) that may be defined as having "symptomatic significance." The events recorded in the case history are just the sort that one would consider "scandalous, defamatory, and discrediting" (Goffman, 1961: 155–159). In *One Flew Over the Cuckoo's Nest,* Big Nurse always carried a small pad of paper in her uniform pocket on which to record select events in her patients' daily life. This information was dutifully filed in each patient's record and referred to during "group meeting" for the purpose of degradation and controlling their behavior (Kesey, 1962: 221ff, 252). Such selective collection and collation of data are a matter of partisanship, serving the interests of organizations that process deviants.

Finally, the content of the case record—the file—often becomes reified and takes on greater importance than the person's actual words or actions. Consider the following account from a prison program coordinator who is responsible for conducting an initial interview and evaluation with prisoners at the state prison at Jackson, Michigan:

> The pre-sentence report is my primary source of information on the prisoner's non-institutional behavior. It is critical that the report be as clear and accurate as possible. Other documents like the county sheriff's report may be critical to my determination. From these documents I develop a treatment plan for each prisoner. I also complete a security classification screen form to rate a prisoner's escape risk and assaultiveness. Factors such as sentence length, previous institutional behavior, history of escapes, predatory sexual behavior, and pending charges are considered. The final phase of the reception process is the classification interview. Classification affects not only institutional placement but eligibility for programming, community placement and ultimately parole placement. (Michigan Judicial Institute, 1991)

As this example shows, institutional procedures are typically governed by the content of the file which is seen as more credible than the behavior of the actor. The file becomes a substitute for the person and takes precedence; this depersonalizes the individual. Letkemann notes that

> the file . . . is personified. The comments of others are perceived of as a more accurate reflection of the person than the person himself. In fact, the

body is perceived of as a false image. "It" may "give you a line," "give you a snow job." In contrast, the file is trustworthy. It contains absolute legal identity, the fingerprints. In addition, it provides us with the body's character—an account of its values and thoughts by way of psychological tests, charts, and reports. The body's ability is also indicated by aptitude and IQ tests. The body's photograph, evidence toward which one is inclined to react in a more personal manner, is tucked away in an envelope at the back of the file. (Letkemann, 1973:18)

Given the process of retrospective interpretation, the establishment of files, and the extraordinary durability of case reports, all of which emphasize the "abnormal" and what is "wrong" with the actor, it may be difficult for one to return to a state of "health" or other socially acceptable status after they have experienced a transformation of character and been labeled (Newberger and Bourne, 1978:601; cf. Whiting, 1977).

It should be noted that, to some degree, rule breakers are constrained to contribute to their own identity transformation (Perrucci, 1974:166). Like others, rule breakers, too, engage in retrospective interpretation. Given their shared cultural resources, rule breakers and accusers may well embrace similar sets of explanations for rule breaking. Assuming this commonality, the rule breaker may easily be persuaded to agree with the accusers' definitions. Moreover, primary deviants who are confused, anxious, and ashamed may be specially vulnerable to the interpretations or explanations offered by control agents. Being vulnerable, they may be more prone to give approval to or concur with other's interpretations, especially when these are professional, assertive, and official. Added to this is the promise of being rewarded for agreement and the threat of greater problems for resistance. Presented with the option of prison or being "out in the sunshine this afternoon," most defendants take the latter course, in spite of its accompanying guilty plea and resultant criminal record.

THE STATUS DEGRADATION CEREMONY

The combined influence of the processes discussed above is never more apparent than in the *status degradation ceremony* (Garfinkel, 1956). Similar to ceremonies such as christenings, circumcisions, puberty rites, bar mitzvahs, confirmations, and marriages, degradation ceremonies signal a change in one's public status and a passage to a new one. However, in the status degradation ceremony, "the public identity of the actor is transformed into something looked on as lower in the local scheme of social types" (Garfinkel, 1956:420). Examples include court trials, juvenile court hearings, incompetency hearings, and psychiatric screening boards. Each is intended to signify a *total* change in actor's identity to a new status that reflects not only what a person has done, but also why they are supposed to have done it.

Status degradation ceremonies also express moral indignation. They are *denunciatory* transformations of an actor's former public identity; actor's moral identity is virtually destroyed and replaced by a totally new stigmatized identity. Thus,

> The work of denunciation effects the recasting of the objective character of the perceived other: The other person becomes in the eyes of his condemners literally a different and new person. It is not that the attributes are added to the old "nucleus." He is not changed, he is reconstituted. The former identity, at best, receives the accent of mere appearance . . . the former identity stands as accidental; the new identity is the "basic reality." What he is now is what, "after all," he was all along. (Garfinkel, 1956: 421–422)

While degradation ceremonies tend, for the most part, to be retrospective, they may also have an anticipatory element and reflect concern over actor's future behavior. Having transformed the actor from a person who engages in deviant behavior to one who *is* deviant results in the prediction that they will continue to behave in ways consistent with their newly recognized "essential" deviant self.[9]

The Court Trial as a Degradation Ceremony

One example of a degradation ceremony is the court trial, where elements of fact, and their definition and interpretation, are struggled over. Viewed as degradation ceremonies criminal trials involve the determination of whether the defendant is the type of person capable of doing the particular crime charged as much as whether they did in fact do it. "In other words, is the defendant a social instance of a thief, murderer, rapist, etc.? Can he be made to represent the crime with which he is charged" (Hadden, 1973:270; cf. Bennett and Feldman, 1981)? Two versions of the defendant's character vie with each other, that of the prosecution and that of the defense. The jury's task is to render judgment as to which interpretation of fact and character is the most valid. In making its decision, the jury gives formal legitimacy to one version of reality. We shall consider the elements of the trial as a process of reality construction.

Prosecutors seek to portray the accused as someone different from the public construction of "normal," e.g., different from people who ordinarily sit on juries. From the prosecutor's perspective, all cases must provide an interpretation of the alleged criminal behavior that jurors may regard as internally consistent. Each of the elements of the story— actor, scene, purpose, agency, and act—must be defined and clearly relate to the crime. It must be shown that the defendant (actor), on a particular date and time and in a specified place (scene), with full awareness and intention (purpose), by use of some specified means such as threats, force, misrepresentation of self, etc. (agency), acted in a manner proscribed by law and that the defendant had a motive for doing so. While the specific tactics used to achieve this consistency will vary from case to case, it is important that all elements be coherent with one another (Bennett and Feldman, 1981:94–96).

To counter this effort, defense attorneys use strategies similar to those used by individuals in their own techniques of neutralization (see Chapter 3). Thus, they seek to establish that (1) the act in question was not deviant (claim to normality), (2) that the defendant was not in control when the act was committed (denial of responsibility), (3) that the defendant did not know the act was prohibited and had no intention of defying the law or producing harmful consequences (denial of intent), or (4) that the defendant is a victim of a vendetta by the state and is, in fact, harmless (condemnation of the condemners) (Hadden, 1973:272). Each strategy is intended to frustrate the prosecutor's effort to create a discreditable image of the defendant and is that much more powerful than it would be if the defendant was saying this alone, since it is translated into terminology acceptable to the court (Scott and Lyman, 1968).

The defense uses a variety of other strategies as well (Bennett and Feldman, 1981:98ff). One, the *challenge*, is intended to refute the prosecution's claim that evidence supports the elements of the story. A second is called *redefinition*; this involves trying to demonstrate that one or more of the story elements provided by the prosecution is ambiguous and, hence, may be otherwise explained. For example, if the defense can show the person accused of burglarizing a store had been drinking heavily and had entered the store to seek relief in a rest room where they fell asleep, it is possible to redefine the element of purpose or intent. A third strategy, *reconstruction*, calls for altering the context in which the action took place. The classic example of this is to have the jury perceive as "self defense" what the prosecution calls murder. This may be achieved by "showing that the defendant could have been at the scene without intending to kill the victim, that the defendant had no prior reason to kill the victim, and that the means of causing death reflected a spontaneous response [not premeditated] to serious provocation" (Bennett and Feldman, 1981:104–105). In the final analysis, whatever tactics and strategy are used, all involve retrospective interpretation. The central role of the process of moral reconstruction to the working of the court is why some observers describe this approach as the "status passage" model (King, 1981). It can be further illustrated by examining the operation of the juvenile court.

CONSTRUCTING MORAL CHARACTER: THE JUVENILE COURT

The moral passage of actors, how they are categorized, transformed, and assigned a moral character through retrospective interpretation, has been revealed in Robert Emerson's (1969) investigation of the juvenile court. As instances of status passage, juvenile court proceedings show how the construction of the offender's moral character is greatly influenced by various court officials, parents, and other witnesses to the alleged rule violation and by the general demeanor of the offender. How, and what, information is presented to the court will eventually result in the status of the adolescent offender being categorized as a "normal" or "abnormal" delinquent.

Pitches and Denunciations

According to (Emerson, 1969:104), information presented to the court as a "pitch" is designed to cast the offender in the most favorable moral light. Like the "claim to normality" discussed in Chapter 3, the pitch is an attempt to have the delinquent defined as "typical," that is, normal. As if to balance the ledger, the youth's socially approved qualities are emphasized while their opposite is ignored, hidden, or normalized. The youth must be shown to have redemptive qualities. Pitches, then, provide a foundation for the attribution of a socially acceptable moral character. They are, in short, a professionally rendered rationalization used when rehabilitation and leniency are desired and to keep the accused from being sent to a detention center or dealt with punitively.

The *denunciation*, in contrast, is intended to "(a) establish that the present act is of a kind typically committed by a delinquent or criminal like character and (b) construct a delinquent biography that unequivocally indicates someone of such character" (Emerson, 1969:105). Emphasis is placed on the offender's lack of redeeming qualities, failings, and social unacceptability. In short, the offender is defined as abnormal. The denunciation is used to stigmatize the adolescent in order to both legitimate punitive sanctions and to demonstrate the futility of rehabilitation.

While having different goals, pitches and denunciations rely on similar techniques in order to establish plausible links between the delinquent act, the delinquent's biography, and the moral character being presented to the juvenile court. We will consider both the act and the biography.

Linking Delinquent Acts and Actors

In juvenile court the bureaucratization of clients and their actions occurs when offenses and offenders are categorized in organizationally convenient ways. Thus, any given delinquent act may be categorized as "typical," "criminal," or "disturbed" (Emerson, 1969:109–110). Associated with each category are distinctive motives (intentions) and distinct kinds of persons (actors). Acts and moral character are perceived to be interdependent. For example, to be perceived as "typical" means that an assault (the illegal act) will be defined as a "fight"—an ordinary event. To be classed as "criminal," the assault must be seen as one-sided in which power and responsibility are concentrated in the hands of the accused who dominates the other who is the victim. If seen that way, the offender's character must be suitably altered and a relevant motive pattern established. It is presumed that one who engages in criminal assault is a qualitatively different "kind of person" from one who engages in ordinary fighting. Finally, the "disturbed" category requires the assault to be perceived as "vicious," lacking sensible motivation and occurring for "no reason." Such acts are seen as particularly dangerous, risking possible loss of life, and the work of a "disturbed" person.

The offense of sexual misconduct by a female may be similarly categorized. If defined as a case of incidental or nonrepetitive sexual contact, the behavior may be regarded as "typical." Though officially frowned on, it is unlikely to be seen as reflecting a morally unique character. However, if the record reveals that the youth's sexual episodes are regular and persistent, they will likely be defined as "criminal," i.e., prostitution. Character would change accordingly. Lastly, if these sexual encounters are reported to involve the client's willing submission to several males in quick succession and be orgiastic, the act and actor would likely be assigned to the "disturbed" category. The act and moral character then are linked and categorized in ways that make sense to the court. Categorization of acts and actors thus rests on a combination of several "indicators" about which meanings are constructed that allow them to be classed as "typical," "criminal," or "disturbed."

Evaluating Biography

Court generated inquiry into the actor's biography (background) also involves the use of the pitch or the denunciation. The pitch will be used to create the image of a youth whose school record, family situation, known delinquent history, etc., show the promise of successful rehabilitation. A denunciation is used to define a youth as showing signs of progressive moral decline and in need of restraint and punishment. In either case, consulting the biography aids in (1) reconstructing the actor's moral character, and (2) helping to "place" the youth in terms of the development of a delinquent career (Emerson, 1969:120–121).

Whether the pitch or the denunciation is used depends on the court personnel's perception of where the youth stands in relation to a delinquent career. That perception rests on (1) the court's definition of the general pattern of delinquent behavior (is it characteristically "typical," "criminal," or "disturbed?"), and (2) the meaning of various environmental conditions (such as family situation) felt to cause serious delinquency (Emerson, 1969:121–132). Concerns over the general pattern of behavior lead to a standard series of inquiries. Is the present offense one of a series? Has the youth had prior contact with the juvenile court? Has the youth had previous commitment to a training school indicating the establishment of a pattern of serious delinquency? Where the presentation is denunciatory, attention will focus on these questions and the details recounted.

Events of a more personal nature will also be investigated. What is the youth's "attitude"? Does the behavior with respect to the police, the court, and the offense reflect a "hard core" delinquent or a person who is amenable to treatment? How does the offender get along with the staff and other students at school? What attitudinal pattern is reflected in the actor's academic record? Who are the actor's friends and how involved are they in delinquent acts? Such information may be available in the offender's file or be available from imputational specialists. Each piece of information is subject to collation and evaluative interpretation in an effort to "make sense" of the instance of deviance under investigation.

Turning to environmental considerations, investigation of the actor's biography tends to focus on issues of causality. In view of its perceived causal importance, consideration is almost always given to family background, particularly parental neglect or other conditions seen as leading to reduced guidance and social control. The amount and kind of parental discipline, general conduct of the home, and whether the parents' behavior conforms to the moral expectations of the court will also influence assessment of the child's moral character and prospects. Basically, the questions posed concern whether the moral stature of the family is reputable or disreputable (Emerson, 1969:133). If the family is deemed disreputable, its stigmatizing power may well be transferred to the youth.

If these inquiries fail to provide information sufficient to "clarify" the actor's character, the court may look outside for assistance from professional case workers or other persons who are "above reproach" (e.g., a clergy, teacher, or psychiatrist). Whether these resource persons are used rests on the perceived need to resolve ambiguities (Emerson, 1969:133–136).

Total Denunciation—The "Hopeless Case"

We have noted that denunciations emphasize the socially negative aspects of actor's behavior and character. Carried to the extreme, such emphasis precludes justification for the behavior and weakens any support the actor may have for retaining a moral identity. Such cases, referred to as *total denunciations* (Emerson, 1969:137), call for constructing a "hopeless case." That is, the actor must be presented as one who has ignored or rejected several opportunities to refrain from rule-violating behavior. If supported, that contention may lead to the conclusion that the youth is a "hopeless case," beyond reform, suited only for punitive rather than rehabilitative disposition. If there were numerous rejections of opportunities to "go straight" then the fault is seen to rest solely with the offender and there are no defenses for the behavior.

Total denunciation also disallows a defense in another way. First, all parties to the degradation ceremony—officials, witnesses, perhaps family—agree that the actor is a hopeless case and fully discredited. Second, disallowing a defense means there is no suitable alternative to detention, which is seen as a logical and reasonable consequence of the youth's failure to take advantage of the available rehabilitative opportunities. This failure is used to mark the actor's essential character as discreditable. Using constructs such as "unresponsiveness to rehabilitation" as evidence, detention is defined as the only reasonable disposition.

Finally, anyone defending the actor as socially redeemable or who would question the propriety of total denunciation of persons written off as thoroughly immoral must also be discredited. Persons likely to support the youth, such as parents, are often encouraged to concur in the denunciation, at least to the degree of conceding that actors should be sent away for their own good. In this regard, total denunciation involves a systematic connection, a *circuit of agents* (Goffman, 1973:100), between court officials, next-of-kin, police, and defense counsel, who engage in *stripping*, the official removal of the symbols of a socially acceptable being.

In sum, degradation ceremonies mark the end point in the process of status passage that restructures one's character and moral status. The moral self is "killed off" and replaced by the immoral. However, this recasting is not an automatic consequence of one's behavior. Consistent with our comments throughout, control agents do not passively respond to objective moral meaning linked to offender's behavior and the accused is not wholly passive in the construction of their new public identity. The moral meaning of the behavior rests on the court's definition of contextual, biographical, and other materials, and in part on the acceptance, albeit often through defense bargaining, of the new moral status. The goal of the process is to establish consistency between the actor's behavior, biography, and presumed character. The outcome is a negotiated, legitimated congruence that is nothing less than the social construction of a new moral status, itself available for future reconstruction.

THE CASE OF TOTAL INSTITUTIONS

The contribution to the "shaping" process by official agencies is most apparent and most significant in *total institutions*. These are organizations that demand (though rarely receive) total subordination of the client population and that severely restrict association between client and "free" population groups (Goffman, 1961:4–5). Examples of total institutions include military boot camps, detention centers, mental hospitals, and prisons. Of special relevance to assuming the deviant identity is the way these institutions remove symbols of one's individual and social statuses and replace them with those indicating uniformity and unacceptability. In view of the power of this process, this type organization deserves special consideration.

Admission to total institutions involves a variety of rituals that reduce or eliminate the uniqueness of self among inmates. Because it is perceived as a threat to agency routines and a contribution to a person's immoral past, inmate's nondeviant identity and prior conception of self are eroded by a "series of abasements, degradations, humiliations, and profanations" (Goffman, 1961:14). For example, as a person enters prison they are fingerprinted and photographed, subjected to a mortifying rectal (and, if a woman, vaginal) examination, stripped of a name in preference for a number, possibly subjected to a haircut of a standard sort, disinfected, and otherwise "cleansed." Called "trimming," "programming," or "being squared away," these procedures shape the actor into an object that can be fed into the administrative machinery of the organization, to be worked on smoothly by routine operations" (Goffman, 1961:16). The following statement on the intake process from an officially produced information video about the state prison at Jackson, Michigan affirms these observations:

> All prisoners enter at a reception center. The prisoner enters the reception area . . . where he is physically processed. That is, he is stripped, searched, showered, given prison clothes, photographed and assigned a prisoner ID number, given an ID card, undergoes "health screening," given a bed robe, is given a personal hygiene package, assigned a cell, given physical and psychological screening and an educational assessment. (Michigan Judicial Institute, 1991)

Shaping is not limited to the admissions period. Mortifying experiences may be imposed at various points during one's incarceration or hospitalization in order to bring obstreperous, boisterous, or otherwise unruly clients back into line. The following account by a prison inmate makes this clear:

> I have never gone a month in prison without incurring disciplinary action for violating rules. . . . I've been subjected to strip-cells, blackout cells, been chained to the floor and wall; I've lived through the beatings, of course; *every* drug science has invented to "modify" my behavior. . . . They've even armed psychopaths and put them in punishment cells with me to kill me. A prisoner is taught that what is required of him is to *never* resist, *never* contradict. A prisoner is taught to *plead* with the pigs [guards] and accept guilt for things he never did. I have had guards I have never seen before report me for making threats and arguing with them. I have been taken before disciplinary committees of guards for things I have never done, things *they knew* I never did. . . . To say you are *not* responsible . . . in the face of your accusers, accusers who also justify their mistreatment of you by those accusations is to be really responsible for your words and deeds. Because every time you reject the accusations, you are held responsible *further* for things you are not responsible for. (Abbott, 1981: 14–41)

The message: defiant clients are not tolerated. The result: exposure to humiliating experiences leading to the deadening or "mortification" of one's individuality and preinstitutional self (Goffman, 1961).

Individuals also experience mortification due to *contaminative exposure.* Persons in total institutions are typically denied the opportunity to protect the self and its symbols from contamination (i.e., "soiling") by association with others. They must excrete, bathe, and sleep "in public," must reveal every discreditable fact about themselves, and are forced to associate with and subordinate themselves to persons they would otherwise shun (Goffman, 1961:24–35). Inmates are denied personal belongings and are issued regulation clothing and equipment. Access to personal belongings, ranging from clothing to cigarettes, is often restricted in conformity to organization rules and their rationale. Even names are replaced by numbers. Going to bed, getting up, working, eating, and playing are at the command of agency personnel. Over time the effect of these experiences is *personal defacement*, i.e., one is "stripped of his usual appearance and of the equipment and services by which he maintains it" (Goffman, 1961:20). Things that are expressions of self and symbolic of identity are denied. The consequence is an ongoing erosion of one's former self and a deepening of one's involvement in a deviant career.

Mutilation of the body may also be included as part of the "shaping" process. Chemotherapy, electroshock therapy, and surgical techniques such as lobotomy have all been officially authorized (Kesey, 1962:269; Jackson, 1973:42ff; Chambliss, 1971). In addition to its prescribed forms, mutilation also occurs informally. Thus, in 1987 New Jersey State Senator Richard Codey "watched [state mental hospital employees] corral and prod patients with a pointer, heard [an employee] brag of sexually assaulting sleeping female residents and was ordered not to intervene when a disturbed patient stuffed cigarette ashes and butts into his mouth" (*Tempe Daily News/ Tribune*, 1987a). Even lacking direct imposition of these forms of mutilation, the simple threat of them may be sufficient to inhibit, intimidate, and control the client population.

Intimidation and control may also be sought by means of verbal humiliation. Being required to address institutional personnel using terms of deference (while similar regard is systematically withheld from the client population) is common. Some prison administrative personnel pride themselves on their ability to know and refer to every inmate by number rather than name. To have one's name stripped away is to suffer the removal of a symbol of one's identity and individuality. It is an assault on self.

Though the precise elements of the shaping process will vary with the agency and the situation, the following lines illustrate the experience and also the resistance to this kind of humiliation:

> Every society gives its men and women the prerogatives of men and women, of *adults*. After a certain age you are regarded as a man by society . . . no one interferes in your affairs, slaps your hands or ignores you . . . you are shown respect. Gradually your judgement is tempered. Your experience mellows your emotions because you are free to move about anywhere, work and play at anything. . . . You are taught by the very terms of your social existence, by the objects that come and go from your intentions, the nature of your own emotions—and you learn about yourself, your tastes, your strengths and weaknesses. You, in other words,

mature emotionally. A prisoner who is not state-raised tolerates the [prison regime] because of his social situation prior to incarceration. He knows things are different outside prison. But the state-raised convict has no conception of any difference. He lacks experience and . . . maturity. His judgement is untempered, rash; his emotions are impulsive, raw, unmellowed. . . . At age thirty seven I am barely a precocious child. My passions are those of a boy. . . . Can you imagine how I feel—to be treated as a little boy and not as a man? And when I was a little boy, I was treated as a man—and can you imagine what that does to a boy?. . . . A guard frowns at me and says "Why are you not at work?" or "Tuck in your shirttail!" Do this and do that. The way a little boy is spoken to. This is something I have had to deal with . . . for eighteen years. And when I explode, then I have burnt myself by behaving like a contrite and unruly little boy . . . the state-raised convict's conception of manhood . . . is a fanatically defiant and alienated individual who cannot imagine what forgiveness is, or mercy or tolerance, because he has no *experience* of such values. (Abbott, 1981:11–14)

As this example reveals, there are numerous ways for a person to suffer a mortification or deadening of self. Overall, however, a person's prior "innocence" and identity are suppressed if not obliterated by being ignored, ridiculed, humiliated, etc. In their place one acquires a deviant identity and is responded to as an "outsider," at least morally, and is dealt with as such. This entails more than assuming an alternative status, however. Being identified as "lower" in the moral order of things serves also to justify "treatment" by practitioners in total institutions.

RESISTANCE TO LABELING

Consistent with the model of human nature discussed in Chapter 1, the above illustration indicates that people do not always submit meekly to status degradation and moral recasting. In this final section we will examine how people resist labeling and what factors appear to assist them in that effort.

Power: Bargaining and Negotiation as Strategies

One major factor influencing the labeling process is the relative power of the labeler (control agents) and the actor who is labeled. As noted in Chapter 4, power is distributed unevenly. But rarely is it so unevenly distributed that one party has all, while another has none. This is especially so when coalitions, exchange of favors, situational advantages, and other factors that enhance one's power position are considered. It should be no surprise, then, that power may be employed in strategic ways by both parties engaged in the labeling process.

One example of the strategic use of influence is *plea bargaining* (Michalowski, 1985:210–215; Newman, 1966) in which defendants in criminal cases plead guilty to reduced charges and reduced sentences; in return, prosecutors avoid costly, full-scale prosecutions. Such agreements account for between 90 and 95% of all criminal convictions in this country (Blumberg, 1967:29; Newman, 1966:3). Plea bargaining demonstrates that guilt and responsibility are human constructs arrived at through negotiation rather than being absolute and objective (Scheff, 1968:3–4).

A second type of "negotiating" involves people's efforts to amass *moral credits* that may be used ("drawn on") at a time when their moral image is jeopardized by public awareness of wrongdoing. (A similar process occurs in the neutralizing role of the "metaphor of the ledger." See Chapter 3.) Having these credits available helps support one's claim to an acceptable social position despite having broken rules. One such case involved the premarital pregnancy of a young woman belonging to an ascetic religious group. Ruling out marriage and abortion, the young woman feared she would be stigmatized when her pregnancy became public. In an effort to neutralize that anticipated consequence she worked to build up moral credits on which to draw when and if necessary. She gave up smoking and the small amount of alcohol she consumed, refrained from even the mildest forms of revelry, did every extra chore at home she could, worked very hard in school to raise her grades, etc. In short, she lived as exemplary a life as she could in order to accumulate "credits" and reinforce her positive moral identity.

Not everyone facing stigmatization needs to "negotiate" in this way; the need is influenced to some extent by the definition constructed about people's social position. For example, the positive characterological attributes assigned to persons of great wealth, power, and high social status are felt to work as mitigating factors when and if they are convicted of crime. Thus, in comparison to the poor and persons of limited social status,

> officials are inclined to believe that "respectable" people are more easily hurt by the . . . embarrassment and discomfort of being arrested or charged. Thus, the rich are more likely to be treated as having suffered enough without resorting to incarceration, . . . "Good families," good jobs, and other visible contributions of defendants to the community weigh in their favor. It also helps for those who can afford it to show that private arrangement have been made for treatment or that defendants

have continued working without incident while awaiting trial. (Pepinsky and Jesilow, 1984:87)

Lacking these "credits," Pepinsky and Jesilow suggest, the poor suffer harsher penalties "by default."

A third way people avoid labeling is by "subverting the system." For example, despite frequent and extensive episodes of drunk driving, many men learn how to avoid being identified as alcoholic and escape being convicted of driving while intoxicated (DWI). Kotarba (1984) discovered that these men frequently swap yarns about how they successfully handle drunk driving problems. By swapping tales with others they learn ways to justify their own behavior, neutralize the impact of admitting such behavior on feelings of self (e.g., the idea that they "can't hold their liquor"), and acquire recipe knowledge concerning how to manage future problems (e.g., damaging consequences for self feelings) when faced with a DWI conviction. In short, subcultural elements shared by these men enable them to "subvert the system" and reduce the negative effects of labeling.

Fourth, people avoid labeling by putting on a "performance" (Lorber, 1967:303), which is always possible when one wishes to influence or control other's conduct toward self. This is accomplished by trying to influence other's definition of the situation and get them to "voluntarily" behave in the desired way (Goffman, 1959:4). For example, those engaged in welfare fraud learn routinely acceptable ways to account for their "need" for assistance. Some claim that they are new in an area, have no friends or relatives, and no means of employment. Although the welfare officers may suspect fraud, such "performances" may be convincing enough to put the agency in a position of compliance based on the general principle of "if in doubt, pay out" (*Primetime Live*, ABC-TV, 1992).

Similarly, an investigation of delinquency among Japanese-American boys (Chambliss and Nagasawa, 1969) revealed that the boys played to stereotypes in an effort to influence police definitions of their behavior. For example, playing on the already existing favorable bias police had of them, these boys would explain their presence on the streets at unusual nighttime hours as a consequence of work or other socially acceptable conditions, e.g., claiming they were detained at a late Boy Scout meeting or other socially acceptable event. During predaylight hours a frequently used excuse was "preparing for newspaper delivery."

Other studies have found that young offenders who display respect for the police and show remorse (both of which may be feigned) are prone to be given a formal or informal reprimand and released, while youth who are "fractious, obdurate, and nonchalant" tend to be viewed as "tough-guys" or "punks" and arrested (Piliavin and Briar, 1964). Further, labels may be withheld or less forcefully applied if offenders are contrite and willingly acknowledge having violated an important rule. By taking a repentant position the violator (1) acknowledges the legitimacy of the rule and, thereby, (2) establishes a moral consensus (albeit counterfeit) between themselves and the control agent (Gusfield, 1967:179). In this way violators are able to influence the behavior of labelers. As Blumstein et al. (1974) show, accounts by those whose behavior is questioned are honored when they confirm the reality of the questioner.

A fifth tactic used by accused persons seeking to obstruct labeling is *counterdenunciation*, i.e., attacking the actions and motives and/or character of one's accusers (Emerson, 1969:156ff), either by "condemning the condemners" or by denying the victim's status as undeserving (see Chapter 4). Thus, men accused of rape frequently try to destroy the credibility of the accusation by claiming the victim is mentally unbalanced, sexually frustrated, or an oversexed, promiscuous whore (Brownmiller, 1975:238). Another counter denunciation is to *appeal to higher loyalties* or resort to a justification. For example, a man on trial for refusing military induction justified his action on the basis of his greater devotion (a "higher" loyalty) to the principles of peace and humanity than to the state's policy of war and destruction (Bannan and Bannan, 1974:25; Parker and Lauderdale, 1980:54ff). In these and other ways defendants try to delegitimate the charges against them and undermine the legitimacy of the prosecution.

Finally, resistance to labeling was noted by Emerson in his work on the juvenile court, where youth display a number of *protective or defensive strategies*. One is to professes technical or factual *innocence* of the charge. This is particularly effective when evidence is conflicting and the physical facts of the case are inconclusive (Emerson, 1969:144–149). A second strategy is to use principled or situational *justifications*. Principled justifications require "placing" the youth in a situation involving a conflict of principles (not unlike an "appeal to higher loyalties"), the resolution of which allegedly resulted in the violation. Situational justifications are used when one cites the contingencies of his or her actual situation. Thus, the act is acknowledged to be wrong, but the circumstances are said to have been such as to permit an exception. A third strategy involves *excuses*, stories designed to reduce the wrongfulness of the act. Well-handled, "reasonable excuses allow the court to form and maintain an acceptable evaluation of moral character and in this way further favorable dispositions" (Emerson, 1969:153). Elements used in excuses include duress, accident, ignorance, or that one was innocently led into an act that was planned and initiated by others (see also Scott and Lyman, 1968).

In these and many other ways individuals seek to limit the capacity of officials to attach labels. This effort is consistent with our model of human nature. As interactive agents, people seek to direct and control the actions of others toward themselves. However, as we will see in Chapter 7, efforts to resist and neutralize the effects of labeling move beyond the individual into the collective and political levels.

Social Distance

A final consideration when seeking to understand the process of labeling is *social distance* (the degree of intimacy and sympathetic understanding between people). As the intimacy and sympathetic understanding between the labeler and the labeled increases (resulting in reduced social distance), the probability of being labeled decreases. For example, Emerson claims that if complaints against a youth are brought by a person of his or her own age, or by a family member (wherein social distance is minimal), counterdenunciation is likely to succeed and the charges will be dismissed. But if the complainant and the accused are socially distant, counter denunciation is more difficult and charges are less likely to be dismissed (Emerson, 1969:160–161). As Rubington and Weinberg note (1973:9), the tendency is to grant rule-breaking ingroup members the benefit of the doubt and withhold the attribution of deviant. Similarly, Newberger and Bourne (1978:601) suggest that physicians are least likely to identify an individual as a child abuser if that person and the physician share similar social characteristics, especially similar socio-economic status. However, if the alleged abuser is perceived to be "socially marginal," i.e., to show signs of poverty, be unemployed, have a large family, be alcoholic, have a low level of education, etc., the probability of being confirmed as a child abuser increases substantially.

A final observation is in order. The power to label and the power to resist can be mutually constitutive such that resistance and control fuse into a new form that satisfies neither controllers nor controlled, destroying both. This is nowhere better illustrated than in the following insight from Jack Henry Abbott:

> No one has the right to take Jack Abbott away from Jack Abbott, not my soul. Yet that is what is being done to me. I have become a stranger to my needs and desires . . . . I cannot imagine anyone with more moral stamina, more psychological endurance and more willpower than I myself have. I have measured all these things and I know. I have seen men around me through the years fall apart morally, seen them go mad in subtle ways, and seen them surrender their will to the routine of prison, and I have resisted it all much longer than others. I know how to live through anything they

could possibly dish up for me . . . starvation was once natural to me; I
have no qualms about eating insects in my cell or living in my body wastes
if it means survival. . . . When they say "what doesn't destroy me makes
me stronger" that is what they mean. . . . But you cannot spit in my face
every day for ten thousand days; you cannot take all that belongs to me,
one thing at a time, until you've gotten down to reaching for my eyes, my
voice, my hands, my heart. You cannot do this and say it is nothing
. . . [when] what faces you is a cesspool world of . . . noxious sewage,
piles of shit and vomit and piss. . . . You do not ignore all this and live
"with it"; you enter it and become a part of it. . . . And after it is all done to
you—what point is served by keeping you in prison? It is no longer
possible to punish you. You have been rendered unpunishable. (Abbott,
1981:23–41)

Labeling, then, is not simply an automatic or inevitable consequence of
rule-breaking behavior, but an ongoing process of construction and reconstruction. Labels or categories may be changed (as in the case of plea
bargaining) or entirely withheld (as at many competency hearings) as
a consequence of the interaction between the rule breaker and the
labeler(s).

SUMMARY

This chapter has focused on "creating deviants," i.e., the informal and
formal procedures by which people come to be regarded by themselves
and others as having a deviant identity. This has required a consideration of deviance as a status, achieved and ascribed, primary and secondary, and the seeming capacity of one's deviant status—a master
status—to obscure one's other roles and statuses.

Extended consideration has also been given to the institutionalization
of deviance, i.e., to how responsibility for responding to deviant persons is assigned to bureaucratic organizations, how these organizations
operate, and their impact on the client population. Of major importance
is how these agencies—especially total institutions—mortify the prior
self and replace it with one consistent with a deviant status. Not the
least important element in this process is the construction of stereotypes. Relying on the work of imputational specialists, and by a process
of retrospective interpretation, a biography of the deviant is constructed
that validates the assigned label. In this way actor's character and behavior are linked and shown to be consistent, and the conduct of the agency
vis-à-vis the client is legitimized. The culmination of much of the labeling process is noted in the degradation ceremony through which a person acquires a new moral status.

Overall, being cast as deviant is a consequence of a process of constructing reality, the outcome of which is problematic, uncertain, and unending. Part of what contributes to this uncertainty is that the decisions reached are negotiable (hence, unpredictable), subject to reinterpretation or confirmation, and altogether resistible.

For all of that, some people are subject to the power of agencies and audiences to construct a negative moral identity, one that is deviant, and to be labeled. What, then, are the effects of a "spoiled identity?" We turn now to a consideration of the consequences of labeling and stigma.

NOTES

1. Context is important here. It is not sufficient for a characteristic simply to be different for it to be the basis for ascribed deviance. The difference has also to be judged as significant. This, in turn, depends on context. Groce (1985), for example, in studying the congenitally deaf of Martha's Vineyard found that because of the commonplace occurrence of deafness among the islanders, those people did not consider being deaf either significant or a handicap.

2. It is important to recognize here, however, that primary deviation is incidental activity to that from which a person derives their public and private statuses. In contrast, secret deviance may include behavior that is central to the person's private status (e.g., heroin addiction or compulsive gambling) even though it is absent from their public status. For instance, employees who systematically and regularly steal from their employer may privately see theft activity as their main source of income. However, unless they are discovered, they remain secret deviants. It is because of this confusion that the concept of secret deviance has been subject to much criticism and is little used.

3. Though this probably is the most notable distinction between primary and secondary deviance, there is reason to qualify it as a universally applicable distinction. Of major importance in positing the need for qualification is the process of symbolic labeling, with which we will deal in Chapter 6.

4. Congress has estimated that the annual loss from street crime is less than 5% of the yearly loss from corporate crime (Coleman, 1989:7; Clinard and Yeager, 1980).

5. This ignores the distinction drawn earlier between symbolic and instrumental goals. The present discussion pertains to instances of the instrumental sort where some kind of control is attempted.

6. Consideration of routines and the theory of office is not intended to suggest that these regulatory elements, rules, and so on, become a "strait-jacket" denying practitioners the opportunity to display individuality or inhibiting the creation and application of situationally specific meanings. Thus, for example, while every social control agency has a theory of office, it is problematic which of its specific elements will be applied to any specific case. Nonetheless, as we will see, regimentation does prevail.

7.   Rapid and efficient processing of court cases is the norm. Research in one jurisdiction revealed that almost three-fourths (72%) of municipal court cases were resolved in one minute or less (Mileski, 1971:479). In another jurisdiction, municipal court cases were, on average, disposed of in about 2.2 minutes (Maynard, 1984:44).

8.   The proliferation of imputational specialists reflects the increasing bureaucratization of social control agencies. Supplementing the work of these people is the advent of electronic data processing, especially the storage of highly personal information (often of a damaging sort) that is readily collatable into central files. "With some 3.9 billion records on persons stored in thousands of federal data systems, there is mounting concern that computers could be manipulated . . . to control, intimidate or harass citizenry" (*U.S. News and World Report*, 1978; Whiting, 1977). This situation is perceived by some as a potential "information tyranny." Other observers, of course, define the situation quite differently (White, 1982).

9.   The predictive element of degradation ceremonies parallels the anticipatory aspect of stereotypes and typification. The similarity is not accidental. In each instance the actor's character is assumed to be consistent with the "kind of person" who could behave as he or she is alleged to have acted. In the case of stereotypy and typification, the characterological properties are assigned informally, while in degradation ceremonies they are assigned in an "official" and formal manner.

CHAPTER

6

Consequences of Stigma

INTRODUCTION

Though not all rule breakers are publicly identified and labeled deviant, those who are labeled find that their public identity is "spoiled" and they are burdened with the consequences of stigma. The present chapter deals with the personal and social consequences of people *being the thing they are named* (Manning, 1975:2). Here we focus on the third phase of the deviance process. We begin with an introduction to the concepts of stigma and spoiled identity and follow with a brief treatment of labeling theory. We then consider the practical consequences of labeling and stigmatization in both personal and social terms. Finally, we will attempt to make sense of conflicting research evidence bearing on disputed aspects of the labeling process.

STIGMA AND SPOILED IDENTITIES

A *stigma* is a mark or brand placed on people (e.g., slaves, criminals and others) to indicate their low social position and their status as "outsiders." Stigmata symbolize one's morally *spoiled identity* or social undesirability and take precedence over other qualities to which one may lay claim. On the basis of the alleged "spoilage" one is rejected. This is demonstrated in the historical practice of branding. For example, in 1356 the English Parliament passed a statute decreeing that "any labourer who left his place of work to seek higher wages should be branded with the letter "F" on his forehead as a sign of falsehood" (Hibbert, 1963:33). Two hundred years later runaway servants, under the English Statute of Vagabonds, were branded on the cheek with a "V" and judged a slave for 2 years. For a second offense "he was branded with an "S" on his forehead and to be judged a slave for ever" (Hibbert, 1963:40). Such branding symbolized moral defect and publicly identified people as mor-

157

ally spoiled. As Goffman notes: "an individual who might have been received easily in ordinary social intercourse possesses a trait that can . . . turn those of us whom he meets away from him, breaking the claim that his other attributes have on us" (1963:5).

Not all stigmata are alike. Goffman suggests three types (1963:4–5). First, are *abominations of the body*, i.e., conditions such as physical deformities resulting from birth, illness, or accident that are regarded as repugnant and are the basis on which others ascribe to them the status of deviant. Examples of persons stigmatized in this way include Victor Hugo's fictional character Quasimodo, the *Hunchback of Notre Dame*, as well as John Merrick, the so-called "elephant man" (Montagu, 1979). Second are *blemishes of character*, i.e., negatively defined traits attributed to people having engaged in proscribed behavior—crime, homosexuality, or political radicalism, attempted suicide, and the like. In such cases character traits and behavior are rendered consistent. As an example, political radicals are often characterologically regarded as dangerous, impulsive, and aggressive, while adulterers are often assumed to be immoral, promiscuous, and insecure (Simmons, 1969:29). Third and last are *tribal stigma*, the "stigma of race, nation, and religion, . . . that can be transmitted through lineages and [that] equally contaminate all members of a family" (Goffman, 1963:4). Examples include skin color and names that have specific religious and/or national connotations. In most cases, these stigmata, like abominations of the body, are matters of ascription rather than achievement.[1] To understand the social psychological consequences of stigma it is necessary to understand how labels are imbued with symbolic meaning through interaction.

CONSEQUENCES OF LABELING: THEORY

Symbolic interactionism stresses the idea that human behavior, personality, and self-image rest on the use of language (i.e., symbols) to transmit meaning and that these meaningful constructs emerge in interaction with others. Cooley, for example, argues that people's self-feeling consists of three elements: (1) how we imagine we appear to others, (2) our imagination of how others judge our appearance, and (3) a resulting self-feeling. As a result, people evaluate their behavior, attitudes, and general appearance partly on the basis of how they think others evaluate them. Cooley noted that "we always imagine, and in imagining share, the judgments of the other [person's] mind" (Cooley, 1902:184–85). From such imaginings we derive self-feelings such as shame, pride, mortification, and embarrassment, among others.

Mead takes a similar position: people see themselves as objects as a result of *role taking*, i.e., putting themselves in another's position and identifying with that person (Meltzer, 1967:9). Taking the role of the other depends on the ability to use symbols to communicate or transmit meaning. By learning the symbols common to one's family, friends, neighborhood, etc., a person learns and internalizes others' meanings and definitions. People are then able to put themselves in others' roles— *take the role of the other*—and have other's perspectives become their own. "The standpoint of others provides a platform for getting outside oneself and viewing oneself as other's do. The development of the self is concurrent with the development of the ability to take roles" (Meltzer, 1967:10). This, as well as the development of a self-image is the consequence of the socialization process. It is through this general process, too, that identity is acquired. As Peter Berger notes, "identity is socially bestowed, socially sustained and socially transformed" (Berger, 1963:98). To better appreciate their relationship to labeling deviants, we need to expand briefly on these theoretical issues.

In Chapter 5 we noted that the major differences between primary and secondary deviants are (1) the degree to which their lives are organized around the facts of their deviance, and (2) the difference in their respective self-concepts. Because the primary deviant's transgressions are unknown to public agencies and are incidental and subordinate to their law abiding identity, they continue to be regarded as "essentially innocent." In contrast, the secondary deviant's rule-breaking is publicly known and is the basis by which their public identity is transformed from "essentially innocent" to "basically evil." An appreciation of this consequence of labeling calls for consideration of the distinction between the concepts of *essential* or *substantial* self and that of *situational* self.

In writing about the self, Mead referred to the "I" and the "Me" as interrelated phases of people's personality (Natanson, 1973:17). Viewed analytically, the "I" roughly corresponds to what others have referred to as the *essential* or *substantial* self, i.e., the elements of self that transcend particular situations and reflect what one is "really" thought to be "in essence," "in the first place," "all along," "in the final analysis," "originally" (Garfinkel, 1956). Similarly, the term *substantial self* has been used to refer to the "complex of meanings—or characteristics—which are imputed to a person as a whole . . . , not as a player of special roles in special scenes and times" (Douglas, 1967:282).

The "Me," in contrast, refers to the *"social self*, the object that arises in interaction" (Charon, 1979:82), or one's *situated self*, i.e., the way people refer to themselves in terms of specific roles and statuses. Theoretically, then, while people have only a single substantial self, they have many situated selves—one for every situation or activity in which they are involved.

Consistent with the idea that the "I" and the "Me" are integrated and interactive, a person's substantial self ("I") is a consequence of their having been assigned a series of situated selves ("Mes") (Douglas, 1967:282). Accordingly, the moral meaning of the "I" reflects the cumulative meanings of the "Mes." Once established, the substantial self ("I") begins to dominate and subtly influences the assimilation of situated selves (Mes) subsequently assigned to the actor. Thus, the assignment of successive situated selves over a prolonged period results in a substantial self. In turn, the perceived nature of that substantial self filters the sorts of situated selves that might thereafter be assimilated by the actor. A degree of "moral harmony" between these selves is then predicted.

The theoretical relationship between the substantial and situated selves and the consequences of labeling may now be made clear. As noted, a person's self (or selves) is reflected in the name(s) used to refer to them; such names as "geek," "nerd," "airhead," "slut," or, at the other end of the moral scale, "stud," "rad," "sweet," and "awesome" are terms by which people are known and refer to the categories to which they are assigned. Thus, names or labels serve to "locate" or place people in the social order and rank them relative to others. So, some names indicate the labeled person has more prestige and value in the local scheme of things, while other names indicate the reverse. *A person's public identity consists of the names by which they are known.*

The names indicating one's identity have several sources including transgressions referred to by verbs such as stealing, dealing, selling, drinking, etc. (Rosenberg, 1979:10).[2] So, for example, if one steals, indulges in drugs, sells sexual favors, or drinks alcohol to the extent they are defined as transgressing, they may be "located" in a category reserved for such rule breakers and identified, respectively, as thief, addict or doper, hooker or prostitute, or alcoholic or drunkard. In each instance the transgression forms the basis of an identity. *When nouns replace verbs [as in "he's a (something)"] and are used to characterize people, labeling has occurred.*

Being known by these labels is related to stigmatization in several ways (Rosenberg, 1979:12ff). First, reflecting the relation between master and auxiliary status, people who are labeled are subject to a set of expectations. As a result, *regardless of whether they satisfy the expectation,* people known as criminals, drug addicts, mental patients, etc., are expected to display the behaviors and traits stereotypically linked to those categories. Second, these names serve as the basis for ranking and evaluating people. Because a person's social worth is reflected in the names by which they are known, those who are assigned morally negative or stigmatizing names tend to be devalued. Third and last, these names or labels impact on how people judge or feel about themselves. Whether they experience correspondingly negative feelings of self or retain a positive and combative self-esteem and resist or challenge the devaluation of their social worth will be discussed in Chapters 7 and 8.

These theoretical considerations suggest that how people are defined, evaluated, and responded to by others is (1) reflected in the names others use to identify them, and (2) has important consequences for their feelings of self. In addition, labeling also has social consequences. To understand these we need to consider the process of deviance amplification.

Stabilization and Amplification of Deviance

We have indicated that labeling can result in people adopting the role of deviant (as contrasted with merely breaking rules). Whether they embrace a deviant status in part depends on whether they are socialized to that position and role and whether they learn the appropriate self-feelings. These considerations have led to a major proposition of the labeling perspective called deviancy amplification (Young, 1971). The *amplification hypothesis* states: "rule breakers become entrenched in deviant roles because they are labeled 'deviant' by others and are consequently excluded from resuming normal roles in the community" (Mankoff, 1971:201). Categorizing and labeling people "dramatize" the presumed evil of the act and serve to perpetuate the conflict between the rule breaker and society, In turn, this has negative consequences for the person's self-image. Tannenbaum writes:

> From the community's point of view, the individual who used to do bad and mischievous things has now become a bad and unredeemable human being. From the individual's point of view there has taken place a similar change. He has gone slowly from a sense of grievance and injustice, of being unduly mistreated and punished, to a recognition that the definition of him as a human being is different from that of other[s] . . . in his neighborhood, his school, street, community. This recognition on his part becomes a process of self-identification and integration with the group which shares his activities. (Tannenbaum, 1938:17)

It was Tannenbaum's view that the critical factor in stabilizing people in the position of deviant was the community reaction rather than a person's behavior or character.

Other sociologists suggest that rule breakers who experience degradation ceremonies are put in a position from which there may be little or no escape. For example, Howard Becker contends that "one of the most crucial steps in the process of building a stable pattern of deviant behavior [i.e., becoming a secondary deviant] is likely to be the experience of being caught and publicly labeled as a deviant" (Becker, 1963:31). The negative moral meaning symbolized by the stigma, and the rule breaker's consequent rejection by the community, reduces their chances to maintain a socially acceptable image of self (Erikson, 1964:17). Community rejection, then, is alleged to be a fundamental element in people becoming secondary deviants. Again, Tannenbaum:

> The process of making the criminal . . . is a process of tagging defining, identifying, segregating, describing, emphasizing, making conscious and self-conscious; it becomes a way of stimulating, suggesting, emphasizing and evoking the very traits that are complained of. . . . The person becomes the thing he is described as being. (Tannenbaum, 1938:19–20)

In short, rather than encouraging conformity, it is theorized that labeling pushes the deviant further from "normal" society. Rejected persons then "tend to develop their own values which may run counter to the values of the parent system, the system which defined them as 'outliers'" (Wilkins, 1965:92). Further, as officials receive added information concerning the behavior of deviant groups, reactions intended to curb that behavior persist, perhaps even increasing in intensity. This action–reaction–action cycle is repetitive in nature and may "continue round and round again in an amplifying circuit" (Wilkins, 1965:92).

The deviance amplification cycle may be stated in slightly different terms.[3] To be labeled deviant is to be cloaked with the mantle of a master status that may obscure a person's morally acceptable statuses and alter their identity (Payne, 1973:36). That master status also contains a set of expectations subtly "calling for" the detested behavior in the sense that it is the behavior the audience anticipates and acknowledges or responds to. By dominating people's perception of the labeled rule breaker, the master status reduces the probability that actor will be credited with other behaviors, especially law abiding behaviors. After all, rule violators are expected to violate rules; they are not expected to do much else!

If the actor conforms to these expectations, the label is confirmed and labeling becomes a *self-fulfilling prophecy*. Conversely, the actor may not be given credit for conducting him/herself in a "normal" manner, i.e., for not conforming to the expectations of the deviant status (Tannenbaum, 1938:477). Accordingly, it is theorized that the meaning of one's deviance may prevent the actor from occupying normal statuses or engaging in normal social intercourse. The actor is regarded as a moral pariah and is so treated.

Second, if others respond to the actor in terms of the master status, and because self-feelings are derived from others' reactions, the actor may develop self-attitudes consistent with the moral judgments expressed by others and symbolized by the stigmatizing label. These self-attitudes, as well as the limitations placed on role-playing opportunities, may then become central facts of one's life, entrenching or "engulfing" one in the role of deviant and leading them to enter the stage of secondary deviance (Lemert, 1967:Chap. 3; Schur, 1971:67ff, 1973:115ff; Becker, 1973:31, 179).

Qualifying Labeling Theory

Before concluding this discussion of labeling theory, it is necessary to qualify our earlier remarks and specify what this perspective does not mean. First, labeling theory does not suggest that secondary deviance or amplification is a simple, automatic result of others imposing their definitions on helpless rule breakers. As our model of human nature suggests, rule breakers and officials are interactive agents defining, ordering, and adapting to elements in their environment. The labeled deviant, then, is not to be thought of as "a pinball inevitably propelled in a deviant direction, or . . . the police [as] . . . the cushions of the machine that will inevitably reflex into a reaction triggered by the changing course of the deviant group" (Young, 1971:34). Nonetheless, negative responses by the community and its representatives are major conditions with which labeled persons must deal. Because labeling "places the actor in circumstances which make it hard . . . to continue the normal routines of everyday life and thus provoke . . . 'abnormal' actions" (Becker, 1973:179), the actor's exercise of self-determination may be reduced. Thus, *though it does not cause rule-breaking behavior*, responses to the meanings of labels may help to intensify, enlarge, and prolong one's involvement in a deviant role or toward the aberration of a nondeviant one.[4]

Second, to say that labeling and subsequent reactions are the foundation for secondary deviance is not to locate the origins of rule-violating behavior in people's response to that behavior. The theory does not imply that mental hospitals drive people insane, that police and prisons force innocent people to engage in crime, or that narcotics treatment facilities make addicts of people. Indeed, labeling theory has nothing to say about the etiology of behavior, per se, either conforming or nonconforming. Rather, the theory focuses on the *etiology of the meanings of a condition and their consequences*.[5]

Finally, the theory should not be interpreted to mean that labeling automatically precludes labeled persons from participating in all forms of normal social interaction (Davis, 1975:174). Whether they do so and the degree to which labeling is an impediment depend on a variety of conditions, which we will consider later in this chapter.

With these qualifications in mind, let us examine the consequences of the labeling process in terms of the everyday life experiences of deviant actors.

CONSEQUENCES OF LABELING: PRACTICALITIES

We have noted that naming may have profound consequences for the person named, especially when it involves assigning morally loaded labels. Children know that some words (labels) can raise serious questions about their own fundamental worth. How cool can one be who is tagged "nerd," how brave or manly one who is labeled a "wimp," how strong one who is dubbed "dork," how attractive one who is referred to as "dog," how feminine one who is labeled "tomboy"? Being intended to disparage, such labels may erode a child's sense of self-worth.

Certainly, such labels are not entirely comparable to those used to formally and officially identify deviants. However hurtful, their effect is apparently short-lived for most people, perhaps reflecting the compensating influence of more positive valuations. However, some children do experience the prolonged and agonizing effects of stigmatization. Consider the following:

> I was 4 years old when I started school. My mother had told them I was 5; I was somewhat precocious, and she may just have wanted to get me out of the house. But butch haircut or not, some boys in the third grade took one look at me and said, "Hey, look at the sissy," and they started laughing. It seems to me now that I heard that word at least once five days a week for the next 13 years, until I skipped town and went to the university. Sissy and all the other words—pansy, fairy, nance, fruit, fruitcake, and less printable epithets. I did not encounter the word faggot until I got to Manhattan. I'll tell you this, though. It's not true, that saying about sticks and stones; it's words that break your bones. (Miller, 1971:48)

In short, we should acknowledge what everyday experience tells us— that the psychological and social consequences of stigma and labeling can be extremely damaging to "emotional bones," if not to physical ones. We can better appreciate this by examining the experiences of persons who have been effectively labeled and stigmatized and who have had their public identity changed. We will first examine the consequences of labeling for self-attitudes and follow with a consideration of its social effects.

Social Psychological Effects of Labeling

Symbolic interaction enables people to have a mental life, to experience self, become the subject of their own thoughts, and to define themselves, at least in part, as others do. As a result, labeling influences the way people define themselves (Matza, 1969:143ff; Lemert, 1967:17). Let us consider the practical meaning of this for secondary and for primary deviants.

The Secondary Deviant.   People perceive and relate to secondary deviants largely, if not exclusively, in terms of their spoiled identity. How that experience may contribute to negative self-attitudes is seen in the labels associated with the three identities of skid row alcoholics—the popular, the medical, and the legal. Regarding the popular identity, these men often are labeled "bums," "derelicts," or "transients," and are seen as "people who fail abysmally, are dependent on society, lack self-control, drink too much, are unpredictable, and often end up in jail for their criminal behavior" (Spradley, 1970:66). These labels serve to (1) assign character traits to these people that (2) may be taken as evidence of their lack of social worth—evidence of their "spoilage." For example, "derelict" refers to one who lacks respectability because of being neglectful, irresponsible, undependable, and unfaithful. "Transient," in the pejorative sense, refers to one who is unsettled, migratory, impermanent, unstable, and who cannot be relied on. These ascribed qualities reinforce the popular belief that the way of life of the skid row alcoholic is "irrational, immoral, and irresponsible," i.e., worthless relative to dominant values (Spradley, 1970:66).

The second identity these men share is the medical, which emphasizes the belief that their objective condition (poverty, nomadism, and so on) stems from their drinking behavior, itself a result of alcoholism, a disease that, unlike other illnesses, is believed to influence one's being. For example, while people suffer various diseases and illnesses, their maladies are seen to be temporary and rarely form the basis of a personal noun or adjective reflecting on the quality of the person. People are not "influensics" or "measlitics." Even where a disease's effects are chronic, e.g., stroke, heart attack, cancer, there are often no personal nouns referring to victims. Nor are those conditions the basis for moral judgment. In the case of alcoholism, however, one becomes an alcoholic. Overeaters *are* obese and undereaters *are* anorexic. Similarly, one who suffers paralysis of the lower limbs *is* a paraplegic, one who cannot see *is* blind, and one lacking hearing *is* deaf. And, at least in American culture, these conditions are fused with people's essential character (Romano, 1982:66–67). It matters little that the criteria for some of these conditions, such as alcoholism, lack specificity. Simply, in the nature of stereotypy, those perceived to suffer the condition are burdened with its popularly associated traits (Spradley, 1970:66), many of which are pregnant with moral meaning. Thus, reflecting the evaluational property of adjectives, people experiencing blindness, deafness, mental illness, alcoholism, and other conditions often are marked as inferior, morally or otherwise (Scott, 1970:258; Nunnally, 1961; Rosenberg, 1979:30).

Finally, skid row residents have a legal identity composed of traits that also indicate the belief that these men are morally "spoiled." "In the view of the experienced patrolman, life on skid row is fundamentally different from life in other parts of society . . . skid row is perceived as the natural habitat of people who lack the capacities and commitments to live 'normal' lives on a sustained basis" (Bittner, 1967:705). The quality of life on skid row, then, is seen as a manifestation of the essentially defective character of the people living there. Thus, police view these men as vagrants who, at the very least, are guilty of the moral offense of public drunkenness (Spradley, 1970:67).

As we have indicated, the stereotypical beliefs about those who populate deviant categories come to be reified, i.e., take on "objective" character, and then constitute the reality that provides the framework for the evaluation, judgment, and actions of "normals" vis-à-vis the deviant. For example, such knowledge, leads some sighted persons to shun the blind (Scott, 1969:24), interferes with the establishment of intimate (perhaps sexual) relations between normals and the physically handicapped (Kriegel, 1974:233ff), encourages some police and others to view the skid row resident with fear and apprehension (Bahr, 1973:231), leads people to view the homeless with disgust and insist that they be segregated in some place with "others of their own kind" (Bahr, 1973:64), and leads to the categorical rejection and condemnation of AIDS victims (*Time*, 1985b).

Alteration of Self Feelings.   Consistent with symbolic interactionist theory, research indicates that many secondary deviants entertain feelings of self that correspond to their public image. For example, a majority of men arrested for public drunkenness reported that the worst thing about appearing in court on a drunk charge was "the public humiliation," including one's physical appearance and the difficulty of maintaining an acceptable social image. Said one man about his appearance, "it is degrading to lay in the drunk tank over the weekend and appear in court— no shave, no comb to even comb your hair, clothes all wrinkled" (Spradley, 1970:191). Another commented, "A person is usually sick and dirty from laying on the concrete floor and to have to appear in front of a lot of people in that condition is very humiliating" (Spradley, 1970:191).

Others mentioned their fear of confronting and being recognized by court spectators. One man summarized the feelings of many with one word: "degradation."

Degrading experiences for these men also include the insulting and defamatory ways they are spoken to by officials. Included are the terms used by police (among others) to refer to these men: "tramp," "wino," "bum," "drunk," "dehorn," "skid row bastard," "loser." Men also have to endure threats to their person when they have to deal with police. Such threats as "Shut up or we will beat the shit out of you" clearly inform the person that he is the power subject and that the police are the power holders, and leave men with the idea that theirs is the identity of an inferior (Spradley, 1970:141).

Also affecting their self-conception is the fact that the police frequently rob these men of their possessions (reported by 23% of Spradley's respondents). This experience informs these men that their claim to respectability and consideration is minimal, at best. In a society where one's identity is linked to material possessions, especially money, the loss of such stuff and the lack of means to effect its return may well have a critical influence on one's feelings of self (Spradley, 1970:145). Added to this is the threat of physical assault by police and/or jailers if men protest against the treatment they receive. Thirty-five percent of Spradley's subjects reported that police "rough you up," "hit you," "take shoes to you," "club you," "shake the hell out of you," "work you over," "slam your face on something," "split your head open," "bounce you off his knee," or "drag you someplace" (Spradley, 1970:148–149). Such experiences leave people with a profound sense of vulnerability. Being denied their autonomy, these men's tendency toward self-assertiveness is diminished or extinguished along with their sense of self-worth (Sykes, 1958:73–76; Spradley, 1970:161).

Such experiences are not restricted to members of America's underclass. For example, a college student reported that when she was 15, and in her "punk rock" phase, she was

> vacationing in San Diego when I decided to attend my first punk gig. I went to the show, paid my money and was let in. Ten minutes later cops were swarming the place. They said I was underage and had to come with them. I tried to explain I had no forewarning that minors were not allowed. One of the cops put me in a choke hold and said, "Listen, you little shit, we'll put you to sleep if you don't shut the hell up," and he threw me in the back of the police wagon. (unpublished)

Largely hidden from view, these experiences, often at the hands of the law ("public servants"), effectively inform people of their powerlessness and perceived lack of social worth.[6] They are crucial in amplifying people's deviance in general and affecting feelings of self. Extended over a prolonged period, repeated experiences of this sort lead to the actor being engulfed in the deviant role.

Role Engulfment. *Role engulfment* refers to the process whereby persons become caught up in the deviant role as a result of others relating to them largely in terms of their spoiled identity (Schur, 1971:69ff). As people respond to the actor more in terms of the deviant master status and less in terms of socially acceptable statuses, the deviant status becomes more salient. Becoming engulfed in this way, then, is a cumulative process, sometimes leading people to define themselves as negatively as others define them.

This process is revealed in the way some blind persons are socialized to the "true believer" mode of adjustment, i.e., to

adopt as a part of their self-concept the qualities of character, the feelings, and the behavior patterns that others [those who can see] insist they must have. Docility, helplessness, melancholia, dependency, pathos, gratitude, a concern for the spiritual and the aesthetic, all become a genuine part of the blind man's personal identity. (Scott, 1969:22)

This socialization is sometimes promoted incidentally to the enforcement of rehabilitation agency policies. For example, reflecting the belief that visual impairment carries with it a psychological component, some agencies have insisted that blind students "pass" a Minnesota Multiphasic Personality Inventory test (which, incidentally, has not been standardized for the blind) as a condition for receiving a college tuition grant. What sighted student must "pass" (even submit to) this kind of test in order to obtain aid? By erecting hurdles, people's opportunities for achieving self-sufficiency via the rehabilitative goal of higher education are frustrated. Indirectly, then, agency policy encourages dependency or engulfment.

In another instance, a college student blind from birth was unable to write normal script and was restricted to braille. Whenever he had to sign a document, he was forced to mark an X. Finding this troublesome and degrading, he tried to get a signature stamp and afford himself a measure of dignity. However, agency personnel insisted he learn to sign his name conventionally, a truly formidable task for one who has never seen handwriting and has no conception of its form. By rejecting use of a stamp, the agency was withholding a measure of freedom the student might otherwise have had and subtly added to his engulfment in the role of the blind person.

Third, some agencies insist the visually impaired use canes rather than dog guides, even though many people regard canes as difficult to handle since they can be accidentally run between the legs of passersby, get caught in revolving doors, become jammed in cracks in sidewalks or sewer grates, are easily bent or broken, and are difficult to handle in automobiles and public conveyances unless they are collapsible. In several ways, then, canes place limits on one's mobility, independence, and sense of freedom. For many blind persons, a desirable alternative is the dog guide. More than promoting mobility, dogs help their masters feel a freedom unavailable with canes. Furthermore, research indicates that dogs (guides and others) serve as a "bridge" between strangers and help reduce anonymity. Interactively, they serve as a substitute for eye contact, a vital aspect of initiating and maintaining social relationships. "Dogs facilitate contact, confidence, conversation, and confederation among previously unacquainted persons who might otherwise remain that way" (Robins et al., 1991:23). Despite these advantages, some agencies reject the use of dogs and opt for reliance on canes (Scott, 1965:136).

Engulfment is also apparent in the approach that some agencies have taken to the employability of visually impaired persons (Scott, 1965:136ff). Clients have been told that they will be faced with problems when they seek a job, that there are few jobs for the blind, that employers are reluctant to hire the blind, and so forth. They have been less often told that there are many visually impaired attorneys, physicists, mathematicians, auto mechanics, farmers, and others, i.e., that blind persons occupy a far wider range of occupational roles than stereotypical notions suggest.[7] To restrict blind persons' awareness of employment opportunities is to encourage the "true believer" mode of adjustment and promote role engulfment.

Engulfment is also experienced by those who are deviant by achievement. Thus, persons known to have engaged in crime, drug use, or other questionable behaviors are systematically denied access to several legitimate status positions both on a formal and informal level. Here again, the tendency is for the master status to dominate and influence the way others relate to the deviant, and to shape the deviant's feelings of self.

STIGMA AND THE PRIMARY DEVIANT

By definition, primary deviants do not know themselves and are not known by others as deviants "in the first place" (Lemert, 1967:17). Accordingly, it is sometimes assumed that if the primary deviant's rule-breaking has any impact on self-evaluation, it is transitory and restricted to the person's situated self. However logical and generalizable, this assumption ignores the important process of symbolic labeling. Let us examine this process in detail.

Symbolic Labeling

Symbolic labeling refers to self-labeling (Trice and Roman, 1970; Warren and Johnson, 1972; Rotenberg, 1974) and is wholly consistent with symbolic interactionist theory. Thus, just as people interact with others on the basis of shared meanings, so do they employ these meanings when they interact with themselves (behave reflexively) and engage in self-scrutiny, evaluate their behavior and/or their condition, and derive self-regarding attitudes. For symbolic labeling to occur, then, calls for (1) knowledge of social rules and their moral meanings, (2) self-acknowledgment that one has engaged in disapproved behavior, and/or (3) a sense of the low esteem in which such rule breakers are held. It is assumed only that (1) the individual shares the dominant or popular definition of their behavior or condition, (2) that there are popular labels referring to such people, and (3) that the actor is generally motivated to conform to social norms (Thoits, 1985:223). The rule violator may then proceed to label him/herself in ways consistent with public meanings. This has been observed in its most extreme form among participants in various 12 Step programs such as Alcoholics Anonymous (Trice and Roman, 1970). The outcome may involve a revision of one's substantial self.

To appreciate this process it is necessary to note that symbolic labeling occurs in a social context replete with expressions of the public meanings of deviant acts and actors. For example, young parents sometimes suffer feelings of guilt and label themselves as abusive because they have "deviated" from a stereotype of the ideal parent (Graham, 1981:48). Similarly, sexually active teenagers, aware of their parents' strong disapproval of premarital sexual conduct, often define themselves in negative terms (Briedis, 1975:482–483). Similarly, the public meanings reflected in jokes about fat people, minority people, the mentally retarded (moron jokes), the physically handicapped, "queers," drunks, persons with speech defects, and so on, constitutes the knowledge leading people to experience humiliation and denigration of self—not unlike the consequences of formal degradation ceremonies. One author describes the consequences of his exposure to such knowledge as follows:

> Sometimes I find myself drawn as if into a net by the abuses and sneers of the hostile world. I hear the vile joke or the calumnious remark, and must sit in silence, or even force a smile as it were in approval. A passenger enters an elevator and remarks, "When I come out of a barber shop, I have

a feeling I smell like a fag. I better watch out or some goddamn queer'll pick me up on the way home." The operator laughs, and I find myself forcing a smile, joining in the humiliating remark that is, unknowingly, directed against myself. (Cory, 1951:10)

People who are obese and those who are short also experience humiliation due to the public conception of their condition. For example, every media ad proclaiming "thin is in" demeans the obese, often leaving such people with conflicting emotions and definitions of their condition. On the one hand, many wish never to have the topic of their weight discussed because of its humiliating potential. However, if they lose weight they want to be complimented, yet dislike the implication of the compliment, viz., that they have been overweight and even that weight should be significant (Millman, 1980:80–81). It seems clear that many obese people define their condition and themselves in the same negative way that so many others do and that obesity is a central fact of their life. Similarly, everyday language indicates the low esteem accorded short people. Included are demeaning expressions such as "putting people down," "belittling people," "being shortsighted," "getting the 'short end' of the stick," and "being shortchanged," among others (Feldman, 1975). We have even had popular songs about "Short People" (Randy Newman). When primary deviants judge themselves in terms of such meanings, they may well experience social psychological difficulties.

Guilt, Shame, Transparency, Bedevilment, and Associational Stigma

Primary deviants face additional difficulties as a result of *guilt* and *shame*. Experienced as negative attitudes such as feelings of self-disgust, and a sometime desire to withdraw from public view ("I could have crawled in a hole and pulled it in after me!"), guilt and shame derive "from a horror of being disapproved of by others, particularly by meaningful or significant others, and from the fact that the values of these others have often been accepted by the rule breaker" (Sagarin, 1975:315). Consider the following illustration from a member of Weight Watchers:

I became very aware that I was unattractive when I was fat and it made me very, very miserable. . . . It meant that when I was fat, wherever I went, I was not conscious of being a woman nor of being a nothing or of being a something or of being a friend or of being a stranger. I was conscious of being a fatty and I felt ugly. . . . Day and night for years it got me that bad. (Robinson and Henry, 1977:49)

Guilt and shame may be expected, then, among those persons who anticipate that others will judge them negatively.

Knowing their behavior is banned also means the primary deviant risks losing social acceptability among some persons if information about their behavior becomes public. Accordingly, they are concerned with *transparency*, i.e., with whether they will be able to keep their secret, from whom the information should be kept, and how to manage their secret (Matza, 1969:150). For example, a sexually active young woman explained that she felt guilty because of her parents' attitude toward premarital sex.

> My parents don't know about my personal life. I imagine they have had their suspicions at times, but my mother is adamant about sexual experience before marriage. It would destroy her if she knew about me, I think. (Denes, 1977:35)

Research also reveals that some primary deviants experience *bedevilment*, i.e., they live in fear of losing social acceptability if their secret is revealed (Matza, 1969:146ff). Some fear that public knowledge of their involvement will bring down the law on them, that family members, friends, or neighbors will reject or condemn them, that they may be expelled from school or lose their job. As a result, they struggle with transparency and try to manage their secret. Such concerns have been observed among men responsible for extramarital pregnancies (Pfuhl, 1978; Breidis, 1975:484–485), "closet" gays and those frequenting "tearooms" and other public places for the purpose of engaging in impersonal homosexual encounters (Humphreys, 1970:26, 131; Corzine and Kirby, 1977; Leavitt, 1987), and among persons seeking to avoid acknowledging their dependency on alcohol (Hough, 1974:17). Humor, deceit, and lying are among the tools used by people to maintain their secret, although others will go so far as to engage in "biographical fabrication" such that they come to believe in their own freedom from the problematic condition.

It is important to note that one's degree of concern over such matters varies independently of the depth or frequency of their involvement in rule violations. This is evident in Rossman's investigations of *pederasts* (or pedophiles), males over 18 years of age who engage in sexual acts with adolescent boys. Many of the men studied by Rossman had engaged in a sexual act with a boy only once or twice in their entire life and, at the time of the research, had not had sexual contact with boys for several years. Nonetheless, these men lived in constant fear that this fact from their past would be revealed with devastating consequences. Caution, fear, and secrecy characterize these men's lives. Publicity, research, or public attention is greatly feared, so much so that some pederasts threatened Rossman's life if he persisted in his investigation (Rossman, 1973:30).

Finally, evidence of self-labeling can be found among victims of rule breakers, who, ironically, sometimes suffer as much guilt and condemnation (by self and others) as offenders as a result of *associational stigma*. For example, some female incest victims suffer a derogation of self-image as a result of the guilt they bear even for having been an unwilling participant. Compounding their sense of guilt is the matter of transparency. As one incest victim related,

> The hardest problem I had was that in the period after I left home I was convinced that anybody who saw me could tell that I was bad and that no man would ever want me because I was so bad. That was one of the hardest things to get over. At times the old conviction that I'm a bad woman comes up. To this day, the issue of whether I'm a good or bad woman is alive for me. (Justice and Justice, 1979:182)

Rape victims report similar experiences. Having been socialized to the idea that rape is a sex crime rather than a crime of violence and a violation of human rights, and having learned the rape-related attitudes and values generated in a male-dominated society, many women blame themselves for their victimization. Included is the theory of victim-precipitated offenses: that women precipitate their victimization by placing themselves in situations that "encourage" a sexual encounter or by behaving in a provocative manner. Adding to their negative self-attitude has been the view that rape victims are "despoiled" or "second hand goods" and no longer "suitable" as "male property" whose value is determined by premarital chastity or marital fidelity. As a result of internalizing these ideas, women very often fail to report their victimization, experience severe self-condemnation in private, and live in fear of disclosure. Simply put, "good women" don't get raped (LeGrand, 1973; Marsh, 1983; Scarpitti and Scarpitti, 1977).[8]

The foregoing examples point out the difficulty of distinguishing secondary from primary deviants on the basis that the former entails substantially altered psychic structure and self-regarding attitudes, while the latter involves only limited changes to one's psychological experience. The distinction is more a matter of degree rather than kind. *The issue of salience, i.e., how central or prominent in one's life rule-breaking is, does not adequately differentiate primary from secondary deviants.* Indeed, among primary deviants with active imaginations, the anticipated consequences of revelation may be at least as great as those faced by publicly identified rule breakers. In the case of both primary and secondary deviants, then, rule breakers organize their lives around the facts of their deviance (Lemert, 1967:40–41). We will elaborate on this matter in Chapter 7 where we consider stigma management.

SOCIAL CONSEQUENCES OF STIGMA

Despite widespread denial by officials and others, the social consequences of stigma are multiple. Labeling impacts on self-other relations, involves the rejection of the deviant by others, and may result in severe restrictions being placed on their participation in the normal social life of the community. In the case of disabled persons, for example, there are several ways that the meanings of such limitations intrude on and influence their relations with the able-bodied. First, physical disabilities may become the *focal point of interaction*, influencing conversation, introducing an element of strain into the relationship, and making the interaction a time of general discomfort. Second, and relatedly, is the *inundating potential* of the disability whereby it overwhelms the interaction. For example, rather than good humor, spontaneity, gaiety, relaxation, and laughter, there may be silence, pity, fear, tension, and avoidance as the stigmatized condition dominates people's attention. Third, the meanings of stigmatized conditions can introduce an *element of ambiguity* into a relationship because taken-for-granted expectations that the able bodied have of one another regarding physical activity are unsuitable when applied to the disabled. As a result, the able-bodied do not know what to predict about the disabled's behavior, interests, and capabilities. Lacking alternative definitions, the able bodied person experiences a sense of ambiguity and strain. Shortly we will again refer to these influences. Fourth and last, stigmatized conditions often constitute a *contradiction of attributes*. Thus, consistent with stereotypical ideas and the concept of moral congruence, persons who have been stigmatized tend not to be perceived as occupants of "normal" roles and statuses and are denied the attributes of those occupants. If the stigmatized person displays the attributes of "normals" relative to occupation, tastes, preferences, interests, etc., a sense of discordance may result (Davis, 1961:123–125).

Labeling and stigmatization raise a further set of social barriers as the deviant's identity becomes that of an "outsider" and is denied access to legitimate (nondeviant) positions (Becker, 1963:1). An example of this is the long-standing practice of denying a variety of roles and statuses to known or suspected homosexuals. Thus, the International Association of Chiefs of Police adopted a resolution opposing homosexuals being hired for police work, arguing that the role of policeman is totally inconsistent with one being an "open, obvious, ostentatious" homosexual (*Arizona Republic*, 1977). Similarly, the armed forces have long sought to exclude homosexuals and lesbians by claiming that "the presence of homosexuals in the service . . . could impair recruitment; other young men might feel anxious about living in close quarters with them . . . homosexuals cannot command respect as officers and non-coms and are prey to blackmailers" (*Time*, 1975a; see also *Time*, 1975b; Berube, 1983). Support was provided for this position by the U.S. Supreme Court in February 1990 when it renewed its refusal to consider challenges to the constitutionality of the armed forces' dismissal of homosexuals even if there is no evidence they have actually engaged in homosexual conduct (*Arizona Republic*, 1990).

Such practices reflect the assumption that people known to be deviant possess traits that render them incapable of satisfying normal role expectations. So, "queers" cannot be good soldiers, athletic coaches, or teachers (*Playboy*, 1978:78), prostitutes cannot make good wives or good mothers, people who have smoked marijuana cannot be allowed to be U.S. Supreme Court justices (*Tempe Daily News/Tribune*, 1987b; 1987c) and are suspect when viewed as candidates for president, and convicted felons cannot be given positions of trust. People are taken to be the same as the thing symbolized by the label; they have a moral defect. The alleged moral defect "fixes" them in the position of "outsider" and helps shape others' responses. As our examples show, a basic response is to avoid contact in order to prevent contamination.

Protection of Territories

To a great extent, the restrictive social conditions faced by many rule breakers reflect people's efforts to avoid the contamination of public, home, interactional, and body territories by known deviants who threaten to violate them (Lyman and Scott, 1967). *Public territories* are those areas to which one has freedom of access by reason of citizenship. Nations, schools, cities, and similar places are examples. Closely related and not always distinguishable from these are *home territories*, places where people "have relative freedom of behavior and a sense of intimacy and control over the area" (Lyman and Scott, 1967:238). Churches, clubhouses, and country clubs are cases in point. Indeed, the phrase "homeboy" literally refers to members of a neighborhood. Third, *interactional territories* are any place where people may engage in social interaction. That is, every interaction occurs in some physical place (someone's apartment, a street corner, a tavern) which, for its duration is enclosed by an invisible socially constructed boundary. The social reality of interactional territories is reflected in people's resistance to their penetration by persons other than the interactants. Finally, there is *body territory*, "the space encompassed by the human body" (Lyman and Scott, 1967:241). The existence of body territories may be inferred from people's discomfort and recoil when norms of physical distance are breached and from the selective rights to view and touch their body given to others. This territory has been described as the most sacred of all, as evidenced by the numerous restrictions that exist concerning the time, place, and relationship between persons who may legitimately view, touch, or kiss the naked body of another, engage in sexual intercourse, and so on. In marriage, of course, body territory ordinarily approximates home territory by granting rights to spouses that traditionally have been withheld from others (Lyman and Scott, 1967:241).

Each of these territories is threatened to be encroached on and misused by those who have been labeled deviant, who thereby increase the potential for *violation* (by making unwarranted use of them), *invasion* (cross their boundaries without entitlement), or *contamination* (pollute, corrupt, or otherwise render them impure by use or definition). Viewed in terms of territorial protection, many of the restrictions imposed on labeled deviants become understandable. Given a sense of the deviant as a *pariah*, i.e., someone who is negatively morally valued, people often feel encroached on in their presence. Thus, because of the stigma of nudists and naturists the presence of nude bathers on public beaches is seen as an invasion of public territory. If such efforts succeed, the encroachment may be regarded as an instance of contamination (Douglas and Rasmussen, 1977).

If the presence of the known deviant is regarded as an intolerable encroachment, any of several reactions may occur. One reaction is *turf defense*. An example of this is the efforts by gangs to resist the invasion of its territory by rival gangs whose members are not seen as individuals but stigmatized ambassadors of "the enemy." Another example is citizen opposition to the location of prisons, jails, halfway houses, detoxification centers, and similar facilities in or in close proximity to residential areas based on socially constructed fears associated with the stereotype of the inmates or clients (*Arizona Republic*, 1980c).

Another reaction to known and labeled deviants in defense of territory is *insulation*, i.e., "placement of some sort of barrier between the occupants of a territory and potential invaders" (Lyman and Scott, 1967:246). Examples include the use of their native language by foreign students on university campuses or by residents of an ethnic enclave (such as a Chinatown) to limit contact with those labeled "outsiders."

The social limitations imposed on stigmatized people go beyond territorial protection and extend into almost every facet of everyday life. Thus, irrespective of the offense, a criminal court conviction substantially reduces one's employability (Schwartz and Skolnick, 1964:108–109; Erickson and Goodstadt, 1979). Labeling has also handicapped the physically, emotionally, and mentally disabled in our society, leading them to be seriously unemployed and underemployed, and to retreat from social interaction, hide, or try to "pass" as "normal." As a result, such persons have become "a hidden minority, impotent, hesitant—and contributing less and less to America" (Bowe, 1978:x; also see Safilios-Rothschild, 1970; Fink et al., 1968).

For many labeled persons the consequences of stigma also extend into the most private arenas of life. For example, subjects in one study of the blind reported feeling "ignored" and "overlooked" by sighted people when they entered restaurants, shops, etc. Overall, in their relations with sighted people, 88% of these blind persons reported they suffered from the prejudices of the sighted. Others commented that they were made to feel like "outsiders" and that they felt "forced into the status of a deviant person" (Meyer, 1981:360).

For homosexuals, being identified as gay is often taken by others as an invitation to do violence on the basis that their spoiled identity denies them victim status. The resulting gay bashing, or "queer bashing" has often ended in the death of the victim (*Rocky Mt. News*, 1988). Additionally, homophobia has traditionally interfered with the proper delivery of health care to the homosexual minority, a situation that has intensified with the discovery of AIDS and its identification as a disease of homosexuality (*Time*, 1985a). For those with defective hearing, limited ability to communicate affects relations with family and friends. So, the hard of hearing man "has trouble understanding what his wife is saying, [while] the wife accuses the husband of inattention, which he denies, [and] complains in rebuttal that she mumbles" (Sataloff et al., 1980:358). Compounding the difficulties of the deaf is the taken-for-granted assumption that people ordinarily can hear (as well as the assumption that people can speak and see) and that sometimes leads to tragedy. Thus, Higgins (1980:150) reports the fatal shooting of a deaf mute by a robber apparently because the victim was unable to hear the robber's commands and failed to respond.

Lastly, physical disabilities also impact on people's satisfaction with the companionate aspect of the marital relation (Fink et al., 1968). For example, while husbands of severely disabled women often attempt to spend more time at home with their wives, they frequently find this unsatisfactory, especially when it calls for a suspension of activities in which both were once pleasurably engaged. Included are mundane but important things such as visiting friends, attending movies, and going on automobile trips. The problems resulting from the restrictions placed on the stigmatized bring us to a consideration of "courtesy stigma."

Courtesy Stigma

The consequences of stigmatization are not limited to rule breakers alone. The term *courtesy stigma* refers to the effects of stigma experienced by those with whom the deviant is intimately associated (Goffman, 1963:30). Included among these are spouses and offspring of mental patients (Yarrow et al., 1955; Freeman and Simmons, 1961), families of mentally retarded children (Birenbaum, 1970), and convicted felons, parents of gays (Miller, 1971), and others who are required to share the discredit assigned to the stigmatized individual. An intimate affiliation with a stigmatized person may become a social psychological as well as a social liability.

Courtesy stigma can result in painful self-examination, self-condemnation, and guilt. For example, based on the idea that homosexuality or disability stems from parental failings, many parents of these persons feel culpable and experience guilt and shame (Bieber et al., 1962; Simpson, 1977; Hobson, 1976; Henderson and Bryan, 1984). Consider the following:

> I blame myself for the fact that my son is homosexual. I know that it is a nearly incurable disease. I confessed my son's predicament—he is 16—to our family doctor, and he said that in rare cases the disease can be cured, but he said that the cure is a long and costly one and would be far beyond our means. . . . He said that while the boy may not be an actual menace to society, there is always the possibility of arrest and disgrace. . . . Do you think we should send him away someplace? Are there hospitals where for a minimal charge he might . . . ? I would hope that he would be well treated. . . . We have never discussed the fact that he is queer. His father refuses to allow the subject to be mentioned in our home. (Miller, 1971:73)

Similar self-blame, torment, and fear accompany having one's spouse declared mentally ill and/or hospitalized. Spouses report being worried that people will be disrespectful, suspicious, or fearful of the husband on his release from the mental hospital. "The wives feared that their husbands would suffer from social discrimination—their husbands would not be able to get jobs; they would be avoided by old friends; their children would be excluded from play groups; and, in general, their family would be looked down upon" (Schwartz, 1956:21).

The effects of courtesy stigma may also be experienced socially. Commonly, parents of gays face problems when they must acknowledge to family and friends that they have a homosexual child. Many worry how that acknowledgment will influence their social life, their business affairs, and whether they will be condemned as defective parents, etc. (*New York Times*, 1983). Research also reveals that with the advent of AIDS, there are now additional stigma effects. Weitz reports that families of AIDS victims either hide the news of their relatives' illness or substitute a "less stigmatized disease" in their explanations:

> A 39 year old floral designer whose Catholic family had all known he was gay before he became ill, reported that his mother refused to tell his brothers and sisters that he had AIDS, and ordered him not to tell them as well. When his siblings finally were told, they in turn would not tell their spouses . . . as one fundamentalist Christian said, "it was an embarrassment to [the family] . . . that I was gay and . . . that I have AIDS." (Weitz, 1993:226)

Not all those closely associated with the stigmatized seek to minimize public awareness of that affiliation and/or of the stigma. Thus, the parents of John Hinckley, Jr., after a period of profound guilt, confusion, and self-blame, entered the field of mental health, made public appearances and gave speeches in support of the mental health movement, and founded the American Mental Health Fund in order to promote public awareness of mental health needs (*People Weekly*, 1984). Others affected by courtesy stigma affiliate with persons similar to themselves in order to overcome their difficulties. Two examples are the Children of Gays/Lesbians and the Federation of Parents and Friends of Lesbians and Gays. The first organization encourages children to come to terms with their parents' homosexuality, to overcome fear of ostracism, to feel free to bring friends into the home, and to view homosexuality as a viable life-style. Similarly, the second organization offers emotional support for parents and children of gays, and seeks to keep family bonds intact. Thus, despite courtesy stigma, there are people who manifest a willingness to accept those who are stigmatized and who strive to achieve a degree of normalcy in social relationships (Birenbaum, 1970).

DEVIANCE AMPLIFICATION

Earlier we noted that negative community responses to the rule breaker may sometimes promote the amplification and perpetuation of deviance. Tannenbaum's (1938) view that the dramatization of evil leads to the perpetuation of rule violations is shared by Erikson (1964), Wilkins (1965), Lemert (1967), Young (1971), and Becker (1973). Each contends that community rejection of the actor encourages *career deviance*, i.e., the sequential shift of an individual's identity and status from that of primary to secondary deviant (Becker, 1973:24–39). However logical, some evidence supports that proposition and some does not. In arguing the case so far, we have drawn on evidence supportive of the process. To summarize, some evidence and commentary based on examination of juvenile delinquents (Davis, 1973; Klein, 1974; Gold and Williams, 1969; Gold, 1966, 1970; Farrington, 1977), the blind (Scott, 1965), polio victims (Davis, 1961), the mentally ill (Scheff, 1966), ex-convicts (Irwin, 1970), the disabled (Davis, 1961), and the alcoholic (Wiseman, 1970) show support for the view that labeling, by a complex interactive process, may result in the entrenchment of people in the role of secondary deviant and stabilize them in that position. But, one may ask, is there no contrary evidence? Indeed, there is. It is important to consider the other evidence since it demonstrates the variability of the outcome of the social construction process.

Examining the Counterevidence

One argument in opposition to the amplification hypothesis is that labeling has no permanent consequence on the deviant and that, at most it is a temporary coping strategy. For example, as a result of his study of physician drug addicts, Charles Winick (1964) notes that few doctors are prosecuted for this form of rule-breaking so they are not officially labeled and, in contrast to the "street" addict, most physicians treated for addiction remained off drugs, were not stigmatized, and maintained a successful professional life.

A study of physicians charged with medical malpractice reported that most of the physicians interviewed "reported no negative effects of the suit on their practice," and a few even reported that "their practice improved after the suit" (Schwartz and Skolnick, 1964:11).

These studies suggest that the protective stance and its related discourse taken by professions toward their members may serve to guard even those formally declared to have engaged in serious violations from the burden of stigma. They contrast sharply with those who lack a significant power base (Hessler, 1974:151; Schwartz and Skolnick, 1964:115). Another factor likely protecting professionals from long-term negative effects of stigma is their high occupational status. Given the popular definition of that status, such as physicians' alleged devotion to service and competence, and the associated tendency of lay people to defer to doctors just because they are doctors, it is less likely that these members of the upper world would be subject to prolonged stigma effects.

Similarly, one cannot help recall the relative lack of deviance amplification in the case of numerous government officials found guilty of political corruption, tax evasion, or complicity such as Spiro Agnew, Charles Colson, and John Dean, or Iran-Contra's General Secord and Oliver North. The case of Oliver North is instructive in that, despite his having violated many rules, including the rule against "negotiating with terrorists," he avoided the lasting effects of stigmatization and even became a folk hero.

> [North] became a media star during the Congressional hearings on Iran-Contra . . . North was the perfect media figure, with a shoulderful of decorations on his marine uniform, which he seldom wore before entering the hearing room. Handsome, articulate, emotionally convincing, and combative, North faced several tiers of congressional accusers, and proclaimed his guilt! He admitted that he had lied to Congress on previous hearings, had destroyed evidence, and had taken numerous evasive actions to throw off investigators. The reason he did it, he stated, was to serve his commander-in-chief—Reagan, and to fight communism at all costs. . . . North became an instant American folk hero. He . . . represented the archetype of our Western mythology, a modern version of David vs. Goliath, the rugged moral individual . . . North was doing what was right even though Congress said it was wrong. (Altheide and Snow, 1991:180)

The case of Oliver North suggests that the potential long-range consequences of labeling may be avoided by the use of positively valued themes as well as symbols of one's "morally impeccable" biography.

A second argument contradicting the amplification hypothesis contends that, rather than perpetuating deviance, labeling may actually reduce it. This argument is consistent with the more traditional view that punishment deters (Sutherland and Cressey, 1978:339–340). In her study of shoplifters, Cameron (1964:151) reports "very little or no recidivism" among adult pilferers who were apprehended by store detectives but not turned over to police or formally charged. Cameron, like others (Ditton, 1977; Henry, 1978a), suggests the adult pilferer does not think of him or herself as a thief prior to apprehension; arrest and interrogation undermine that self-conception. Where this is accompanied by fear, shame, remorse, and a lack of support from friends and family, the destruction of these illusions as "front work" encourages pilferers to regard themselves as others do, i.e., as rule breakers. Cameron suggests that for some people the horror of that perception is enough to deter further violations (1964:161–166). Apparently, however, the self-image of these people is markedly affected, at least temporarily.

A second example of how labeling may interrupt the course of rule-breaking is the case of members of Alcoholics Anonymous. Research has repeatedly shown that symbolic and formal labeling combine to aid the alcoholic in achieving sobriety through developing a new way of life (Maxwell, 1967; Henry and Robinson, 1978a). First drinkers must accept the definition that they have a drinking problem they cannot control alone and that the first stage of recovery requires total abstinence. This amounts to acknowledging and accepting the label and identity of alcoholic. Second are the associated feelings of disillusionment and despair. As many alcoholics say, they feel "licked," "down and out," "beaten," that they have their "backs to the wall," are at "the end of their rope," and have "reached rock bottom." Such despair, however, is frequently followed by hope from sharing common experiences, relief from finding others "in the same boat," and the realization that they are not alone with their problem. Recovery begins with the hope that it is possible to do something about the situation that is realized by replacing former drinking friends with fellow AA members who together construct a "new way of life" outside and beyond the bounds of the meeting (Henry and Robinson, 1978a, 1978b; Robinson and Henry, 1977; Robinson, 1979)

RESOLVING THE PROS AND CONS

The contradictory arguments and evidence bearing on the validity of the amplification hypothesis are resolvable by noting that while labeling does sometimes lead to amplification and career deviance, the social construction of meaning occurs in a variety of contexts that shape the outcome of that process. Several aspects of this process deserve brief consideration.

Ascribed vs. Achieved Deviants

Whether labelling has long-term consequences depends in part on whether one's deviant status rests on ascription or achievement. In the case of the highly visible ascribed deviant, such as the obese, the dwarfed, the blind, or the physically disabled, social reaction may be all that is required for one to become entrenched in the deviant role. Such persons "are not handicapped because their physical and/or visible traits prevent them from playing any particular roles, but rather because of the invidious labeling process and the absence of factors which might tend to mitigate its effects" (Mankoff, 1971:207). Given the nonvolitional character of these people's condition, their status is a result of audience reaction to a condition they are in. Therefore, in the case of the ascribed deviant, labeling may be considered *sufficient* to stabilize people in a deviant career.

In the case of achieved deviants, however, the relationship between labeling and amplification or career deviance is less clear. On the basis of evidence derived from examination of embezzlement, marijuana use, and homosexuality, Mankoff notes that people frequently become involved in deviant careers withoutever being publicly labeled and stigmatized. Thus, he contends, social reaction and formal labeling do not always precede (are not necessary conditions of) career deviance. Stated differently, one may become a habitual rule breaker without, or prior to formal labeling, and one may become largely (if not entirely) law-abiding despite having been labeled.

Neither is formal labeling always followed by career deviance. Labeling is not a sufficient condition (one that is always followed by its effect) of career deviance. Many achieved deviants who are formally labeled adapt to this condition in ways unavailable to the ascribed deviant (Mankoff, 1971:209–211). In short, career deviance is more likely to be associated with labeling in the case of the ascribed than the achieved deviant.

Official vs. Unofficial Labeling

Several studies suggest that amplification of deviance most frequently (*not* always) occurs when deviant actors experience registry and processing by public social control agencies, especially by the police and courts. Conversely, amplification is least likely to occur when actors are dealt with unofficially, e.g., by parents, friends, and relatives and by representatives of private organizations such as employers or store detectives in the case of shoplifting. By and large, persons caught up in the bureaucracy of official deviance processing agencies are more likely to be indelibly influenced by that experience. The reasons for this are numerous and interrelated. First, being specialists in imputation, such agencies tend to be more "expert" in their trade and, as creators of official files, have a more extensive and lasting impact on the identity of their clients. Second, given their governmental status, the stamp of disapproval applied by such agencies tends to carry more authority, an authority toward which people are inclined to be most deferent. Third, the interests and mandate of formal social control agencies lead them more often to perpetuate than to discontinue stigmatizing labels. For example, unlike Weight Watchers, whose ostensible purpose is to assist their members to eliminate obesity and extinguish the visible basis for labeling, police, courts, and prisons perpetuate the reality of the actor's presumed defective character. Recall, the "file" is permanent, represents truth, and its content helps promote the legitimacy of the agency's activity. As a matter of organizational interest, then, it is predictable that formal/public social control agencies would have a more amplifying effect than mutual aid and self-help groups., even though *both* use labels and stereotypical categories. Whereas self-help groups such as Weight Watchers and AA set out to deconstruct the label through a variety of "replacement discourse," formal control agencies do the reverse, intensifying what is already a restricted category. Again, however, such agencies do not operate in a vacuum. Their influence can be moderated by the actor's ability and opportunity to negotiate with and influence both how they are labeled and agency actions. With that in mind, let us consider power and socioeconomic status as elements that may help us make sense of seemingly contradictory evidence.

Power and Socioeconomic Status

The ability and opportunity of the labeled deviant to avoid becoming involved in career deviance are greatly enhanced by power, i.e., the control he or she may exert over other's behavior by whatever means available, but especially the use of economic wealth and political influence. Even the briefest examination of everyday life reveals their immunizing effects. As a result, "the rich get richer, while the poor get prison." For example, *"for the same criminal behavior*, the poor are more likely to be arrested; if arrested, they are more likely to be charged; if charged, more likely to be convicted; if convicted, more likely to be sentenced to prison; and if sentenced to prison, more likely to be given longer prison terms than members of the middle and upper classes" (Reiman, 1979:97; emphasis in original). When the element of race is added, the situation becomes even more bleak for the underclass. Thus, convicted "blacks have a poorer chance than whites of receiving probation, suspended sentence, parole, commutation of a death sentence, or pardon" (Sutherland and Cressey, 1978:138). Not only are the poor and minorities more likely than others to be formally processed for their rule breaking, but the long-term consequences are greater.

In addition, we have individualized the responsibility for crime and deviance (Reiman, 1979:143ff; Simon and Eitzen, 1990:321). When we ask which individuals are responsible, the answer reflects the stereotypical image of the villain (see Chapter 4). Accordingly, the justice system pursues violent and blue-collar crime with vigor, while traditionally giving a relatively lower priority to crimes of the elite (Simon and Eitzen, 1990:31). This same set of priorities informs the disposition of cases. So, while we will occasionally see a John Mitchell (U.S. Attorney General under former President Richard Nixon) go to jail, it is most unlikely that we shall ever see a Michael Milken (the junk bond "king") or a Charles H. Keating, Jr. (of S and L fame) on their knees being clubbed by police officers. Such treatment is reserved for the "real thugs" who happen to be powerless (Coleman, 1989:189–190).

Lastly, the dominant social reality of crime and deviance is ambivalent regarding the appropriateness of applying criminal sanctions and stigmatizing offenders in cases of elite crimes such as consumer fraud, price fixing, formation of monopolies, false advertising, environmental pollution, etc. Simply stated, there is a distinction between the legal code, on the one hand, and people's moral codes, on the other. In a heterogeneous society these codes are very unlikely to be wholly consistent with one another. As a result, there will always be some measure of disagreement with the operation of the justice system. To alter that system, however, will necessitate a revamping of the American consciousness and its priorities with respect to crime and deviance. In short, what may appear to be a consequence of a power game needs also to be considered to be the result of the interaction of power and several other factors, not the least of which is the conflicting elements of social reality in a heterogeneous society.

Motives

Whether labeling promotes career deviance also hinges on the motives for the behavior. The motives that underlie the actor's decision to engage in rule-breaking do not necessarily cease after the initial violations occur. On the basis of enduring motives (considered here as recursively constructed meanings) people may persist in rule-breaking and even pursue a "deviant career" despite the absence of formal labeling and regardless of an opportunity to refrain from rule breaking and/or to reassume a nondeviant status. Thus, the Cantonsville Nine, tried for (admittedly) destroying government property (military draft files) as an expression of their opposition to United States involvement in Vietnam, were described as being "proud" of what they did and that they perceived their actions as "one of the shining moments in their personal lives" (Bannan and Bannan, 1974:129). It seems apparent that the motives of these defendants, founded on religiously based opposition to war, are unlikely to be deterred by public condemnation. Consequently, it seems reasonable to suggest that some people are likely to persist in a pattern of rule-breaking because of ideological commitments, because they like what they are doing, or for other reasons (Mankoff, 1971:211–212). Believing it is acceptable to go to jail for something they believe in these persons are likely to define their label either as a "badge of honor" or as a "price" they are willing to pay. In either case, stigmatization as a control device is meaningless.

Other Factors

On the basis of their own and other's research, Thorsell and Klemke (1972:397–402) suggest that a variety of other conditions may influence the process of deviance amplification. First, they propose that when labels are assigned confidentially (as by private organizations rather than public agencies) to people who have limited commitment to deviant behavior (many shoplifters, for example), the probability of deviance amplification is reduced. Second, they suggest that when labeled persons identify with the labeler, and share the labeler's general moral sense, labeling is most likely to retard further deviance. This proposition is consistent with the work of Maxwell and Henry and Robinson on alcoholics cited earlier, and that of Carol A.B. Warren (1974b). Contrary to the amplification hypothesis, Warren reports that negative labeling by former members of the stigmatized category (such as ex-cons, ex-drug users, and ex-alcoholics) promotes identification between the labeler and the labeled and stimulates a change in the deviant's life-style and behavior. Third, labeling that occurs within relatively small, voluntary membership groups (such as a weight loss group) is more likely to promote a positive change in the labeled person's behavior and identity than when labeling occurs in total institutions such as jails or prisons (Warren, 1974b:307–308). Unlike degradation ceremonies, labeling in voluntary (often therapeutic) self-help and mutual aid groups, is intended to promote "positive" changes that the labeled person is seeking and is engaged in by persons with whom the actor identifies. Further, these labels are transitory; they are applied in an effort to promote abandonment of (rather than engulfment in) a morally questionable condition. Often, too, such labels are stripped of heavy moral meaning and are reconstructed positively. In Alcoholics Anonymous, for example, alcoholism is medicalized; it is a disease to be treated and controlled rather than a moral defect and "alcoholics" are redefined as "some of the nicest people you would ever want to meet" (unlike drunks).

Third, Thorsell and Klemke suggest that the nature of community response to the labeled deviant is critical as an insulator against the labeled becoming entrenched in the deviant status. Especially important are positive, supportive relations with significant others (e.g., family and friends) that help to maintain social integration between the labeled and the larger community. The disintegrative potential of formal labeling is thereby eliminated.

Finally, these writers propose that when labels can be relatively easily removed, as in the case of "closing" records of juvenile delinquents or "sealing" other public documents, the actor has less chance of becoming involved in career deviance. When such records are no longer visible they cannot shape relationships between offenders and others. Offenders are given a "second chance."

SUMMARY

The aim of this chapter has been to examine the social–psychological and social consequences of stigma and identity spoilage. Employing a social constructionist approach, theory suggests that the construction of stigmatizing categories as symbolic labels, and behaving toward persons in terms of the moral meaning of those labels may result in a substantial transformation of both their public identity and self-concept. The evidence we have examined supports the contention that many persons who are publicly labeled do, indeed, suffer social–psychological consequences, specifically a decline in self-feelings. For the most part we may say that such feelings reflect (1) the social relations between persons judged deviant and the audience as their condemners, (2) the actor's internalization through coconstruction of the moral meaning linked to his or her deviant status, and (3) the fact that deviant actors are often responded to by others rather exclusively in terms of their deviant, i.e., spoiled, identity.

These consequences are not limited to those who are publicly labeled. Through the process of symbolic labeling undetected rule breakers—primary deviants—may label themselves and experience the burden of guilt and shame, as well as the fear of public disclosure. Called role engulfment, these social–psychological consequences are the result of an ongoing cumulative process.

In addition to social–psychological consequences, stigmatization may also have social consequences of varying intensity and duration, extending not merely to the deviant actor but, by way of courtesy stigma, to those with whom they are intimately associated.

Most important, we have attempted to show that these consequences stem not from any indelible characterological or other defect possessed by the actor, but from the audience's definition of the deviant as unacceptable, morally defective, and, hence, difficult to relate to in normal ways. These definitions are sustained by negative stereotypy. Consistent with such meanings, we have seen that "normals" often erect barriers to avoid contact with and contamination by those they regard as defective. These barriers obstruct normal social interaction and, in turn, may encourage some stigmatized persons and groups to become more deeply involved in the deviant role, i.e., to have their deviance amplified.

Evidence bearing on the validity of the deviance amplification hypothesis and the permanence and universality of labeling effects is conflicting. Nonetheless, by refining our perspective it is possible to make sense of the broad and conflicting claims. Consistent with that, we examined several factors that research and experience indicate have an influence on the amplification process. Included are the distinction between ascribed and achieved deviance, the labeled person's ability to wield power and his or her location in the social structure, the motives underlying one's involvement in rule-violating behavior, as well as a host of other influential elements.

Taken together, these considerations suggest it is inappropriate to make unqualified claims that labeling, in and of itself, has either positive or negative effects on target populations. In the final analysis, labeling and stigmatization are socially constructed processes, and because of this are open to construction in different ways by different human agencies. These agencies are particularly influential on the actor's ability to manage stigma. Our concluding chapters focus on that final phase of the deviance process.

NOTES

1.   Some apparently "tribal" stigma result from voluntary behavior and so are due to achievement. One example is the development and display of large, well-defined muscles and veins by women engaged in competitive body building. In the view of some people, such body types are contrary to traditional expectations and norms regarding the female body type and are stigmatizing (Duff and Kong, 1989).

2.   Rosenberg (1979:10–12) suggests five other categories of identity: (1) social statuses based on people's age, sex, occupation, etc.; (2) membership groups, including those based on ethnicity or cultural background, religion, sociopolitical affiliation, friendship groups, interest groups, and other categories such as race; (3) derived statuses, those positions one occupies on the basis of prior statuses such as war veteran, ex-con, divorcee, etc.; (4) social types, referring to the names given people as they are located in standard categories based on their interests, attitudes, behavior, etc., including such typifications as egghead, nerd, stud, etc; and (5) personal identity, usually referred to by people's unique name or, in some cases, a social security number or fingerprint.

3.   As with the term "amplification" in electronics, the louder sound is obtained by repeatedly selecting and reproducing the same signal, so it is with

deviance amplification where other behavioral possibilities are filtered out, restricted, or closed off, resulting in an intensification of the deviant activity.

4. When persons classified as offenders or mental patients are released from institutional settings after sentence or treatment, we construct for them an abnormal "normal" status. Unlike those not publicly labeled and who are "allowed" to participate in primary rule-breaking (which *is* normal), excarcerated rule breakers are expected not to participate in *any* deviance (an impossible position) since doing so will invoke renewed moral condemnation and resurrection of their deviant status.

5. In this sense theory has more to say about the persistence and reproduction of patterns of rule breaking and deviance than it does about why people break rules in the first place (primary deviance).

6. Not all such experiences are kept out of the public eye. The much publicized case of Rodney King who was kicked, stomped, shot with a stun gun, and bludgeoned with billy clubs by Los Angeles police—while being filmed by a man with a video camera—is a case in point. But King's case seems to be only the "tip of the iceberg" since the southern California branch of the ACLU has reported that they receive about "55 police-related complaints each week from black and Hispanic citizens" (*Newsweek*, 1991).

7. This range will soon expand even more as the provisions of the Americans With Disabilities Act are implemented (Koral and McLanahan, 1990).

8. One consequence of the feminist movement has been the reform of rape law in our society—especially the revision of the definition of that offense from one involving infringement of a property right (that of the male) to one involving infringement of a personal right (that of the victim). Unfortunately, given prevailing stereotypes, situational or rational choice theory perpetuates the idea that women can avoid victimization by avoiding "provocative" styles of dress and make-up, and places that are supposed to attract rapists.

CHAPTER

7

Responses to Stigma

INTRODUCTION

Throughout this book we have emphasized people's active role in creating reality and shaping their destiny albeit in conjunction with others, and have suggested that people rarely allow themselves to be buffeted about willy-nilly by sociocultural forces. We noted people's efforts to resist or modify other's attempts to label them. Once derogatory moral meaning has been created, however, the central issue becomes *stigma management* or *stigma transformation*. This is the effort made by individuals or groups either to (1) control information about their spoiled identity, (2) alter the meanings attributed to them in order to reduce the social significance of their deviance, or (3) transform the public meaning of a deviant category through the politics of deconstruction and reconstruction. In this chapter and the next we will examine the techniques people use to manage and transform stigma. This constitutes the final element of the deviance process.

Before considering stigma management or transformation, we must acknowledge that such efforts are neither universal nor uniformly successful. First, stigma is simply inapplicable to some people. For a variety of reasons some people are insulated from and undisturbed by the demands and condemnation of others. Stigma is ignored (Goffman, 1963:6). Second, some deviants concur with public attributions and accept the associated stigma and shame, such as minority group members who express self-hatred (Vander Zanden 1983:326–328), or AIDS patients who believe they deserve the disease (Weitz, 1989). In these cases, then, people do not seek to manage or transform their stigma.

In contrast is the tendency of many stigmatized people to deal more directly with their stigma and to minimize the consequences of the differences. For example, some experiencing paralysis or loss of limbs refuse to accept their disability and struggle to walk, run, or engage in athletic activity characteristic of "normals." Transsexuals submit to radi-

cal surgery, psychotherapy, hormone injections, and socialization to reduce the ambiguity of their gender and/or sex identity (Humphreys,
1972:137; Kando, 1973). In contrast, the stigma-managing and transforming techniques we will examine are more social-psychological and
political. They concern the "management of information" others have
(or may acquire) about one's condition, and range from efforts to avoid
disclosing damaging information, making disclosed information less ob-
trusive and stigmatizing, and/or to the politics of changing the customary public meaning of one's stigma. Regardless of the techniques used,
each effort involves an attempt to reconstruct or influence the social
construction of reality.

Further, the public nature of stigma varies, partly because some stigmatizing conditions are not necessarily visible or known to others. Examples of the resulting secret deviants include impotence or sterility in a
male, infertility in a female, one's ethnic origin, or that one is a former
mental patient or prison inmate. Such cases may be described as the
discreditable, i.e., people who likely would be discredited were their deviance to become public. In contrast are cases in which the stigmatized
condition is self-evident (blindness, obesity, a physical handicap, skin
color) or is or may be assumed to be known by others. These cases
represent the *discredited*. In this chapter our analysis will follow this
distinction as it pertains to individualized efforts to manage or transform stigma. Chapter 8 will focus on collective efforts to achieve these
same ends.

THE DISCREDITABLE DEVIANT

Secrecy and Information Control

Persons we define as discreditable face the problem of whether "to
display or not to display; to tell or not to tell; to let on or not to let on; to
lie or not to lie; and in each case, to whom, how, when and where"
(Goffman, 1963:42). They must consider the possibility that those who
accept them unwittingly might reject them if the stigmatizing behavior
or condition became known. To avoid this, those with undisclosed information concerning stigmatizing conditions have an understandable
need for secrecy that may be sustained for many years before discovery.
Consider the following letters written to advice columnist Ann Landers
regarding men engaged in cross-dressing (*Daily Interlake*, 1988).

> I had been secretly cross-dressing since the age of 11, and at 18 I was
> buying women's clothing by mail order. When my mother discovered my

secret she hit the roof. She was sure I was a homosexual, possibly a child molester and that I would end up in prison.

It took a long time for my mother to cool down and then only after I promised to give up my "hobby." Of course, I didn't stop. I was just more careful from then on. But my relationship with my mother was never the same.

And the following from an Ohio woman.

I was married to a man for seven years. Although our sex life was just so-so for the first five years, I thought he was basically normal. Then he told me his big secret. Since he was 11 years old, he had cross dressed in private. He thought I would accept it and that our marriage would be wonderful. I agreed until he brought it into our sex life. It turned out that he could not become aroused unless he was wearing a lace bra and a garter belt. That was too kinky for me and I got a divorce.

People's concern over information control compounds life's diffi- culties. This is revealed in the following letter.

I have been working on this letter and trying to send it for more than three months now. . . . I have been married for over 20 years, have a daughter who is 20 and in college, and another who is 18 and will start college in the fall. We have a beautiful home and, I feel, a good life together. My wife is my best friend, but she has a very Victorian view of sex; it is performed more as a duty than anything else. . . . For me the thrills, excitement and beauties of sex have always come from men. I don't like the lying, the hiding, the excuses that go on because of my situation. I would like to open the door and have gay friends to my house and have the knowledge accepted. Has this ever been done successfully? If so, how? How can you change a person's mind when "homosexual" is a very dirty word, al- though they have lived over 20 years with one, lovingly? Any ideas, please? (Miller, 1971:69)

Clearly, management or control of information about one's self is a per- sistent concern for some deviants.

Information control takes a variety of forms. One of these is avoidance of contact with *stigma symbols,* signs that call attention to or reveal one's debased or deviant condition (Goffman, 1963:43). For example, histori- cally, for a black person to establish a totally white identity (i.e., "pass") called for "sociological death and rebirth." It required the person to sacrifice his or her educational credentials if they were acquired at a black school, to abandon all contact with family and friends so as to avoid the risk of being identified, and to suffer the loss of work and other references that might reveal one's racial identity (Drake and Cayton, 1962:163). Among transsexuals, passing may require name changes, a move to a new community, as well as new friends, jobs, etc. (Kando, 1973:98; Bogdan, 1974) and having their birth certificate altered to conceal their former sex. (*Arizona Republic*, 1981c)

A second form of information control involves the use of *disidentifiers*, symbols used to prevent one being conceived of as deviant (Goffman, 1963:44). For example, research has revealed the widespread use of disidentifiers by covert male homosexuals in Mexico where concern over disclosure stems from the tight grasp held by Mexican families over their unmarried males. Because of this, these men fear being seen in the company of effeminate males or entering or leaving places where known homosexuals gather—either of which is likely to be taken as evidence of one's own homosexuality. To avoid disclosure, the men frequently maintain social contacts with women, periodically engage in heterosexual intercourse with prostitutes, and publicly whistle or make sexually suggestive remarks at passing women (Carrier, 1976).

The use of disidentifiers and the maintenance of secrecy may become woven into the fabric of one's life. For example, research indicates that maintaining secrecy for some lesbians necessitates adjusting patterns of speech (Ponse, 1976). As a result of having cultivated a self-protective sensitivity, one lesbian admitted becoming so accustomed to anticipating her utterances that she lost much verbal spontaneity and at times became inarticulate. Others cultivate speech patterns and discuss topics intended to misinform their audience. For example, to establish and maintain a heterosexual image, some lesbian women will speak publicly about boyfriends or unrequited love affairs, while others establish relationships with a man so as to have a male companion on select occasions. Another device is to habitually dress in ways suggestive of their being "super feminine" or straight. In all these ways people seek to avoid displaying any sign of their discredited sexual orientation.[1]

The need to use disidentifiers is so widespread as to sometimes make it profitable for others to provide such services. Thus, one state university student established an "Alibi Service" for her female classmates. Limiting herself to 10 customers at one time, she provided a bogus mailing address and phone number for young women living with boyfriends despite their parents' objections. The service included collecting and delivering mail to subscribers, as well as answering the phone and giving callers the appropriate message or alibi for each person. She charged $20 per month (*State Press*, 1980).

Third, managing undisclosed stigma often prompts people to lead a *double life* in which severe restrictions are placed on one's choice of associates and friends. This is designed to resolve the tensions and anxieties that accompany unrestricted intermingling. For example, some gay persons refuse to have any association with heterosexuals other than highly impersonal, instrumental contacts. Having a drink after work with a co-worker or dropping by a neighbor's residence to talk are to be scrupulously avoided for fear of revealing sexual orientation. When homosexuals and heterosexuals do interact, there remains the questions of disclosure and deception. The success of double lives is debatable.

> Oh boy, I've lived a double life like you wouldn't believe all my life and sometimes the pressure was so enormous I thought I was going to explode. We'd sit around and have coffee, the girls in the office, and they'd say . . . this woman looks like a man . . . Omygod that's a queer and I'd sit there and listen to this kind of stuff and . . . until I'd just get violent sometimes. And there's been a few times when it's been all I could do just to keep from jumping up and saying, "Look you guys have lunch with me, we've socialized together for fifteen years. I'm queer!" I've wanted to do it so bad that you know, I uh, almost explode! Because you know . . . Why? I mean, what would I have accomplished anyway—I would have lost more than I had gained. (Ponse, 1976:327–328)

The foregoing suggests that the preservation of secrecy requires the development of "a more heightened awareness and a sharper perspective on ordinary affairs and everyday encounters than [found among] those for whom concealment is not an issue" (Lyman and Scott, 1970:78). Conditions of ordinary social interaction that "normals" take for granted often must be given considerable attention by those seeking to conceal their stigmatized conditions or behaviors. As we have seen, families of mental patients and AIDS victims (Weitz, 1993) go to great lengths to conceal the stigma. Similarly, stutterers may develop tricks to disguise their speech problem such as anticipating the inclination to use "difficult" words and then selecting a less troublesome substitute (Petrunik and Shearing, 1983) and ostomates (those having a surgically formed fistula connecting the bowel to the outside) find it necessary to select a theater seat so as to provide quick and easy access to a lavatory. In each case the paramount concern is to never relinquish control over information about self.

The maintenance of secrecy and information control is not without unintended consequences. For example, precisely because it helps them to maintain a heterosexual image, the reliance on a male companion may frustrate some lesbians' desire to become more involved in the gay community. The price of a heterosexual image, then, is at least limited association with one's reference group. As Ponse remarks, "the veils of anonymity are often as effective with one's own as with those from whom one wishes to hide" (1976:319).

Another consequence of "hiding" is the strain and tension secrecy imposes on what would otherwise be quite ordinary and relaxed situations. Thus, referring to the 4 years he served prior to "coming out" (publicly revealing one's homosexuality), a gay police officer indicated "it was very stressful to keep it hidden. What I'm going through now [being dismissed from the police force and seeking reinstatement]— with all the publicity—is stressful, but not nearly so stressful as keeping it hidden for so long" (*Arizona Republic*, 1980d). Taken-for-granted activity such as casual conversation with co-workers or others about friendships, about how one spent a weekend, or the types of leisure activity one engages in may be the basis for heightened tension for fear one might slip and reveal their deviation. One cannot afford to be free and open; one must always be circumspect. As Weitz's research on AIDS victims shows, hiding one's condition "carries a high price." Persons with AIDS (PWAs) may lose their job because they cannot reveal the reason for their increased absences from work. Those who choose not to tell friends are denied support and,

> must . . . endure the emotional strain caused by the secretiveness itself. As one man said, "I want to tell. I'm not used to hiding everything from everybody . . . I'm basically an honest person and I don't like to lie." Finally, PWA's who keep their illness secret risk hearing painfully disparaging comments about how AIDS "serves those queers right." On such occasions, PWA's may feel that they cannot respond without risking exposure. A 33 year old salesperson . . . said: "I was at my desk and three secretaries telling AIDS jokes were standing right behind me. It cut and it hurt. I grit my teeth and said nothing. (Weitz, 1993:232)

To have the desired effect, then, secrecy may require a person to lead a double life, replete with alienation, isolation, dissonance, emotional pain, and uninterrupted vigilance.

The Role of Others

In many cases, successful management of discreditability is achieved only with the assistance of others. Quite often this involves *counterfeit secrecy*, i.e., a mutual pretense between the deviant and others (Ponse, 1976:323). In such cases people tacitly agree to preserve the fiction that there is nothing different or unusual about the deviant or his or her actions. For example, despite abundant evidence to the contrary, a facade of heterosexuality was maintained between a lesbian woman and her mother, neither of whom was willing to discuss the situation. Mother-daughter conversations excluded topics such as boyfriends, marriage, childbearing, and other things that might risk acknowledgment of the unmentionable (Ponse, 1976:325–326). This same strategy has been noted among some male homosexuals in Mexico, many of whom live in the parental home long after custom suggests they should have established their own residence. Between such men and their families, and even when their homosexuality is known to several members of the family, there may exist a "conspiracy of silence" or "counterfeit secrecy."

> The homosexually involved individuals . . . act [so as not to] expose themselves to unknowing relatives, neighbors, or friends. They may continue to maintain the fiction, for example, that some day they will marry and have children; and social occasions at the house may be organized as though their interests were heterosexual. (Carrier, 1976:367)

Similarly, a 33-year-old woman who is obese suggests that "other people put fat people in the closet. They don't talk about it and don't acknowledge it. No one will use the word *fat* in front of you. They use circumlocution, like *zoftig* or *heavy*, or say that you have a pretty face" (Millman, 1980:14–15, emphasis in original). Weitz's research on AIDS shows that such secrecy can be facilitated by others who work with PWAs to conceal the condition from others. She showed that to protect clients from possible legal, social, and financial repercussions and to avoid the resulting stigma, "physicians may circumvent the reporting law" and thereby avoid job loss or insurance problems. This can be done by subtle manipulation of the diagnosis, using highly restrictive definitions of AIDS, and by diagnosing each opportunistic infection rather than full blown AIDS (Weitz, 1993:230).

As with leading a "double life," counterfeit secrecy demands a price. Obscuring one's stigma and one's identity in this way may reinforce the idea of one's unacceptability and promote self-alienation. It also may serve as the basis for erecting barriers between self and others from whom one might conceivably obtain emotional support. As a result, areas of interaction may become highly attenuated and social relationships may become strained unless they are replaced by other networks more supportive. The tension one seeks to avoid may be intensified by the very means employed to reduce it.

> To maintain the privacy of perversity . . . requires the highest levels of self and personal control, and a spurious rationality that enables the individual to calculate each and every situation in order to estimate the degree to which he can reveal himself. Spontaneity invites sanctions and defeat. (Bensman and Lilienfeld, 1979:59–60)

Indeed, the dilemma of concealing or revealing results in "learning to predict how others may react" and "learning when to tell" (Weitz, 1993:232).

THE DISCREDITED DEVIANT

In contrast with the discreditable, the discredited face the problem of reducing the relevance of the *known* stigmatized condition by attempting to maintain a positive, if not normal, self-image and public identity. A variety of tactics are used in seeking this goal.

Destigmatization: Purification and Transcendence

Destigmatization refers to the processes used to negate or expunge a deviant identity and replace it with one that is essentially nondeviant or normal. Warren (1980) proposes two methods whereby individuals may achieve this change in identity. These are purification and transcendence.

Purification refers to the process whereby one's defective self is replaced by a moral or "normal" self, either by sacred or secular means. In the sacred method, one is transformed from "sinner to saint." One experiences "rebirth" and, in being reborn, the effect of stigmatization is erased. Accordingly, purification involves reversing the effect of status degradation, allowing a "lower order" self to be exchanged for one of a "higher order." This exchange is achieved by the actor extinguishing the condemned behavior and/or engaging in behavior that is defined as having a spiritual base, e.g., charitable works involving self-sacrifice. One example of this rebirth is that of Malcolm X, once a leading figure in the Black Muslims, who rose from hoodlum, thief, dope peddler, and pimp to become one of the most dynamic leaders of the Black Revolution in the United States. In Warren's terms Malcolm X "became an abstinent, educated Black Muslim from being a wild-living, uneducated atheist." Similarly, Charles Colson of Watergate fame "passed from being a 'crooked, power-hungry politician' to a 'humble and repentant Christian'" (Warren, 1980:63). Purification by means of assuming a repentant posture is also used by many of the 12-step organizations—Fattys Anonymous, Cocaine Anonymous, Overeaters Anonymous, etc.—based on the 12 steps developed by Alcoholics Anonymous (Trice and Roman, 1970:542).

In contrast with purification (which is limited to achieved deviants), destigmatization by *transcendence* applies mainly to the ascribed deviant. Thus, while in purification the old, defective self is "erased," in transcendence the old self (or its symbols) persist. The achievement of destigmatization, then, requires the deviant to "rise above," i.e., transcend, their condition by means of some persistent type of action that is unexpected among people of their type. In short, transcendence calls for one to display a "better" self rather than to eliminate the former self (Warren, 1980:64–65).

Examples of destigmatization by transcendence are abundant. John Merrick, the Elephant Man (Montagu, 1979; Warren, 1980:65), author, lecturer, and humanitarian Helen Keller (deaf and blind), President Franklin D. Roosevelt (polio victim), English poetess Elizabeth Barrett Browning (an invalid due to spinal injury), Russian author Fyodor Dostoyevsky (epileptic), comedian Jerry Jewell (cerebral palsy) (Gliedman and Roth, 1980:41; Graves, 1980), and Stephen Hawking (paraplegic theoretical physicist). For these and other ascribed deviants (the spinal cord injured person who skis, the wheelchair bound hiker, the blind and legless horseman, the postpolio gymnast, the lame swimmer, etc.), one way they may experience destigmatization is to become expert in areas of endeavor ordinarily closed to persons such as themselves (Goffman, 1963:10). In a real sense, they are repudiating stereotypes.

Deviance Disavowal

Another stigma managing tactic used by the discredited (achieved or ascribed) is *deviance disavowal*, i.e., denial that their behavior or condition is abnormal (Davis, 1961). Deviance disavowal is used by the stigmatized to redefine the abnormal and immoral as normal and acceptable (Davis, 1961:126).[2] It is achieved by casting off the affected part of the deviant identity as "not really them." If successful, disavowal may normalize relations between the deviant and others.

Disavowal has been observed among convicted child molesters who frequently allude to the influence of alcohol as an explanation for their behavior and as a way of normalizing the situation. The following remarks reflect that effort.

> "If you been drinking a lot your passions get aroused."
> "I was intoxicated and couldn't account for myself."
> "I was drunk. I didn't realize their age and I was half blind.
> "I've always been a drinker."
> "Drinking is the reason. I could always get women. I can't figure it out.
>   A man's mind doesn't function right when he's got liquor on it."
>   (McCaghy, 1968:48)

Essentially, these men deny responsibility for their actions and contend that the offense would never have occurred had it not been for their intoxicated condition and that it is not extraordinary for alcohol to have this affect on people. They claim alcohol *caused* them to do what their "true character" would not otherwise permit. They argue that while they sometimes drink to excess and then do "stupid things," such behavior is not symbolic of their substantial self. Thus, these men simultaneously attempt to explain their wrongdoing, absolve themselves of responsibility for it, and avail themselves of the image of a normal, socially acceptable, moral person possessing the same positive social attributes as others. In short, they seek to "normalize" their identity while acknowledging, though not accepting, responsibility for their rule-breaking.

Disavowal rests on a three-stage interactional process between the deviant and others. Stage one, *fictional acceptance* of the deviant as normal and equal to others, involves politeness and privacy in interaction. Ordinarily one may expect people to exhibit some curiosity about others' differentness, be it obesity, a physical handicap, a record of wrongful behavior, and the like. Despite this curiosity, norms supporting the value of privacy require that people "refrain from remarking or otherwise reacting too obviously to those aspects of [deviant] persons which in the privacy of our thought betoken important differences between ourselves" (Davis, 1961:126). People generally tend to honor the norms of privacy and conduct themselves according to the standards of politeness. Feigning avoidance amounts to *civil inattention*, the practice of which is evidenced by the horror that sometimes arises when it is not maintained.

By maintaining the fiction of "no difference," interaction between deviants and others may persist to the point that the second stage of deviance disavowal commences—*the facilitation of normal role taking*. Here the interaction is no longer guided by the stereotypical definitions linked to the deviant master status but by other nonstigmatized statuses. Terms such as blind, crippled, and so on, can be used without embarrassment or tension when talking with a blind or paralyzed person. This stage is actively promoted by the effort of the deviant to project images, attitudes, and concepts of self other than those of the stigmatized. Weitz found, for example, that persons with AIDS reduce stigma through putting on a show of bravado "in order to convince others of the reality that they are functioning and worthwhile human beings" (Weitz, 1993:234). She describes how AIDS sufferers would go to neighborhood bars and act "like nothing was wrong" to "show these people that we can live with AIDS, that we can have a good time. That we can dance, that we can socialize, that we're not people with plagues" (Weitz, 1993:234–235).

Facilitation of disavowal also calls for reciprocity and negotiation between the deviant and the normal. As the deviant disavows his or her "abnormality" and attempts to redefine self, the nondeviant must respond so as to support that effort if it is to be successful. This also helps to promote "normalization" of the traits that were the basis of the actor's stigmatization. When the deviant condition is no longer regarded as a restriction on interaction, one may be said to have "broken through" the limitations imposed by the master status (Davis, 1961:128). Interaction may then become spontaneous and natural rather than forced or artificial.

Facilitation leads to the third stage: sustaining *normalized relationships*. This does not mean that the special condition of the deviant is ignored but that it is acknowledged and worked into ordinary relationships. This stage is reached by "over normalization" or "defiance." *Overnormalization* occurs when one no longer perceives the "deviation" to be at odds with normal standards. (Davis, 1961:130) It exists when a person schedules events, appointments, activities, and so on, that are inconvenient, embarrassing, or uncomfortable for the deviant. A case in point is making dinner reservations at a usually crowded restaurant without thinking to tell the management that one of the diners will be in a wheelchair. In short, the deviant is being encouraged to "give up" his or her abnormality.

In the second method, the nondeviant joins the deviant in *defiance of stereotypic definitions* and affirms his or her belief in the deviant's capabilities (Gowman, 1956:71). An able-bodied person might jokingly chide a paraplegic friend for being "so damned helpless," or they may ask a hearing impaired friend when they last "cleaned out their ears." While some regard such remarks as violations of "good taste" others regard them as evidence that the disability is defined as a "small part" of the individual (Levitin, 1975:552).

These comments are not to suggest disavowal or normalization is a panacea for the ills of the stigmatized person, or that all instances of apparent acceptance constitute genuine cases of normalization. As Millman (1980:78) notes regarding the case of some overweight women, acceptance of the obese by others in certain roles (e.g., confidante and friend) does not necessarily extend to their being accepted in other roles (e.g., competitor in the dating game). Indeed, in some instances, the fact of one's obesity serves as the basis for friendship. To the insecure female seeking to be active in the dating game, the fat girl who is felt to be unable to compete favorably is a "safe" friend and an enhancement of their own relative attractiveness. In short, what appears to be normalization may itself be counterfeit. Further, disavowal may constitute a

catch-22. If the deviant assumes others accept them as normal and behaves accordingly, they risk rejection. "On the other hand, if they never
take the risk of presenting themselves as normal, they relinquish any
chance of ratification [of normalcy], of participating in the world and its
pleasures" (Millman, 1980:78). Clearly, the management of stigma poses
some difficult problems.

Deviance Avowal

Some attempt to manage their stigma by *deviance avowal*, i.e., acknowledging their condition or wrongful action while simultaneously working
to maintain a positive social identity and playing legitimate social roles
(Turner, 1972). For example, people who are temporarily physically disabled sometimes proclaim that the condition "will not always be me"
(Levitin, 1975:551) thereby seeking to discourage the idea that the application of any such label is appropriate.

Avowing one's deviance while making a bid for normality may demand considerable time, effort, and imagination. It may require a physically disabled person, for example, when telling their story, to place
emphasis on the expectation of early recovery (even when this is not
medically justifiable), thereby emphasizing the temporary nature of the
condition. This was nicely dramatized by the temporarily disabled person who painted "Houdini" on his wheel chair. The basic message is
that "this handicap will *not always* be who I am" (Levitin, 1975:554).
Another device is to inquire about other's past illnesses or disabilities,
thereby reminding them that they, too, may have once been afflicted.
The objective here is to limit other's opportunities to "draw lines" separating the nonstigmatized and the stigmatized or to erase these where
they seem to exist.

This same effort is engaged in by the permanently handicapped who
seek to convey the basic message that their "handicap is *not all* of who I
am" (Levitin, 1975:554). To emphasize this, messages of avowal often
carry information about the untainted aspects of self. By broadcasting
details of one's "normality" and providing cues that permit others to
relate in terms of a nondeviant role, normal role taking is facilitated (as
in the second stage of the disavowal process). Should this effort be
successful and the proffered definition be accepted by nondeviants, relations between deviants and others are normalized.

In addition, avowal seeks to separate the deviant *condition* from the
deviant *role*. For example, alcoholics who have their drinking under
control acknowledge they are alcoholics, but stress that they no longer
are drunks. In making the separation between condition and role, it is

possible to overlook, forget, or redefine their prior "failing." Indeed, as we noted earlier, one's prior, now controlled, deviance becomes the basis of a derived status, a position based on one's prior condition.

Accounts: Excuses and Justifications

Public knowledge about a person's deviant status can lead those who are stigmatized to manage their moral burden by using *accounts*. These are statements designed "to explain unanticipated or untoward behavior" (Scott and Lyman, 1968:46). As we saw in Chapter 3, such devices are also referred to as *vocabularies of motives* (Mills, 1940), "verbalization" (Cressey, 1953) and "neutralization" (Sykes and Matza, 1957), and comprise ways of talking intended to neutralize the wrongfulness of actions or their consequences prior to an act's contemplation or commission. Here, however, we are concerned with how such words and phrases are used *after* stigmatization as part of negotiating a respectable identity and for separating apparent behavior from self-conception. Accounts either excuse or justify the questioned behavior.

Excuses are verbal tactics used by people to redefine and soften their moral breach and/or relieve themselves of responsibility for the deviant condition (Scott and Lyman, 1968:47). These include (1) the *appeal to accidents*, used to claim the conduct in question resulted from chance events over which they had no control (e.g., an environmental hazard or a momentary bodily weakness); (2) appeal to *biological drives* in which behavior is attributed to conditions over which people are believed to be predisposed through no fault of their own; (3) *appeals to defeasibility* in which responsibility is denied by claiming the act was based on "misinformation arising from intentional or innocent misrepresentation of the facts by others" (Scott and Lyman, 1968:48); and (4) *scapegoating*, whereby one's behavior is excused on the basis of less desirable traits displayed by others such as them being liars, jealous, or trouble makers (Lewis, 1961:143). To the degree that one or more of these claims is convincing, the questionable behavior becomes understandable and the actor is less blameworthy. Whether they are convincing will depend on whether they confirm the view of reality held by the questioners (Blumstein et al., 1974). The consequences of *not* confirming the questioner's reality are reflected in Anita Hill's remarks concerning the judgment of the Senate Judiciary Committee in the confirmation hearings concerning Clarence Thomas' nomination to the U.S. Supreme Court.

> Because I and my reality did not comport with what [the senators] accepted as their reality, I and my reality had to be reconstructed by the . . . committee members with assistance from the press and others.

In constructing an explanation for my marital status as single, I became unmarriageable or opposed to marriage, the fantasizing spinster or the man-hater. An explanation of my career success had to be introduced which fit with their perceptions about the qualifications of people of color, women and the myth of the double advantage enjoyed by women of color.

I thus became aloof, ambitious, an incompetent product of affirmative action and an ingrate who betrayed those who had worked to insure my success. (*Ann Arbor News*, 1992c)

A second category of accounts, *justifications*, also serves to "neutralize an act or its consequences when either is called into question" (Scott and Lyman, 1968:51). The unique feature of justifications is that they acknowledge the wrongfulness of the act in question while seeking to have the specific instance defined as an exception. For example, taking the life of another person is generally wrong, yet it may be justified as self-defense.

People may employ a variety of justifying ideas to account for their past behavior. In addition to those words and phrases that served to neutralize the moral bind of law prior to the act (see Chapter 3) are the sad tale and self-fulfillment. "The *sad tale* is an (often distorted) arrangement of facts that highlight an extremely dismal past used to 'explain' the individual's present behavior" (Scott and Lyman, 1968:52; see also Goffman, 1961:150–151). As an example, Greenwald (1958:32–36) relates the case of a prostitute whose biography included poverty during the depression of the 1930s, being confined in an orphan asylum, being sent to a series of foster homes (in one of which she was allegedly forced to perform fellatio on the foster father and in another where she was regularly punished for things she had not done), loneliness, and so on. These circumstances were said to have led her to engage in sex for material reward.

In *self-fulfillment* one justifies the rule violation with the claim that it is a means to an end such as the explanation for the ingestion of some drugs (such as peyote, marijuana, LSD) on the ground they "expand consciousness" and enhance one's sensibility to others and things in the environment.

Covering

A final technique used to manage a discredited condition, minimize one's stigma, and ease any associated tension is *covering* (Goffman, 1963:102–104). Covering can involve displacing one form of stigma by another lesser form. For example, Goffman cites the blind person who wears dark glasses symbolizing his or her blindness, in an effort to cover defacement or disfigurement in the region of the eyes (Goffman, 1963:102–103). Covering also includes the "necessity defense" used by some peace and pro-life activists charged with trespassing as a result of their protest activity. As in the "appeal to higher loyalties," these activists claim that the crime they are trying to prevent is worse than the crime they committed. Therefore, they are actually moral rather than guilty. A third form of covering calls for the discredited person to avoid displaying "failures" that expose the stigma. Thus, the near blind might refrain from reading in public thereby avoiding obvious difficulties that would thereby call attention to the disability (Goffman, 1963:103). Quite similar is the case of some obese people, especially women, who wear stylish clothes and have their hair stylishly cut, etc. in order to ease the tension they sometimes feel when appearing in public situations (Millman, 1980:9).

It should be noted that the specific techniques used for impression management, if they are to have a reasonable probability of success, must be selected with an awareness of the social context of their use, as well as of the properties of the offense, the offender, and the condemner (Benson, 1985:598ff). For example, to refute the idea that an act was extraordinary, tactics must lead it to be defined as a "normal, everyday practice" or, alternatively, an "aberration" or a mistake. This makes it difficult for a behavior in which the accused has been involved for years, e.g., embezzlement, to be explained as a temporary "aberration" or a random error.

Similarly, the ability of the deviant to resist being cast as characterologically flawed will, to some extent, rest on the nature of the offense as well as one's biography. Thus, a one-time tax violator might reasonably seek to excuse their behavior as an inadvertent error, the sort of thing anyone might commit. However, it might be difficult to explain a systematic pattern of evasion on the basis of inattention or ignorance. It might be more useful to explain the behavior as due to "extraordinary pressures" imposed on an ordinary person who "understandably collapsed under the pressure" (resort to a version of the sad tale). To the extent such an explanation is accepted by one's condemners, the consequences of stigmatization can be avoided or reduced. Moreover, whether such an account will be accepted will often depend on the detailed information provided by others as to how the rule violator responded at the time of the behavior or its discovery. Thus the person who claims to have seriously injured a partner accidentally, during a pushing and shoving altercation, will be more believable if she took him to the hospital and showed concern, rather than simply disappearing from the scene.

Lastly, in addition to countering negative characterizations of their behavior and themselves, those constructing these varieties of "impression management" (Goffman, 1959) may also seek to characterize their condemners so as to "turn the tables" by raising questions about the propriety or merit of the condemner's actions. Attention is thereby diverted from the accused to the accuser. For example, an offender may allege they are the "victim" of a "power hungry" prosecutor or of a "vendetta" engaged in by a prosecutor motivated by personal (e.g., career) goals. Alternatively, a white-collar offender may (often correctly) allege they are being "individually singled out" and held accountable or scapegoated for systemic conditions in an industry. Again, however, these devices are not universally available. To succeed, tactics must be consonant with the context and be perceived as credible.

SUMMARY

In this chapter we have examined the diverse means by which individuals seek to deal with stigma. To facilitate our analysis of this process we drew on a distinction between the discreditable and the discredited. Among the former, stigma management appears to involve a rather universal set of properties, including the manipulation of stigma symbols, a reliance on disidentifiers, and the occasional complex and stressful practice of leading a "double life." We saw that such techniques have varying success, depending on the circumstances and social context in which they are used. However, in the case of counterfeit secrecy, the use of these devices sometimes bears a substantial cost, not least of which comes from the substitution of one set of tensions for another.

Considering the discredited, we described the use of the techniques of deviance disavowal and deviance avowal, and the role of invoking excuses and justifications to put a spin on the meaning of stigmatizing conditions. The use of these techniques is intended to absolve actors of the responsibility for, and to promote a morally acceptable definition of, their discredited behavior or condition. At first sight these uses of diversionary discourse seem to be little different from the neutralizations and verbalizations discussed in Chapter 3. However, as we have seen, there is the critical issue of timing. With the stigmatized the deed has been done. The issue is one of social rationalization. The stigmatized deviant works to repair the broken relations that his or her behavior or condition symbolizes. In short, as Goffman (1971) has said, the deviant engages in "remedial work" designed to transform the offensive into the acceptable.

To the extent that they are manipulable such devices may be used to reduce blameworthiness, frustrate the aim of degradation ceremonies, and negate the primary function of the stigmatization process—the symbolic separation of the offender from the community. As we shall see in the next chapter, however, this attempt at separation is often countered by deviants forming their own community. This leads us to consider the collective management of stigma.

NOTES

1.   Some may object to using homosexual men and lesbian women to exemplify instances of secrecy and misidentification, since such usage contradicts the aim of "liberation." However, "liberation" seems not yet at hand. Thus, the National Gay and Lesbian Task Force Policy Institute reports a 42% rise in anti-gay violence and harassment in San Francisco and five other cities in 1990 (*San Francisco Examiner*, 1991). It is also estimated that for every "liberated," avowed lesbian women, "there are 200 . . . who can't afford to be visible or who won't be" (Yollin, 1991:22).

2.   This is similar to the "claim to normality" that was discussed under neutralization is Chapter 5. The crucial difference, however, is that deviance disavowal comes *after* the activity or condition, as an attempt to reduce stigma, whereas the "claim to normality" can be part of the discourse that when invoked prior to committing deviance becomes part of the motivational context, allowing deviant behavior to happen.

8

Transformation of Stigma

INTRODUCTION

In the previous chapter we examined the ways that individuals attempt to cope with behavior or conditions others deem problematic, questionable, and stigmatizing. For many deviants, however, support is needed to effectively manage their stigma. This support typically comes from others in similar situations who share common experiences, wishes, and hopes. In this chapter we shall be concerned with the psychosocial processes used by stigmatized persons who form or join groups and organizations to transform their situation. We will look at the nature and goals of such associations, why and how they form, their recent proliferation, their attraction to those stigmatized as deviant, and, importantly, how they mobilize their members to inwardly combat the effects of stigma while simultaneously transforming the public definition of the problem. In considering the latter issue we will return to where we began: the politics of defining deviance. We will explore the tactics of deviants as moral entrepreneurs: how they construct new moral meanings of their situation through a form of "replacement discourse" and how they can be instrumental in changing public policy. Finally, we will examine arguments about the dangers of romanticizing the political impact of such groups, and consider whether their limits in light of problems of internal fragmentation and external cooptation.

COLLECTIVE RESPONSES TO STIGMA

In discussing the group management of stigma we first need to distinguish between people who join with others primarily to continue their deviant behavior and those who do so to obtain relief from the society's response to that behavior. Illustrative of the former are members of delinquent subcultures, gangs, homeboys, clubs, and other groupings whose organized form historically was the "secret society." The purpose of such groupings is to facilitate the commission of their members' questioned behavior. Examples include loose affiliations of criminals, gangsters of the 1920s and 1930s who gathered in speakeasies, restaurants, and cigar stores (Sutherland, 1937; Taylor, 1984), vagabonds and hobos (Anderson, 1923; Reitman, 1937), homosexuals, lesbians, and strippers, and more recently skin heads, covens of white and black witches, and satanists. The more organized versions of these deviant associations include the national Ku Klux Klan (U.S), the Shining Path (Peru), and the international Chinese and Asian secret societies. Such societies have sometimes provided a base from which to launch protests against oppression. Typically their members, who are recruited from individuals rejected by society, are rarely concerned with the problematic nature of their stigmatized status but with developing, reaffirming, and enlivening their deviant practices. Inadvertently, however, some of the benefits accruing to the membership are the same as those found in stigma management and change groups. Thus the secrecy of the groups (1) obscures their members deviant behavior, providing protection from public scrutiny (MacKenzie, 1967), (2) fosters a sense of mutual confidence and trust through "sharing," (3) heightens their specialness, honor and status through a kind of "aristocratization" (Simmel, 1950:346–365; Warren, 1980:67), and (4) creates the social space for freedom of action without censure or condemnation. Further, the secret society permits one to abandon the managed images of self and take down "fronts" (Goffman, 1959:22ff), with all the relief from tension that such a freedom to deviate implies. Secret societies provide the sense of "brotherhood and sisterhood" found in other forms of "community" (Warren, 1974a:13). "By joining a secret society, an individual acquired a sworn fraternity of comrades, a protective group, and the force to counter the strength of the traditional societies" (Lyman, 1974:41).

Voluntary Self-Help and Mutual Aid Groups

In contrast to the secret society, in recent years there has been a growth and proliferation of a vast array of *voluntary associations* that have emerged specifically to deal with the problems of almost every kind of deviance from those of "short-term crisis," to those with a "permanent fixed stigmatized condition," to those trapped in a habit, addiction, or self-destructive way of life" (Bean, 1975:38). Demone has said:

> It matters not what you call them—self-help, mutual aid, support systems—they are the fastest growing component of the human service industry. Nor is it surprising. Man is a social animal who throughout his

history has banded together for problem solving and survival. . . . Thus they are as old as man in one sense or a contemporary solution to a complex problem in another. (Demone, 1974:3)

While these groups are defined and classified in various ways,[1] the most significant distinction for our purposes is the one originated by Edward Sagarin (1969) in his now classic work on societies of deviants called *Odd Man In*. Sagarin observed that in forming, supporting, or joining a group, a stigmatized person with physical or social problems seeks, "either (1) to conform to the norms of society, or (2) to change those norms to include the acceptance of his own behavior. In the first instance the person renounces deviant behavior, in the second he changes not himself but the rule making order" (Sagarin, 1969:21). The first type has been referred to as "inner focused" (Katz and Bender, 1976) or "ameliorators" (Steinman and Traunstein, 1976), who acknowledge their members' problems and gear their primary activity to providing help through direct services (Tracy and Gussow, 1976:382). The second type is described as "outer focused," where the predominant interest is outside the immediate welfare of members (Katz and Bender, 1976). The primary activity may be organizational self-promotion through research support or fund raising (Tracy and Gussow, 1976) or as activist "redefiners" who reject social definitions of their members' situation and seek to persuade others to redefine the practice or condition (Steinman and Traunstein, 1976). It has been shown that most groups start by being totally concerned with supporting their members and gradually become involved in wider change, legislation, and broader social issues. In their major survey of mutual aid groups Steinman and Traunstein (1976) found that over half the urban and almost three-quarters of the rural organizations that they studied in a particular geographical area said that their most important objective was to change the public's *and* their own membership's image of their condition from being "deviant" to being "different." However, they also found that the large number of ameliorative services provided by two-thirds of all of these groups conflicted with the goal of changing the stereotypical view of the problem.

The Emergence and Growth of Stigma-Focused
Mutual Aid Groups

Although mutual aid groupings have had a long history, the particular form that they have taken since the mid-twentieth century owes its emergence to the confluence of several macrolevel trends. Five of these stand out. First, is the growing isolation and alienation of individuals

stemming from industrialization and urbanization. This change saw societies move from an era of extended families, kinship networks, and
face-to-face multiplex relations to one based on simplex, contractual relations, that celebrated the "cult of the individual" and allowed a freedom
to be different while moving social control to the margins of personal
experience. Thus, rather than deal with problems of difference through
ongoing, albeit often repressive face-to-face interaction, social reaction
was centralized and appropriated to specialist government and private
agencies.

Second, and related, was the growth of centralized bureaucratic government policy on a variety of social issues. Not only did private troubles become public issues, but public policy was formulated in such a
way that differences between people became "medicalized" problems
(Illich, 1975; Zola, 1972; Conrad, 1979). Beginning in the 1920s and 1930s
Americans began to see rule-breaking behavior as a reflection of an
underlying emotional, or psychological disorder. On the coattails of
medicine's generalized success in curing disease, developments in psy-
choanalysis, psychology, and psychiatry were seen as the scientific
solution to problems of the mind whose symptoms were manifest as
deviance. The explanation of deviant or odd behavior "as the product of
childhood traumas that might have happened to anyone . . . helped the
public to absolve [some] deviants of responsibility for what they do"
(Becker, 1970:343). In one sense, then, this decline of blame and its
attendant moral condemnation allowed deviance to be tolerated. It also
promoted the idea that rule breakers were in need of help rather than
punishment, sympathy rather than condemnation.

Third, individuals' freedom to maintain relative anonymity as deviant
identities was concealed within the urban jungle. More than ever, "outsiders" could gather with like-minded others and indulge their appetites
despite opposition from public morality. This was facilitated by increased geographic mobility that allowed quick trips to nearby urban
places.

Fourth was the social protests of the 1950s, 1960s, and 1970s over civil
rights, women's issues, and the Vietnam War (Altman, 1971) as well as
other movements from fat liberation to the "quiet revolution" among the
disabled. Together with numerous other groups and associations these
social formations have been said to form a humanitarian movement
(Mauss, 1975:45),[2] which showed that it was possible to challenge authority with impunity, and that to do so successfully one must organize,
engage in civil disobedience, and press for social and political change.

A not unrelated and crucial fifth development was the growing awareness of the limits of science, and particularly of the new helping professions. The therapeutic vision that had liberated personal problems from
moral blame was slow to deliver the promised cures. Not only had

traditional coping solutions of the family and church been replaced by new caring professions, and rule-breaking become individualized as sickness, but when the solutions to these problems proved evasive, the problem was cast off. Thus persistent and chronic problem sufferers, with "the most taboo of psychological traits, the inability to control certain of one's behavior such as gambling, drugs, alcohol, sexuality, mental illness and obesity" (Zola, 1975:xv) not only placed a burden on resources but crucially did little for those who now believed their deviance was disease.

Indeed, studies report that two recurring themes accounting for the rise of modern mutual aid groups was "disillusionment with existing helping services and the decline of supportive social institutions" (Robinson and Henry, 1977:8). For example, Zola (1975) argues that mutual aid groups grew up around people who were abandoned by the helping professions as embarrassing failures or who had socially unacceptable problems. Others have pointed to the general lack of trust in professional help and of rational solutions to social problems (Back and Taylor, 1976:302). For Levin this has accompanied the shattered dream of an inegalitarian world, the visible rape of the environment, the realization of supracorporate control of international relations, the disillusionment with government, and the general sense that "the world has moved too fast, is too big, too much, too indifferent to quality and the human need for integrity and dignity" (Levin, 1975).

In summary, the growth of mutual aid groups is arguably no accident and as a social form their emergence is in part the product of major societal changes, most of which have been summarized by Katz and Bender:

> Industrialization, a money economy, the growth of vast structures of business, industry, government—all these have led to familiar specters: the depersonalization and dehumanization of institutions and social life; feelings of alienation; powerlessness; the sense for many people that they are unable to control the events that shape their lives; the loss of choices; feelings of being trapped by impersonal forces; the decline of the sense of community, of identity. These problems are compounded for many by the loss of belief—in the church, the state, progress, politics and political parties, many established institutions and values. These same conditions give rise to many of the important social movements of the day—nationalism and ethnic consciousness, the civil rights struggles, Women's Liberation—all of which countertrend against the dehumanization and atomization, the discrimination and the lack of nurturance in social institutions. (Katz and Bender, 1976:3–4)

It is in this context, then, that mutual aid groups for stigma sufferers have emerged. As we shall see, such groups not only provide their socially outcast and abandoned members with empathetic understanding, and immediate concern, but provide the means to reconstruct meaningful lives from their personal chaos and do so *in spite* of condemnation and rejection by nonmembers. Little wonder that some have seen them as "the emerging church of the twenty-first century" (Mowrer, 1971:45).

How Groups Form

As well as the broad trends that constitute the sociopolitical context for the emergence of mutual aid groups, there are several specific and localized conditions that make participation together to combat stigma more desirable than survival alone. In the previous chapter we saw how those stigmatized because of their deviance suffer emotional and interactive problems beyond those specifically associated with their behavior or condition. According to evidence from studies of mutual aid groups, these form when four localized conditions occur. First, there is a sense of dissatisfaction with the existing situation that arises out of their individual and collective experience (biography).[3] Given the stigmatized burden of being discredited through public expressions of shame concerning people like them and what they do, many are "driven out" of legitimate society. Some will literally go home after a bad public experience and not go out for weeks afterward, fearful of the next demeaning encounter. Such experiences may take the form of legal, physical, occupational, financial, or ego destructive oppression or they may result from prejudice or discrimination. Second, before forming a group, a stigma sufferer must come to recognize the value of sharing their experience and despair with fellow problem sufferers—those "in the same boat" or the same situation. It is with such recognition and shared consciousness that people are led to a new level of awareness and sensitivity to their oppression and the need for some kind of change (Levine and Perkins, 1987). Such persons may be said to be *susceptible* (Toch, 1965:12–13), meaning that they are sensitive, alert, suggestible, and oriented to change. As a result they are more than ordinarily prone to see others' proposals as promising vehicles of change. Third they must either decide, or are typically encouraged by friends, relatives, or a concerned professional, "to do something about" their situation. Where a group already exists they may respond to its members' appeals and affiliate. Such appeals are typically couched in simple and concrete terms relating to some relief that "joining" will bring, such as the appeal to "trim down" or weight watching organizations offer to potential members of being relieved of the "disease" or "sin" of being overweight (Allon,

1973). Similarly, the Little People of America offer potential members medical knowledge, help with occupational problems, and the opportunity to expand their social life (Weinberg, 1968:67; Truzzi, 1968). And COYOTE (Call Off Your Old Tired Ethics), the union of female prostitutes, offers such services as bail and counseling for arrestees and child care for "working" mothers (St. James, 1987). However, since new stigmas are endlessly constructed around differences, for many no group exists. In such circumstances a problem sufferer may begin one. Fourth, the personal revelation that solace is available from a public "banding together" is facilitated by media human interest stories, either a feature focus on the problem or, typically, a letter to a newspaper. Indeed, the role of the mass media is very significant to self-help groups not only in their formation but, as we shall see later, in their ability to redefine their situation for themselves and for others.

In summary, the formation of mutual aid groups for deviants arises out of the same general conditions that give rise to the formation of other action-oriented groups: dissatisfaction with the status quo, a perception that the existing situation is intolerable, a desire to do something about it, and the vision that this may be best achieved with like-minded others.

Initially, associations of deviants for mutual support tend to be small, loose-knit, relatively unstructured, and lacking definite character. As they grow they become more complex and politically self-conscious, though not necessarily politically active (e.g., Alcoholics Anonymous, Recovery, Inc. and other 12 step programs). In the next section we shall explore their inner workings, addressing the question of how they make a difference and how they bring about change.

THE DYNAMICS OF MUTUAL AID GROUPS

Once formed, groups of deviants who seek to solve their stigma problems have been shown to share the features of self-help and mutual aid groups in general: "by pooling misery, anger and frustration, the groups act as a catalyst for precipitating the relief from knowing one is not alone with the problem and the common interest which leads to a desire to change the situation" (Henry, 1978b:654). Several common characteristics have been identified (Killilea, 1976; Robinson and Henry, 1977; Gibbons, 1986; Levine and Perkins, 1987; Levine, 1988) that operate to deconstruct the stigma. First there is the *common experience of the members*. This is the belief that the other members of the group have the same problems; that no one is separate, superior, or professional, unless they are also problem sufferers. For example, all members of Alcoholics

Anonymous have drinking problems. This is important because, unlike professional–client relationships, members of mutual aid groups have an empathetic understanding of the problems of their members; they "have been there" and have "experienced it." Moreover, by excluding professionals the separation of stigma sufferers from others within the group is dissolved.

Second, this shared situation and *empathetic understanding* that is exemplified by descriptive instances of one's own experience through which another can identify gives *relief* from knowing you are "not alone with the problem." This lifts the burden of self-imposed failure, resentment, guilt, and helplessness that Levine (1988:40) refers to as "self-ostracization." The centrality of the stigma is lessened in the presence of others with like problems. In other words a person might be deviant and suffer stigma, but so do many others with the result that they can begin to feel "normal" in the company of like others. Thus the stature of little people is less noticed when everyone is short of stature. Obesity is less evident when others are of similar shape and weight. Such normalization is an essential step in deconstructing stigma. Related to this, the public moral meaning of the stigma is suspended with the result that interactive stress is reduced: "interactions with others are likely to be less strained, more rewarding, and more intimate than relations with non-stigmatized people" (Gibbons, 1986:141).

Third is the principle of *mutual aid and support*, which means that a stigmatized person is a member of a group that meets regularly to provide mutual aid to deal with their problems. However, formal meetings do not preclude informal contacts and, because all members are also helpers, the feeling that support is ever ready is bolstered and this matches the nature of the problem, which is enduring and isolating. Thus the overweight can call each other anytime a problem or temptation to eat arises or feelings turn negative. Unlike professional help, no appointments have to be made. Unsolicited help is offered. This often occurs before a specific problem arises, thereby removing the onus of the problem sufferer always asking for help. In this way it is made unremarkable to have and be concerned with problems that further deconstructs the stigma.

Central to mutual aid groups is a fourth characteristic described as *the helper-therapy principle* (Riessman, 1965). This draws attention to the feeling that in a situation in which people help others with a common problem, it is the helper that benefits most from the exchange. As Levine (1988:42) says, "The role of helper alleviates the degraded social identity experienced when the member is enmeshed in a deviant role." The previously negative experiences associated with others' reaction to drinking, gambling, depression, homosexuality, disability, and so on are no longer wasted but actually are helpful to another, which further deconstructs the stigma. As one observer to a group of mentally ill commented:

> Many of them said, "When I get involved with someone else I come home feeling high. I feel God, *I* helped this person." Their whole self-system is kind of slowly reconstructed; because "well I'm a dummy. I'm a sicky. I'm dependent." This whole self-picture starts being questioned. (Robinson and Henry, 1977:77)

Put succinctly, a group for relatives of the depressed explained to researchers: "If you've been through hell it helps to know that you can use that experience in some way and that it's not going to be wasted. Knowing you're being useful to somebody is the best medicine in the world" (Henry, 1978b:654). Moreover, the ability of members to help others and thereby demonstrate their ability to cope serves as a role model to newcomers demonstrating that "someone not too different has overcome a seemingly insurmountable problem" (Levine, 1988:42).

Related to this characteristic and to the common experience in general is Sutherland and Cressey's principle of *differential association*, which in this context, as Killilea (1976) says, emphasizes the reinforcement of self-concepts of normality, which in turn hastens the individuals separation from the commitment to their previous deviant identities. For example, being affirmed as construction worker, restauranteur, hair stylist, and so on has helped San Francisco's Delancy Street ex-cons to dissolve the stigma of their former prison experience, replacing it with a new sense of self and a commitment to an alternative life-style. As one of the members of the Delancy Street project said: "All I had ever done was destroy things. This has shown me another way." This is facilitated by *collective will power and belief.* This is the principle that Killilea says is the tendency of each member to look to others in the group for validation of feelings and attitudes.

Deconstructing Stigma and Reconstructing Lives

Robinson and Henry (1977:94) have argued that mutual aid groups are "not merely a forum for deconstructing members' problems by coping with practicalities and coping with stigma." They are also a "positive process, enabling members to reconstruct a new way of living through project work." Two final characteristics are of crucial importance to the operation of mutual aid groups in the correlated processes of deconstruction and reconstruction: the *importance given to information* and *constructive action toward shared goals* (Killilea, 1976). The first of these refers to the emphasis given by many groups to a factual understanding of the problem condition. Members of these groups share not only experiences but diverse collections of data. This is particularly relevant to the first stage of a three-stage process that constitutes *project work* (Robinson and Henry, 1977; Henry and Robinson, 1978a, 1978b). In this stage, central difficulties are defined simply and practical information is shared about how to cope with and manage day-to-day problems, which may include information on agencies that provide services, on legal rights, and on the dispersal of stigma. Research on some groups demonstrates that the members have superior coping skills in crisis situations (Rychtarik, 1986). Central to this communication of practical coping skills is building up a body of expertise about the problem, typically validated from scientific and medical research. This information elevates members into their own authority and simultaneously provides them with the resources to combat the ignorance of others in everyday encounters; for example, the AIDS sufferer who corrects the errors of fellow workers concerning their fears of transmission by citing evidence of studies on how the HIV virus is transmitted.[4] Coping with stigma then involves continuous support, a reeducation of the members and of the outside world. However, in order to be successful, project work must involve selecting from among all the problems confronted, those that are simple, clear, and manageable. These are then used to demonstrate to the members that they can control aspects of their everyday life and ultimately their own destiny.

The second stage of project work involves *constructive action toward shared goals* based on the philosophy that members learn by doing and are changed by doing. While information exchange comprises some of this activity, projects involve working jointly with others toward a goal that enhances the group for the members. A project may be anything from typing letters about a future activity, photocopying or mailing, to organizing a campaign or conference. The most significant projects are those relating to helping other fellow problem sufferers. It is through such projects that the third stage of the reconstruction process is reached and that is going beyond the group to form a network of friends.

Many groups such as Alcoholics Anonymous and Parents Anonymous have sponsorship systems that make forming friendships that much easier. The overall purpose of the third stage of project work is to help the person give up relying on the all-embracing support of the group and to help them to form new friendship networks in the community. This "ends social isolation and replaces it with a social network, which enhances the individual's opportunities for receiving coping assistance" (Levine, 1988:42; Thoits, 1986). Thus project work at this level is crucial to developing a new life through the stigma:

The project method, based on a shared appreciation of the need to structure time and transmitted through "group talk," is not *just* a matter of doing, it is a matter of being. It is a matter of being in the group but it is also a matter of being outside the group. Groups emphasize their problem, their projects, their way of doing things, but the real purpose, the hidden agenda, is to transform people. (Robinson and Henry, 1977:102–103).

This transformational aspect of mutual aid groups is what makes banding together a different response to the stigma of deviance than that which can be accomplished alone. In reconstructing life to replace that spoiled by stigma,

the problem is integrated with life; the treated is the treater and the treatment is to find a new way of living, incorporating the problem into one's everyday experience. This is done by providing a continuous form of care and concern through a network of friendships that itself permeates everyday living and having problems. Thus rather than *living* everyday life and *having* problems self-help group members live their lives *through* their problems. All of the changes in perception about the severity of the problem, the availability of help, the significance of asking for help, of not discontinuing help, require people to change their everyday lives. This is what we mean when we say self-help groups transform people. (Robinson and Henry, 1977:121)

For many groups, reconstruction through project work that transforms one's self identity is the end in itself leading to a new way of life (Henry and Robinson, 1978a). For many others, however, reconstruction involves a more public form of project work. It involves the transformation of the public definition of the deviant behavior or condition. As Levine argues,

This can lead to a redefinition of one's problem as a matter of social oppression as it becomes clear to members that forms of legal or institutional discrimination or powerlessness is related to the problems members experience. The new consciousness can provide a basis for social and political action to relieve oppression, either by seeking an increase in the allocation of resources to the group's cause, by working for a change in the public's definition of the problem, or by seeking relief through litigation and legislation. (Levine, 1988:41)

In short, it involves the deviant as moral entrepreneur and it is toward an understanding of this process that we now turn.

THE DEVIANT AS MORAL ENTREPRENEUR

As we mentioned earlier Sagarin has observed that some attempts to combat the stigma of deviance are concerned less with changing selves than with changing the norms and the rule-making order. From the ranks of those who perceive their situation to have more to do with others than with themselves are drawn those who seek a quest for change. They achieve this change through moral entrepreneurship. Of primary importance to the success of the collective enterprise are goals and strategy. Goals, in their simplest form, are no more than expressions of ideology. As used here then, *ideology* refers to the beliefs a group of people hold in common and the goals that they expect to achieve collectively (Toch, 1965:21). Such ideological statements define the group or organization. For example NORML (The National Organization for the Reform of Marijuana Laws) identifies its goals as seeking an end to all criminal penalties for possession and use of marijuana. The National Association to Advance Fat Acceptance seeks to change the public perception of obesity to the view that "fat is beautiful." The American Sunbathing Association, a nudist organization, identifies its goals as the cultivation of healthy bodies, while the goal of the National Gay and Lesbian Task Force is nothing less than the complete elimination of prejudice against persons based on sexual orientation. The ideology "provides a viewpoint and at least the outlines of a program for overcoming the problems of everyday living with the core issues and the common problems that emerge" (Levine, 1988:41). How these groups' various goals may be brought about is through the development of a set of objectives to be achieved by the use of several interrelated strategies. While each of the objectives and strategies is part of the overall process whereby groups reconstruct reality, it is worth reiterating that the overall aim of many groups is to counter popular beliefs and stereotypical assumptions concerning the causes and consequences of the problematic condition or behavior that is their deviance, and to expose the myths that perpetuate such views. Let us examine some of these objectives and strategies.

Objectives and Strategies of Change

Just as the basis for the deviant's initial involvement in moral entrepreneurial activity parallels that of nondeviants, so too does the objectives and tactics employed to bring about change. Primarily, the concern of mutual aid groups of deviants is to transform personal troubles into public issues, legitimate their members' lives, expose myths and redefine the public's perception of the problem, promote the visibility of their oppression, and, finally, as the ultimate confirmation of their effort to reconstruct reality, to alter public policy. We shall give brief consideration to each of these objectives and the related strategies for achieving them.

Converting Personal Troubles to Public Issues. We saw earlier (Chapter 4) how moral entrepreneurs had to raise their concerns to the level of a public policy debate *before* they could make progress toward societal change. Similarly, for deviants, converting personal troubles into public issues is a critical issue. One way of achieving this is to demonstrate that existing public policy regarding a specific type of deviance is contrary to the popular values and the public interest. Persons who might not view themselves as part of the problem (they are not gay, not handicapped, do not have a substance abuse problem, etc.) are encompassed by the groups' framing of the problem. There are several methods to achieve this. For example, it is sometimes suggested that the cost to society of maintaining and perpetuating the ban on certain behaviors is excessive and counterproductive and that the most effective course of action would be to decriminalize or eliminate the controls on that behavior. It is claimed, for instance, that the criminalization and imposition of harsh penalties for drug use and possession result in increased unnecessary violence, an overburdened criminal justice system, and lost tax revenue. NORML has argued that the zealous enforcement of marijuana laws diverts significant numbers of law enforcement personnel and other resources away from more important and socially harmful offenses such as violent crime (NORML, n.d.:1). Similarly, COYOTE (Cast Off Your Old Tired Ethics) has claimed that the ban on the sale of sexual services forces sexually frustrated males to prey on the community, a practice that legal prostitution would reduce.

Gaining Legitimacy. As part of the overall strategy to deconstructing the stigma of their condition, deviant moral entrepreneurs seek to improve their social legitimacy. One way to achieve this is by calling attention to the similarities between themselves, their goals, and those of socially respected persons and collectivities. If sustained, this challenges the distinction that is the basis of stereotypes by narrowing the "moral gap" between deviant and respected groups, thereby leading to an altered group identity.

Another tactic used to promote legitimacy is to secure the support of prestigeful and respected others. This is achieved by eliciting sympathetic responses from respected professions, such as NORML's use of an Advisory Board on which it lists prominent physicians, attorneys, educators, and religious personalities. Another example of this tactic is the

support lent to the gay liberation movement by psychologists' opposition to the designation of homosexuality as "abnormal behavior," and by
the American Psychiatric Association's opposition to classifying books
on homosexuality under the subject of "sex perversion" on the grounds
that such a designation was "inaccurate, bad librarianship, and oppressive to homosexuals" (Spector, 1977:52; Spector and Kitsuse, 1977:13–
14). By withdrawing the attribution of "abnormality" and "perversion" a
degree of reconstruction of the official definition of the offending condition is effected. The hope is that the stigmatizing designation will be
replaced by one that is at least morally neutral.

Challenging Myths.   A central objective in any attempt to reconstruct
reality is to undermine established myths about deviance carried by the
popular culture. A classic instance of this is the redefinition by Alcoholics Anonymous of alcoholism, whose public meaning was transformed from a moral weakness to a medical condition: an allergy that
some people (those who became alcoholics and others who eventually
would do so) carried to ethanol. This was given legitimacy by academic
researchers culminating in E. M. Jellineck's work *The Disease Concept of
Alcoholism* (1960) and the popular view of alcoholics as "problem drinkers" (McCaghy, 1976:271–272).

   But professions are not always cited favorably; sometimes, for example,
they are the source of the problem. Several groups of controlled drinkers,
for example, have arisen to challenge the preeminence of the disease
model. Instead of the allergy-abstinence model, controlled drinkers, who
gain their legitimacy from psychology, believe that the disease model *is*
the problem and that it prevents people learning how to become social
drinkers. Similarly, the medical definition of the positive consequences of
dieting is challenged by the Fat Underground. This group believes that
dieting serves no lasting purpose, is not an aid to better health, and may
actually wreck people's health by contributing to increased stress and
high blood pressure. They also contend that in the United States weight
reduction "is a $10 billion dollar industry. Someone is making a lot of
money off the public's fear of fat. Your (temporary) loss is their gain and
they want to keep it that way" (*Before You Go On a Diet,* n.d). To be
successful in any of these challenges to established myths it is necessary
to direct considerable energy toward the opinions of non-deviants.

Communication and Publicity.   To successfully achieve any of these objectives, it is imperative to communicate. Groups of deviants generally
have three ways to do this. They can personally engage in public speak-
ing, they can print and distribute their own literature, and they can
capture the existing mass media.

One method of communication, for example, that is popular with the gay community is to provide speakers for educational, professional, religious, and community occasions and to facilitate face-to-face communication between representatives of the gay and straight communities.

Among the most frequently used means of transformation, however, is the generation and distribution of written materials outlining a group's position in relationship to its deviance. This not only provides a focus for the all-important member-directed project work, and gives an outstretched hand to potential newcomers, but its very existence, if handled well, makes the claim that groups are more than their stigma. Much of the material generated and disseminated by these organizations consists of *bureaucratic propaganda* i.e., material "produced by an organization for evaluation and other practical purposes that is targeted at individuals, committees, or publics who are unaware of its promotive character" (Altheide and Johnson, 1980:5). Viewed as official information, this propaganda is intended to advance the cause of the respective organizations. It typically includes a history of the organization and its basic goals and philosophy. The propagandistic nature of the history, for example, is revealed by those who have studied such groups:

> A good "history," then, is not one that in some way reveals how things *really* happened but one that "makes sense" to the writer and his audience. So whatever actually happened in those early days of particular self-help groups, an acceptable way of accounting for it is to say that things happened, "as a reaction to the failure of existing services" or "because the media highlighted a particular unmet need." These are acceptable things to say. For a group to say that it was set up "because of the megalomanic tendencies of Joe Soap, the founder" or "because Fred Snooks had nothing better to do with his time" would be less acceptable. It might be more *accurate* but it would be less acceptable since histories, as many of the groups themselves are perfectly well aware are the tales of times past produced for today's audiences. (Robinson and Henry, 1977:26)

Indeed, literature published by the groups serves the dual purpose of public "education" and private support. Group published journals, magazines, and newsletters are a central vehicle for group members to communicate with each other and as such, form part of the ongoing support that maintains the patterns of socialization and inner strength. They are also sent to government agencies and political representatives. Publications such as *The Advocate* and *Alternate*, which serve gays, *Grapevine*, the official newsletter of Alcoholics Anonymous, and *Paraplegia News* and *The Disability Rag* for the disabled, heighten people's awareness of their collective strength, promote interaction, and encourage project work, such as letter writing and campaigning for the cause. For example, the *Paraplegia News* contains articles written by "insiders" to help handicapped persons cope with their condition, find fulfillment, and handle distressing encounters with nonhandicapped persons. One such article, Sue Odgers'(1978) "Sex on Wheels," outlines, for disabled females, what "kinds of men" may be encountered and how they may be dealt with. In much the same way that the able-bodied characterize the disabled, Odgers characterizes the well meaning but ill-informed able bodied men she had encountered, including "Mr. Curious," "Mr. I Understand and Can Help," and "Mr. I Have the Remedy." Odgers also indicates how these occasionally clumsy persons and their attendant awkward encounters can be handled with dignity and presents her own romantic fantasy, which serves to normalize sexuality among the disabled, countering the tendency of nondisabled to desexualize such persons.

Capturing of the Media.   Perhaps more than any other means to facilitate moral entrepreneurship in the transformation of stigma is the use of the mass media. We have already seen that for many groups the media plays a key role in highlighting problems and act as a catalyst to the formation of groups. However, it is as a resource in the politics of morality transformation that newspapers, radio, and television are most exploited by groups of deviants.[5] To improve their visibility, attract adherents, and solicit support for change, the sensationalizing cost of the media has to be traded for the necessary exposure of reconstructed meanings. Without a visible, morally neutral or positive image, the probability of achieving legitimacy is likely to be limited. This means that how materials concerning stigmatized groups, their issues, and incidents are portrayed in the media is critically important. For this reason establishing friendly relationships with sympathetic journalists is a necessary strategy, since it can greatly affect the amount and "slant" of coverage media provide. In view of this, spokespersons for deviant interests have often found it necessary to employ contrivances to gain access or to "capture" the media. One device used for capture is for deviants to establish an office (more symbolic than real) specifically for presenting their perspective to the media. Thus in the case of the nude bathers,

> The most effective nude beach power organization by far [was] the Committee to Save Eden Beach. It consisted of a handful of people willing to help get petitions signed and such at various times, but at its core were just two people who appointed themselves as the committee . . . and then proceeded to present their positions as if they somehow represented the beach people. (Douglas et al., 1977:218)

Another device designed to elicit media coverage, though less controllable than the tamed journalist, is to stage events that have a high probability of being defined as newsworthy. Thus acts of civil disobedience, protest marches, and demonstrations intended to promote confrontation with authorities are sometimes staged by groups, such as ACT UP's (1992) prepresidential election vigil outside the White House to gain media attention for the rights of people with AIDS. Such actions bring the group's message to the attention of a larger audience on both sides of the "moral fence" (Shuey, 1978:3, 25). However, the consciousness produced by media coverage is also influenced by how the information is presented i.e., by *media logic*. Critically important in this is format, i.e., "how material is organized, the style in which it is presented, the focus or emphasis on particular characteristics of behavior, and the grammar of media communication" (Altheide and Snow, 1991:9). Thus we are not suggesting that sympathetic consciousness or transformatory effects are simply a matter of capturing individual journalists. Rather, the issue is a matter of capturing the discursive resources to penetrate existing social constructions and to replace these with new forms.

Replacement Discourse. Reaching the nondeviant public through the media with a message is a necessary part of the transformation process. Crucial is what is being said. While it is clear that the aim is to alter the public meaning, which often means to show the suppressed side of persons with stigma, it also means playing a semantic device that can be crucial to the eventual outcome. In other contexts this has been referred to as the constructive side of the postmodernist theory of deconstruction, under the term *"replacement discourse"* (Henry, 1987; Henry and Milovanovic, 1991, 1992; Milovanovic and Henry, 1991), referring to the process of developing alternative terms and phrases for a phenomenon that recasts the meaning of what is being described. As Levine says,

> Each group tends to develop its own language and conceptual tags for common experiences. . . . As members discuss their experiences, they are interpreted within the group in terms of the group's ideology, language and slogans. . . . The concept, as represented by the language or the slogan, enters a member's consciousness. The concept is used to interpret new situations, to reinterpret continuing ones, to guide choices and actions, and in consequence to affect feelings. (Levine, 1988:41)

The simplest illustration are the slogans of Al-Anon such as "Keep It Simple," "One Day At a Time," and "Live and Let Live." However, at a publicly oriented level are examples such as the women's movement success in substituting the address "Ms." for "Miss" and "Mrs." With deviant groups the common theme has been to bring back the concept that they are first and foremost people. Thus we have "Little *People*," "*Persons* of Color," and *People* with AIDS. So extensive has been the adoption of this approach that it has been formulated into a movement under the title "Political Correctness" or "PC." Political Correctness, however, is itself a label that others have used to classify the more vigorous attempts at replacement discourse by those who feel that failure to observe the wishes of minority groups of various sorts can be grounds for taking legal action under various antidiscrimination legislation on the grounds of race, sex disability, etc.

Altering Public Policy. Ultimately, for many deviants, as for other moral entrepreneurs, to be consequential the transformation of public meaning will need to be met with changes in public policy reflected in law. While many of the ways to achieve this are similar to those discussed in Chapter 4, it is worth briefly considering what has been accomplished in the cases of marijuana, homosexuality, and disability, which are illustrative.

Marijuana use has been subject to considerable redefinition and some alteration in public policy as a result of pressure by those who consume the substance. Labels used in the 1930s and 1940s such as "dope crazed killer," "moral degenerate," etc., are seldom heard and the replacement "dope head" does not have the same moral import. Despite the fact that American drug law enforcement continues to focus on marijuana (Dennis, 1990:130), groups working to alter those earlier definitions (e.g., NORML) have been quite successful. During the 1950s, 1960s, and 1970s it became fashionable to regard pot smoking as a relatively harmless source of pleasure. Problems associated with its use were seen as infrequent and superficial (Goode, 1972:183). As a result, groups and organizations began to push for a reduction in criminal penalties for marijuana possession. They appear to have succeeded in several jurisdictions where the penalty for marijuana violations has been reduced to a fine. This has occurred in Oregon, Alaska, California, Colorado, Maine, and New York. And, though the initiative was defeated, in 1986 Oregon held the first state election on the total legalization of marijuana for private use (*Arizona Republic*, 1985). Reform proposals have also been considered due to the growing recognition of the medicinal value of marijuana for victims of glaucoma, multiple sclerosis, chronic pain, and cancer patients undergoing chemotherapy. Reflecting these changes, New Mexico legalized the therapeutic use of marijuana in 1978 and in 1991 a Florida appeals court ruled that a married couple infected with the HIV virus, contracted as a result of the husband's hemophilia, may legally be able to smoke marijuana for therapeutic purposes. Likewise, the Washington, D.C. based Alliance for Cannabis Therapeutics, persuaded the Food and Drug Administration to allow a disabled man to use marijuana to control muscle spasms (*Arizona Republic*, 1991b). Finally, nonenforcement of possession laws has been adopted as the informal policy in some jurisdictions. In other places the marijuana lobby has succeeded in effectively declaring decriminalized areas, such as Ann Arbor, Michigan, which until 1990 had a $5 fine for possession, and as a reaction to the growing tide of antidrug sentiment in the state, increased the penalty to $25!

Despite some change in perception among the public and some softening of law enforcement policy concerning marijuana, the U.S. policy regarding so-called "hard drugs" (i.e., cocaine and heroin) continues to be described as a "war" involving vigorous "eradication and interdiction" at an annual cost estimated at about $30 billion over all levels of government (Dennis, 1990:129; Blair, 1990:7). However vigorous, this policy has also been subject to variable interpretation, and its merit subject to considerable criticism (Johns, 1992). Notable in this regard is the proposal to legalize drug distribution and possession. Largely led by the Washington, D.C. based Drug Policy Foundation, the proposal calls for the decriminalization of drug distribution and possession just as the repeal of prohibition in 1933 decriminalized alcohol distribution. This proposal—which is not to be equated with granting moral legitimacy to drug use—has received endorsement from a variety of notables: former secretary of state George Schultz, Congressman George Crockett, federal judge Robert Sweet, Baltimore mayor Kurt Schmoke, former New York City police commissioner Patrick V. Murphy, economist and presidential advisor Milton Friedman, William F. Buckley, Princeton University professor Ethan Nadelmann, astronomer Carl Sagan, and former Chicago Mercantile Exchange member Richard Dennis (Sullivan, 1990). In addition, major newspapers (e.g., *San Francisco Examiner*) have editorialized in favor of controlled drug legalization. Although decriminalization has it critics (Dennis, 1990:130–132) it is significant that, without pressure from groups of deviants, the legalization issue would not likely have become part of the debate.

Homosexuality has also been subject to widespread public and official attention over the past few decades (Adam, 1987). In several jurisdictions gay candidates have been elected to public office on the local and national levels. Ordinances have been passed giving official support to goals consistent with the interests of gay people (e.g., in housing and job discrimination), and steady pressure is being applied to the military to lift its ban on gay men and women (*New York Times*, 1992e) in part through the move to expel ROTC from university campuses. In universities, gay candidates have been elected to student office (University of

Minnesota) and at least one university (UCLA) has given official recognition to a sorority formed by lesbians. In San Francisco, California and Ann Arbor, Michigan, unmarried couples, gay and straight, are now able to register their partnership, thereby bringing the legal and moral status of such relationships into closer harmony with traditional marriage (*New York Times*, 1991). Likewise, lesbian and gay couples are increasingly experiencing parenthood by means of artificial insemination.

The activism and sometime militancy of minority peoples is not confined to groups concerned only with achieved deviants. Equally active are the ascribed groups such as the disabled who have been identified as an "awakening minority" that is "finally making (itself) heard by lobbying for bills that will aid their cause, by attending city council meetings, and by addressing service clubs" (Watson, 1978:20). Following the model established by other instrumental groups, the disabled have brought great changes in public policy as a result of lobbying. Of major importance are several laws including the Rehabilitation Act of 1973,[6] The Education for All Handicapped Children Act (Public Law 94–142),[7] and, most recently, the 1990 Americans With Disabilities Act (ADA), a bill identified as "the Emancipation Proclamation for disabled persons in America" (Tucker, n.d.). The 1990 Act seeks to end discrimination against the disabled in public and private agencies and businesses nationwide in employment and as a consumer. For example, ADA prohibits discrimination against the disabled in places such as restaurants, bars, stores, and numerous other places of leisure and business as well as on new bus and rail systems, which are required to be fitted with ramps or lifts and spaces for wheelchairs. Given these provisions, there is little doubt that the passage of the ADA represents a monumental victory for disabled persons working to overcome the consequences of their having been isolated from the mainstream of public life.

Taken together, these examples of policy change, many of which rest on the efforts of nonvalued people to challenge their deviant status, reflect the increasingly politicized nature of deviance in our society that ranges from rule violation, civil disobedience, and violent protest, to politically organizing to satisfy their collective interests (Horowitz and Liebowitz, 1968; Schur, 1980). We will conclude with a consideration of that issue.

DEVIANCE AS POLITICS

To consider deviance as politics is to end where we began. Understanding deviance requires that we understand the conflict between competing interests for power, leadership, and dominance in the enforcement of public policy, what Schur (1980) has referred to as "stigma contests." The politicization of deviance recognizes that the deviance process is dialectical, part of an ongoing power struggle in which competing interests vie with one another for an official stamp of legitimacy:

> one of the best ways of thinking about the entire area of deviance is in terms of what might be called *stigma contests*. In these continuing struggles over competing social definitions, it is relative, rather than absolute power that counts most. The power of either side may be subject to change not only through external causes but to an extent by conscious effort. . . . Deviance-defining is not a static event but a continuous and changing process. This is so because, as we have seen, it is a way of characterizing and reacting, exhibited by individuals and groups whose interests and favored values, and their ability to impose them, vary greatly and in many instances change over time . . . the distribution of power among persons and groups crucially shapes deviance outcomes. To study stigma contests or deviance struggles is, then to study the sources and uses of power. (Schur, 1980:8, 66)

As Schur notes, to suggest deviance is a power struggle rather than a morality play, means that issues of deviance are everlastingly negotiable. Thus traditional moral meanings, such as those concerning sexual matters, are likely to be defined as problematic and subject to challenge and change, revision, and rerevision. So called "public standards" are mere snapshots in an endless unfinished movie; alone they tell you little of the plot, nothing of "who done it," and provide few clues as to what the next frozen frame will look like. Viewed as a political struggle, public standards become relative, authority is questionable, and the existing structure of rules and control takes on a new meaning (Horowitz and Liebowitz, 1968:296).

Such a perspective raises questions about how some persons' definitions of morality are elevated to a position of dominance over others. We contend that the politics of deviance results from the moral heterogeneity of society, is shaped by clusters of interests, reflects the uneven distribution of power, and that the processes of "intentional organizing and campaigning . . . are probably much the same whether the attempted crusade aims to impose or expand deviantizing . . . or, on the contrary, seeks to overturn stigma-laden definitions and reactions" (Schur, 1980:190). Indeed, while those subject to domination have always protested their treatment (Gamson, 1975) it has not always been the case that they have sought to transform their position (Becker, 1970:240), or sought to have it publicly legitimized using the mass media and political lobbying tactics. Increased use of these forms since the

1960s reflects the fact that "deviants have become more self-conscious, more organized, more willing to fight with conventional society than ever before. They are more open about their deviance, prouder of what they are and less likely to be treated as others want to treat them without having some voice in the matter" (Becker, 1970:344). These developments reflect elements in what we described earlier as the intercursive power model.

The expression of this voice can be seen in the rejection by many groups of being "ministered to" in therapeutic terms in the name of "help" or "care," recognizing what Foucault depicted as the thin line between care and control. For example, the disabled repudiate the idea that "being different" is pathological (Gliedman and Roth, 1980) or that it calls for "correction" by psychiatry, surgery, social work, or other helping professions. This repudiation reflects increasing self-acceptance among those defined as deviant. Evidence for this is found in books such as *Enabling Romance* (Klein and Kroll, 1992), a "how to" book on sexuality for the disabled, and the attack by a group called "Jerry's Orphans" (*Missoulian*, 1992) on the alleged tendency of Jerry Lewis and the Muscular Dystrophy Association to promote pity for victims of the disease and to infantilize victims by referring to them as "kids" regardless of their age. Indeed, some sociologists studying disability and stigma have argued for a new approach to deviance called a "sociology of acceptance" (Bogdan and Taylor, 1987), which accommodates to instances when the disabled are accepted rather than rejected by others (Schwartz, 1988:36). They argue that the sociology of acceptance is directed at understanding how people with deviant attributes come to be accepted in personal relations, groups, organizations, communities, and society (Groce, 1985). The sociology of acceptance considers "incidents where human service programs integrate people who might otherwise be isolated, excluded, or segregated from typical people" (Bogdan and Taylor, 1987:35). Instead of studying processes of stigma and exclusion this approach looks at caring relationships between people who are different and others, and at successful attempts at their integration.

Finally, due to the politicization of deviance, there has been a significant shift in the boundaries between what was once considered public and private. Thus, we have become more free to express publicly what in previous times was subject to repression and, if expressed at all, was confined to the most private arenas. This is evident in modern dress and speech. Nowhere is this shift in boundaries more evident than in the daytime television talk shows such as Sally Jessy Raphael, Oprah, and Donahue, where "dirty" family laundry is hung out for national viewing and where private suffering becomes public fodder. Such freedom is also seen in demands for the legitimation of social relationships, forms of intimacy, and love that in times past "dared not speak its name" (LaMarche and Rubenstein, 1990). It is evident, too, in women's demand to be free of "sexual terrorism" (Morgan, 1989) and sexual harassment. Such changes can neither be accounted for nor adequately explained by attributing them to "moral decay." Rather, they are the outcome of the ongoing conflict between our conception of the private and public self (Bensman and Lilienfeld, 1979:ix), and the shift in power in our society. What these shifts do not promise is an end to repression. In the ongoing dialectic of deviance, they provide only that the liberated of today will likely be the oppressors of tomorrow. Before we leave the politics of deviance it is important, therefore, to reflect on the limits of transformation.

Limits of Transformation

Recognizing that defining and controlling deviance are political processes brings us to consider the issues of fragmentation and cooptation as countervailing forces mitigating in favor of the status quo. While many accomplishments are possible by collective efforts that would not have occurred by individuals coping alone, we should not be blind to the forces of dissention and the power of dominant groups to undermine movements for change. There are several ways this comes about.

Fragmentation and Fissioning. While many stigma-transforming groups are the outcome of marginalization from the larger society, others are themselves the result of exclusion by already marginalized groups. For example, the various organizations for prostitutes such as COYOTE (Call Off Your Old Tired Ethics), ASP (Association of Seattle Prostitutes), PONY (Prostitutes of New York), CAT (California Association of Trollops), and PUMA (Prostitute Union of Massachusetts Association) (variously, sponsors of Hookers Conventions, Hookers Balls, the Trick of the Year, and the Vice Cop of the Year Awards) (Schur, 1980:123) were formed partly to counter the critical position taken by some radical feminists on prostitution. Margo St. James, founder of COYOTE, argues that the radical feminist view of the female prostitute as "victim" and "sexual slave" is patronizing and condescending believing that instead of being sex objects they are deviants engaged in a stigmatized sexuality (St. James, 1987:86; Beirne and Messerschmidt, 1991:158). Similarly, pedophile organizations, such as the British PIE (Pedophile Information Exchange) formed as a result of the oppression from other gays who were members of the Scottish Minority Group that campaigned for homosexual equality:

> they were put down as much by gays as by straights, you see, in fact probably more so . . . the gays are often labelled with the term "child molester" because it's assumed that most male homosexuals and even some female homosexuals like children. That's often an assumption, just society's. And so they, the gays, want to get rid of that. And the way to get rid of it, lots of them think, is to kick . . . out the pedophiles. (Robinson and Henry, 1977:15–16)

So groups of deviants, regardless of their original reason for forming, once established begin to fragment. This phenomenon has been described as *"fissioning,"* referring to some members' splitting off to form new groups "when there is persistent internal conflict" (Taylor, 1982:92). Even if these groups do not break up, they rarely join together either. They tend to be narrowly focused on removal of their members stigma, rather than addressing the stigmatizing process in general. Thus they remain separated and isolated from each other. For example, Alcoholics Anonymous makes a point of never joining with any other groups or organizations to take a public stand. This raises questions about their ability to operate as a political force.

A Reluctant Movement: Cooptation and Danger.   The fact that marginalized persons come together around their mutual interests does not necessarily mean that they constitute a movement (Mowrer, 1976), are "signs of an evolving more democratic society," or are a form of countercultural protest with a "power to the people" political stance (Vattano, 1972:7). As Katz (1975:9) has argued, such a claim, "does not stand a moment's analysis . . . the philosophy, values or internal operations of groups like Alcoholics Anonymous or Recovery, Inc. . . . is exactly that of assisting their members to conform to the values of the dominant middle-class society." There are several reasons for this.

First, groups of deviants who band together for the purposes of transforming their stigma focus on their problems and those of their members, but rarely do they focus on the wider social context in which their problem is framed. As such "they are often more a response to symptoms than to the underlying problems. In some instances they may even lead to an exacerbation of the deeper problems" (Sidel and Sidel, 1976:67).

Second, such groups exist in dependent relationships with professionals who are relied on to solve their technical problems and to obtain legitimacy. This allows professionals to reciprocally rely on them as "support groups," which coopts them to a subordinate role within the structure of existing power relationships. In such circumstances some of the more vociferous advocates for political change may be palliated, if for no other reason than having their energies diverted to self-serving rather than transforming work. A similar problem arises as a result of groups' ambivalent relationship with the media, which they need to convey their message, but which often charges the price of sensationalism and trivialization: "Although the media's record is on the whole good, publicity may be detrimental since the essential seriousness of the group is often undermined. The inevitable overstatement of the deviant case and its stilted presentation often puts off potential joiners" (Henry, 1978b:655). Ironically, the attempt to expose deviance can repel those who share the same behavior or condition but do not recognize the label applying to them. As George Orwell recognized long ago: "I imagine there are quite a lot of tramps who thank God they are not tramps. They are like trippers who say such cutting things about trippers."

Third, these groups can readily be undermined and controlled through their relationships to the outside world:

> The most obvious way of preventing a successful group from developing a sufficiently firm power base to be in a position actually to threaten the established professional or political order is, quite simply, to take it over. There is no need to "facilitate," "regulate," or "cooperate," when you can "eliminate." As Jack Geiger has crisply described it, "when the counter culture develops something of value, the establishment rips it off and sells it back." (Robinson and Henry, 1977:137)

Finally, the very attempt by some groups to bring about change in their members is one that discourages critical questioning. Newcomers are discouraged from questioning basic principles and those who are disruptive are dismissed as "sick." Members who stray are frowned on and the groups exert extreme pressure to inner loyalty through shaming and ostracism. They may even suppress the controversial behavior itself, which can result in a harsher condemnation of deviance than is found in society and a reaffirmation of the process of stigmatizing. In some weight control groups, for example, people who fail to reach their goal weight are labeled as "pigs." They are fined if they miss meetings and can ultimately have their membership revoked by the group (Henry, 1978b:656). In less coercive groups subtle comments can force the undesirable to feel unwelcome. The critical question is, where do all those deviants go who are rejected by the wider society *and* by groups of fellow deviants?

In summary then, our examination of the politics of deviance shows the dialectical nature of transformation. Transformation is a complex interwoven process in which attempts to change others result in changes to selves and as a result the outcome of any deliberate strategy is unpredictable, at the very least.

SUMMARY

In this chapter we have examined collective methods of transforming stigma. Consideration was given to voluntary associations for self-help and mutual aid, their origins, their continuity with secret societies, and their recent increase in number and visibility in American society. Of most immediate importance in explaining their present status are the political upheavals experienced in the United States between the 1960s and the present. Most significant has been the general humanitarian social movement begun during that period and the more specific movements emerging from it.

We also examined the activities of these associations and the social conditions with which they relate: the experience and definition of conditions as intolerable and the sharing, relief, vision, and hope resulting in a desire to pursue change. We distinguished between groups oriented to personal change of their members and those directed at transforming society. We saw how the rejection that accompanies stigma can be softened by the group, as a result of sharing experiences, information, and knowledge of problems of stigmatization and, more broadly, of everyday living. It is through this shared consciousness that people were shown to develop a new level of awareness to their oppression and the need to change. Easing of problems experienced by participating in the mutual aid group is not, however, the final solution. The easing of problems must be sustained in life outside the group and this is accomplished through project work that allows the stigmatized deviant to lead a new way of life through their problem. A significant component of such project work can involve political action to transform the public meaning of deviance and if this direction is taken the group shifts from inner focused to outer focused activity.

In describing the tactics used by those groups that are outer focused toward political change, several similarities were noted between them and other moral crusaders. That such similarity exists reflects the widespread institutionalization of the means to alter public policy and create "new moralities" by collective effort. Most important, these activities reflect a fundamental change in the nature of deviance in this society—a shift requiring that deviance be viewed as a political rather than a moral and therapeutic issue. We concluded by observing that the politics of change is a dialectical process and that in seeking to bring change, groups may be more changed than changing as they become subject to internal fragmentation and external cooptation.

NOTES

1. As has been noted elsewhere (Killilea, 1976; Robinson and Henry, 1977:31–33) the range of schemes for classifying such groups is vast and varied, being based on criteria ranging from the nature of the problem they confront (Bean, 1975), to the services offered (Tracy and Gussow, 1976), the styles of managing deviance (Sagarin, 1969), the basis of coming together (Hansell, 1976), their purposes and composition (Levy, 1976), and their primary focus, depending on whether this is personal growth, social advocacy, alternative living, coping with "rock bottom," or some combination of these (Katz and Bender, 1976). Such classifications can get quite bizarre, such as that by Steinman and Traunstein (1976:352) who distinguish between "Anonymous" groups focused on group encounters, "Underground" groups that oppose official help, "Masqueraders" who appear not to be self-help organizations, and "Big Timers," which are "sophisticated in their operations"!

2. Women's suffrage and gay and lesbian movements substantially predate the 1950s and 1960s (Adam, 1987:17ff). By the time of World War II, however, these early movements were largely dormant. Their reemergence after World War II, and especially during the 1950s and 1960s, is part of the more general movement of that time involving a general shift in the values of people (Blumer, 1955:200). This seems especially so with respect to the plethora of self-help organizations that have emerged over the past half century, although as we shall see later, it is questionable whether these groups constitute a social movement.

3. This should not necessarily be equated to a dissatisfaction with existing services, however, since research indicates that many members are highly satisfied with these as well as with their mutual aid experience (Bates, 1988), which might reflect a distinction between those who form groups and those who join them.

4. Weitz (1993:232) points out the limits to this approach for the person with AIDS who does not publicly reveal their identity, since to appear too knowledgeable might lead to unwanted attention including questions about *how* they know so much, and suspicions about their health.

5. These deviants are simultaneously exploited by the media, as is testified by the numerous TV talk shows, such as Donahue, Oprah, and Geraldo, whose focus seems almost exclusively on the shocking, the outrageous deviant lifestyle. We will return to this theme when discussing the politics of deviance below.

6. This requires affirmative action hiring of disabled workers, ensures physical accessibility of the handicapped to public and private buildings, requires affirmative action among large contractors working for the federal government, and bans job discrimination against disabled in federally funded agencies (Gliedman and Roth, 1980:267).

7.   This stipulates a "free appropriate public education in an environment that would be the least restrictive for the handicapped child's normal development. The handicapped student would no longer be an exile" (*NEA Today*, 1983). The All Handicapped Children Act reflects a significant change in public policy concerning disabled children since it is designed to eliminate hasty and detrimental labeling of the disabled (e.g., the identification of a dyslexic child as "lazy" or "retarded") and promotes the mainstreaming or integration of the disabled into the life of the community (Hoye, 1983).

Epilogue

Our goal in this book has been to examine and understand the phenomenon of deviance as a human creation and the product of an unending social process. For those weaned on the idea that deviance consists of stuff that is substantively different from nondeviance, or that moral rules are absolute and unquestionable, this may have been a challenging experience.

As for the supposed substantive difference between deviance and respectability, we are reminded of the critic who asked what the difference was between saliva and spit? Would they appear to be different if examined under a microscope? If not, what leads to the distinction implied by these labels? And why are they responded to in different ways? These same questions may be posed regarding deviance. For example, we have suggested that deviance and nondeviance arise from the same motivational sources, including a desire to have fun, to satisfy one's curiosity, to boost one's ego, to make money, to be part of a group, to beat the system, to meet a challenge, to defend an ethical position, or some combination of these and other things. Further, history and anthropology reveal that what people define as moral, right, virtuous, ethical, etc. is anything but stable, universal, or uniform. But one need not read history to learn that; the daily media provide ample supporting evidence that one man's perks can be another man's fraud, or that one woman's coping can be another's dependence. Our argument is that in the absence of a label, deviance is indistinguishable from normality.

In support of this idea and its ramifications we have drawn on the work of several generations of theorists and researchers and tried to validate their conclusions using examples drawn from everyday life, including that of our students. That evidence supports the idea that deviance and respectability are products of peoples' unending effort to create social order in a world that appears to be without inherent meaning, i.e., a world that is absurd (Lyman and Scott, 1970). In creating that ordered world, people seek to control persons and situations they regard as threatening or distressing. That control effort leads to the creation of new moralities, portions of which may become institutionalized as a part of public law. In that regard, the deviance process is largely political.

A second output of the effort to produce order is the creation of several categories of "outsiders," i.e., people who display attributes defined as offensive, are perceived to have broken public rules, and are regarded as qualitatively different. Viewed in this way, the phenomenon of deviance originates neither with rule breakers nor with moral entrepreneurs acting alone. Rather, it stems from the interaction between them (Scheff, 1979). Deviance is nothing if not a socially constructed phenomenon.

To say that deviance is a social creation is not to reduce it to a mere matter of attributing meaning. Our model suggests it entails far more than semantics since it is only by naming and defining that people are able make sense of their sociocultural world and organize their responses to it. To suggest the social construction of deviance reduces to mere semantics (as if that were nothing) is to ignore people's objectification of meaning and to trivialize the struggle of those seeking to extricate themselves from its constitutive clutches.

But what conclusions can we draw from our study of deviance as a social creation? Are we to conclude that the elimination of deviance lies in abandoning rules? That is, if deviance results from rule-making, should we then repeal all rules and ban moral entrepreneurship? Of course not. First, as we have seen, rule makers are no more responsible for deviance by banning than rule breakers are by nonconformity; *both activities are mutually constitutive and codetermining of the phenomenon.* Second, the absence of rules will not prevent people from developing interests and preferences. Nor will it eliminate fear and its companion, social control. Even in a society of "saints" there will be "sinners."

Another reading of our perspective might prompt the conclusion that it leads to advocating the principle of "anything goes." That is, society's ills and deviance can be eradicated by refraining from interpreting others' actions and/or conditions, or perhaps by normalizing the variations in the human condition. Practically, that suggestion lacks merit since it ignores the idea that reality is multiple and that people's tendency is to assign cosmic importance to its many facets. To suggest a policy of normalization is to expect that people will cease to be evaluative, judgmental creatures, and refrain from the conflict generated by defending their interests and values. To advocate normalization, then, runs contrary to the perspective used throughout this book. The only defensible conclusion to be drawn is that deviance and respectability have the same origins and are inextricably linked. Unless we eradicate respectability, we need not look for the elimination of deviance.

In the final analysis, deviance is both a celebration and condemnation of diversity. Diversity enables us to adapt to changing circumstances. It gives us the possibilities to survive. Conformity is tied to what is. Reproducing conformity provides continuity and control. But we need to recognize that reproducing what is desirable of existing constructions need not limit the energy required to construct something new. We need not be completely bound by the constraints of existing constructions. Moreover, or own energy *can* make a difference. What you or we think *does* matter. That the difference made is one that some, or even many, find offensive should not blind us to the importance of the struggle we all endure to make a difference. It should alert us to the fundamental importance of societal institutions to facilitate the means of individual recognition, for claims on that space will emerge if we try to suppress it and its emergence may not please us.

What is learned from this study of deviance will depend in part on our values and interests. It will also depend on how far we are able to suspend moral judgments in order to appreciate the meanings of those who are doing things we find offensive and objectionable.

Does this exploration of deviance mean, therefore, that we cannot make moral judgments? Of course it does not. We can make much more informed judgments than those we would have made without the appreciation and understanding of the meanings of those who take part in deviant behavior. To understand the meaning of a deviant activity and then to weigh that activity in the light of a wider social context is to make a responsible judgment about the activity. Failing to understand that to which we object is taking the same irresponsible attitude that we find offensive in others. We do not care. Why should they?

At the same time we may now appreciate that while we are in some important senses capable of shaping/changing the world we live in, even when we strive to be different our interaction with others binds us to conform. That most of us do not wholly conform to wider societal morality and law is no evidence that we do not conform, for our very joining with others who share our deviant activity is an indication of the force of those around us. We declare independence when we say that we do not care what others think, but we reveal our vulnerability in our sensitivity to what friends and fellow deviants think. We are individuals but we are also social beings. We might be able to tilt the balance, but it is only the truly *deviant* deviant that is unaffected by those considerations. However much we may pretend it is otherwise, to be in the social world is to be connected with others. It is to engage in a world of socially constructed meaning based on distinctions and judgments of difference. The challenge to humanity is for each person to recognize the active role he or she plays in building the structures through which lives are lived, and avoid having the authority over those constructions float from our grasp. This involves being aware of the connections we have to others, not only in making structures, but also in *unmaking* them. It is not enough merely to know that we construct our social world together. We need also to acknowledge that we can *deconsruct* that which oppresses and, most importantly, that with others we can *reconstruct* that world, just as groups of deviants who escape the stereotypical yoke of other's intentions and the resultant public policy have reconstructed theirs. The first stage in such a process is to go back to our fundamental assumptions, to the perspective of our umpire who said "they're nothing until I call them." Now we may see that we can call them differently, call them ourselves, call them with others, and, most importantly, recall them.

Bibliography

Abbott, Jack Henry. 1981. *In The Belly of the Beast*. London: Arrow Paperbacks.

Achievement, The National Voice of the Disabled. 1981. "An Open Letter to Jerry Lewis." November: 2.

Adam, Barry. 1987. *The Rise of a Gay and Lesbian Movement*. Boston: Twayne Publishers.

Adler, Patricia, and P. Adler. 1978 "Tiny-Dopers: A Case of Deviant Socialization." *Symbolic Interaction* 1(Spring):90–105.

Allen, Brandt. 1975. "Embezzler's Guide to the Computer." *Harvard Business Review* 53 (July/August):79–89.

Allon, Natalie. 1973. "Group Dieting Rituals." *Society* 10 (January/February):36–42.

Allport, Gordon. 1938. *Personality*. London: Constable.

Altheide, David L. 1976. *Creating Reality, How TV News Distorts Events*. Beverly Hills, CA: Sage Publications.

Altheide, David L., and J. M. Johnson. 1980. *Bureaucratic Propaganda*. Boston: Allyn and Bacon.

Altheide, David L. and R. P. Snow. 1991. *Media Worlds in the Postjournalism Era*. Hawthorne, NY: Aldine de Gruyter.

Altman, Dennis. 1971. *Homosexual Oppression and Liberation*. New York: Avon Books, The Hearst Corporation.

Anderson, Nels. 1923. *The Hobo, The Sociology of the Homeless Man*. Chicago: University of Chicago Press.

Anderson, Robert T. 1968. "From Mafia to Cosa Nostra." Pp. 269–279 in Marcello Truzzi, ed., *Sociology and Everyday Life*. Englewood Cliffs, NJ: Prentice-Hall.

Ann Arbor News. 1992a. "Rape Vastly Underreported," April 26:1.

———. 1992b. "Violent Crime Increases 5%, FBI Reports," April 27:1.

———. 1992c. "Anita Hill Gives Retrospective on Last Year's Senate Hearings," October 17:3.

Anonymous. 1986. *An Organizational View of the Creation of Knowledge*. Arizona State University.

Aptheker, Herbert. 1943. *American Negro Slave Revolts*. New York: International Publishers.

Arizona Daily Star (Tucson, AZ). 1987. "'A Jazzing Shock' Bureaucrats Show No Appreciation for the Double Entendre," February 27:A-17.

Arizona Gay News (Tucson, AZ). 1978. "Perspective." November 23:4.

Arizona Republic (Phoenix, AZ). 1976. "Officers Call on Legislators to Examine Smut for a Day," April 26:A-1, 12.

_____. 1977. "Chiefs of Police Oppose Homosexuals as Officers," October 7:A-8.

_____. 1979. "Housewife Grimly Pursues Pornographers," December 27:C-1.

_____. 1980a. "Series of Sex Killings Worry Californians," September 21:B-15.

_____. 1980b. "Jean Harris and the Scarsdale Diet Doctor," (Andy Rooney), March 27:A-18.

_____. 1980c. "Glendale Residents Oppose Halfway House Despite Switch," February 26:A-5; March 1:B-1.

_____. 1980d. "Fired Gay Police Officer Plans Fight to Regain Job," September 10:B-1.

_____. 1981a. "Coalition Determined to Clean Up 'Sodom and Gomorrah'," February 11:A-2.

_____. 1981b. "John W. Hinckley, Jr., a Wanderer with Nowhere to Go," April 6:A-1 and A-3.

_____. 1981c. "Transsexuals Seek Changes in Birth Records," October 4:AA-7.

_____. 1982a. "Conscience Haunts Purse Thief," May 2:B-8.

_____. 1982b. "Junkie Doctors 'Adept' at Hiding Habit," February 17:B-10.

_____. 1982c. "Reagan Urged to Decree Anti-pornography Week," October 21:A-16.

_____. 1983a. "Addicted Doctors Saved by Self-help," February 14:A-1

_____. 1983b. "Special-Interest Funds Listed for 80 Freshmen in Congress," October 2:A-12.

_____. 1984. "Churches Take Stock Against Nuclear Ads," January 5:A-3.

_____. 1985. "Oregon Voters Will Get Chance to Legalize Pot," November 23: D-2.

_____. 1987. "Chicago Lawyer Admits to Bribing up to 24 Judges," April 24:A-4.

_____. 1989. "Gay Parents Reshaping Family," March 3:A-2.

_____. 1990. "Court Turns Down Gay Rights Cases," February 27:A-3.

_____. 1991a. "Capital 'Sting' Roll Call," February 11:A-8.

_____. 1991b. "Paralyzed Man Allowed to Smoke Pot," April 18:A-11.

Ashman, Charles R. 1973. *The Finest Judges Money Can Buy and Other Forms of Judicial Pollution*. Los Angeles: Nash.

Aytemiz, Ohran. 1992. "Deviance and the Disabled." Unpublished Master's paper, Ypsilanti, MI: Eastern Michigan University, Department of Sociology, Anthropology and Criminology.

Babbie, Earl. 1989. *The Practice of Social Research*, 5th ed., Belmont, CA: Wadsworth.

Back, K. W., and R. C. Taylor. 1976. "Self-help Groups: Tool or Symbol." *The Journal of Applied Behavioral Sciences* 12:295–309.

Bahr, Howard M. 1973. *Skid Row, An Introduction to Disaffiliation*. New York: Oxford University Press.

Bannan, John F., and R. S. Bannan. 1974. *Law, Morality and Vietnam*. Bloomington, IN: Indiana University Press.

Barber, Bernard. 1973. "Resistance by Scientists to Scientific Discovery." Cited in W.J. Chambliss, ed., *Sociological Readings in the Conflict Perspective*. Reading, MA: Addison-Wesley.

Bates, D. 1988. "A Review of the Research Literature on Mutual Help and Support Groups." Unpublished Paper. Department of Psychology, SUNY Buffalo, cited in Levine (1988).

Bay, Christian. 1967. "Civil Disobedience: Prerequisite for Democracy in a Mass Society." Pp. 163–183 in D. Stolz, ed., *Political Theory and Social Change*. New York: Atherton Press.

Bayley, David H., and H. Mendelsohn. 1969. *Minorities and the Police*. New York: Free Press.

Bean, Margaret. 1975. *Alcoholics Anonymous*. New York: Psychiatric Annals.

Becker, Howard S. 1960. "Notes on the Concept of Commitment." *American Journal of Sociology* 66 (July):32–40.

_____. 1966. *Social Problems, A Modern Approach*, ed. New York: John Wiley.

_____. 1970. *Sociological Work, Method and Substance*. Chicago: Aldine.

_____. 1963. *Outsiders, Studies in the Sociology of Deviance*, New York: Free Press.

_____. 1973. *Outsiders, Studies in the Sociology of Deviance*, rev. ed. New York: Free Press.

Before You Go On a Diet. n.d. Fat Underground, Venice, CA.

Beirne, Piers, and J. Messerschmidt. 1991. *Criminology*. New York: Harcourt, Brace Jovanovich.

Bell, A.P., S. Weinberg, and S.K. Hammersmith. 1981. *Sexual Preference, Its Development in Men and Women*. Bloomington: Indiana University Press.

Bell, Daniel. 1962. *The End of Ideology*, rev. ed. New York: Free Press.

Bell, Robert R. 1976. *Social Deviance, A Substantive Analysis*, rev. ed. Homewood, IL: Dorsey Press.

Bennett, Lerone, Jr. 1965. *Confrontation: Black and White*. Baltimore: Penguin Books.

Bennett, W. Lance, and M. S. Feldman. 1981. *Reconstructing Reality in the Courtroom, Justice and Judgement in American Culture*. New Brunswick, NJ: Rutgers University Press.

Bensman, Joseph, and R. Lilienfeld. 1979. *Between Public and Private, Lost Boundaries of the Self*. New York: Free Press.

Benson, Michael L. 1985. "Denying the Guilty Mind: Accounting for Involvement in White Collar Crime." *Criminology* 23(4):583–607.

Berelson, Bernard, and P. J. Salter. 1946. "Majority and Minority Americans: An Analysis of Magazine Fiction." *Public Opinion Quarterly* 10 (Summer):168–190.

Berg, Bruce L. 1989. *Qualitative Research Methods for the Social Sciences*. Boston: Allyn and Bacon.

Berger, Peter L. 1963. *Invitation to Sociology, A Humanistic Perspective*. New York: Doubleday Anchor.

Berger, Peter, and T. Luckmann. 1967. *The Social Construction of Reality*. New York: Doubleday.

Berube, Allan. 1983. "Coming Out Under Fire." *Mother Jones* 8 (Feb/March):23–29ff.

Best, Joel. 1990. *Threatened Children, Rhetoric and Concern About Child Victims*. Chicago: University of Chicago Press.

Best, Joel, and G. Horiuchi. 1985. "The Razor Blade and the Apple: The Social Construction of Urban Legends." *Social Problems* 32(June):488–499.

Bieber, Irving, et al. 1962. *Homosexuality, A Psychoanalytic Study of Male Homosexuals.* New York: Vintage Books.

Birenbaum, Arnold. 1970. "On Managing a Courtesy Stigma." *Journal of Health and Social Behavior* 11 (September):196–206.

Bittner, Egon. 1967. "The Police on Skid-Row: A Study of Peace Keeping." *American Sociological Review* 32 (October):699–715.

Black, Donald J. 1968. "Police Encounters and Social Organization: An Observation Study." Ph.D. dissertation. University of Michigan.

———. 1976. *The Behavior of Law.* New York: Academic Press.

Black, Donald, and A. J. Reiss. 1970. "Police Control of Juveniles." *American Sociological Review* 35:63–77.

Blair, D. 1990. "Drug War Delusions." *The Humanist* 50(Sept/Oct): 7–9, 40.

Blumberg, Abraham S. 1967 *Criminal Justice.* Chicago: Quadrangle Books.

Blumer, Herbert. 1955. "Collective Behavior." Pp. 165–222 in A. McC. Lee, ed., *Principles of Sociology.* New York: Barnes and Noble.

———. 1956. "Sociological Analysis and the Variable." *American Sociological Review* 21(December):683–690.

Blumstein, P. et al. 1974. "The Honoring of Accounts." *American Sociological Review* 39(4):551–556.

Bogdan, Robert. 1974. *Being Different: The Autobiography of Jane Fry.* New York: John Wiley.

Bogdan, Robert, and S. Taylor. 1987. "Toward a Sociology of Acceptance: The Other Side of a Study of Deviance." *Social Policy* 18:34–39.

Bohannon, Paul. 1973. "The Differing Realms of Law." Pp. 306–317 in D. Black and M. Mileski eds., *The Social Organization of the Law.* New York: Seminar Press.

Bordua, David J. ed. 1967. *The Police: Six Sociological Essays.* New York: John Wiley.

Bowe, Frank. 1978. *Handicapping America, Barriers to Disabled People.* New York: Harper and Row.

Box, Steven. 1971. *Deviance, Reality and Society,* New York: Holt, Rinehart & Winston.

———. 1977. "Hyperactivity: The Scandalous Silence." *New Society* 42 (December 1):458–460.

———. 1981. *Deviance, Reality and Society,* 2nd ed. New York: Holt, Rinehart & Winston.

———. 1983. *Crime, Power and Mystification,* New York: Tavistock.

Brennan, William C. 1974. "Abortion and the Technique of Neutralization." *Journal of Health and Social Behavior* 15(4):358–365.

Briar, Scott, and I. Piliavin 1965. "Delinquency, Situational Inducements and Commitment to Conformity." *Social Problems* 13 (Summer):35–45.

Briedis, Catherine. 1975. "Marginal Deviants: Teenage Girls Experience Community Response to Premarital Sex and Pregnancy." *Social Problems* 22 (April):480–493.

Brodie, Fawn. 1945. *No Man Knows My History*. New York: Alfred A. Knopf.

Brown, Claude. 1966. *Manchild in the Promised Land*. New York: Signet Books.

Brown, J.W., D. Glaser, E. Waxer and G. Geis. 1974. "Turning Off: Cessation of Marihuana Use After College." *Social Problems* 21(April):527–538.

Brown, Richard H. 1977. "The Emergence of Existential Thought: Philosophical Perspectives on Positivist and Humanist Forms of Social Theory." Pp. 77–100 in Jack D. Douglas and John M. Johnson, eds., *Existential Sociology*. New York: Cambridge University Press.

Brownmiller, Susan. 1975. *Against Our Will: Men Women and Rape*. New York: Simon and Schuster.

Brunvand, Jan H. 1984. *The Choking Doberman and Other "New" Urban Legends*. New York: W.W. Norton.

Burt, Martha R. 1980. "Cultural Myths and Supports for Rape." *Journal of Personality and Social Psychology* 38(February):217–230.

Calley, William L. 1970. *Lieutenant Calley: His Own Story*. New York: Viking Press.

Cameron, Mary Owen. 1964. *The Booster and the Snitch, Department Store Shoplifting*. New York: The Free Press of Glencoe, Macmillan Company.

Carrier, J.M. 1976. "Family Attitudes and Mexican Male Homosexuality." *Urban Life* 50(October):359–375.

Carson, W. G. 1974. "Symbolic and Instrumental Dimensions of Early Factory Legislation: A Case Study in the Social Origins of Criminal Law." Pp. 107–138 in Roger Hood, ed., *Crime, Criminology and Public Policy*. London: Heinemann.

Chambliss, William J. 1964. "A Sociological Analysis of the Laws of Vagrancy" *Social Problems* 12:67–77.

————. 1969. *Crime and the Legal Process*. New York: McGraw-Hill.

————. 1971. "A Visit to San Miguel." *The Humanist* 31 (July/August):24–25.

————. 1975. *Criminal Law in Action*. Santa Barbara, CA: Hamilton.

————. 1979. "On Lawmaking." *British Journal of Law and Society* 6:149–171.

Chambliss, William, and R. H. Nagasawa. 1969. "On the Validity of Official Statistics: A Comparative Study of White, Black, and Japanese High-School Boys." *Journal of Research in Crime and Delinquency* 6(January):71–77.

Chambliss, William J., and R. B. Seidman. 1971. *Law, Order, and Power*. Reading, MA: Addison-Wesley.

————. 1982. *Law, Order, and Power*. 2nd ed. Reading, MA: Addison-Wesley.

Charon, Joel M. 1979. *Symbolic Interactionism: An Introduction, An Interpretation, An Integration*. Englewood Cliffs, NJ: Prentice-Hall.

Chatterton, Michael. 1976. "Police in Social Control." Pp. 104–122 in J. F. S. King, ed., *Control Without Custody?* Cambridge: Cambridge Institute of Criminology.

Chernin, Kim. 1981. *The Obsession, Reflections of the Tyranny of Slenderness*. New York: Harper and Row.

Chicago Tribune (Chicago, IL). 1984. "Neighborhood Crusader, Saluting the Lady Who Took on City Hall." October 15 (Section 4):1–2.

Choate, Pat. 1990. *Agents of Influence*. New York: Simon and Schuster.

Clark, Brian. 1978. *Whose Life Is It Anyway?* New York: Avon Books.

Clausen, John A. 1976. "Mental Disorders." Pp. 103–139 in R.K. Merton and R. Nisbet, eds., *Contemporary Social Problems*, 4th ed. New York: Harcourt, Brace Jovanovich.

Cleland, Max. 1982. *Strong at the Broken Places*. New York: Berkley.

Clinard, Marshall B. 1983. *Corporate Ethics and Crime: The Role of Middle Management*. Beverly Hills, CA: Sage.

Clinard, Marshall B., and P. C. Yeager. 1980. *Corporate Crime*. New York: Free Press.

Cohen, Albert K. 1955. *Delinquent Boys: The Culture of the Gang*. Glencoe, IL: The Free Press.

Cohen, Stanley. 1980. *Folk Devils and Moral Panics*. New York: St. Martin's.

Coleman, James William. 1989. *The Criminal Elite, The Sociology of White Collar Crime*, 2nd ed. New York: St. Martin's.

Collins, Randall. 1981. "On the Microfoundations of Macrosociology." *American Journal of Sociology* 86:984–1014.

Conrad, Peter. 1975. "The Discovery of Hyperkinesis: Notes on the Medicalization of Deviant Behavior." *Social Problems* 23 (October):12–21.

———. 1979. "Types of Medical Social Control." *Sociology of Health and Illness* 1 (1):1–11.

Cooley, Charles Horton. 1902. *Human Nature and the Social Order*. New York: Charles Scribner's.

Cory, Donald Webster. 1951. *The Homosexual in America: A Subjective Approach*. New York: Greenberg.

Corzine, Jay, and R. Kirby. 1977. "Cruising the Truckers: Sexual Encounters in a Highway Rest Area." *Urban Life* 6(July):171–192.

Cox, Jenny. 1990. "Naturist nudism." Pp. 122–124 in Stuart Henry, ed., *Degrees of Deviance: Student Accounts of Their Deviant Behavior*. Salem: Sheffield.

Cressey, Donald R. 1953. *Other People's Money*. Glencoe, IL: Free Press.

———. 1969. *Theft of the Nation, The Structure and Operations of Crime in America*. New York: Harper and Row.

———. 1970. "The Respectable Criminal." Pp. 105–116 in James Short, ed., *Modern Criminals*. New York: Transaction-Aldine.

Daily Interlake. 1988. "Ann Landers," December 19:B-1.

Davis, Fred. 1961. "Deviance Disavowal: The Management of Strained Interaction by the Visibly Handicapped." *Social Problems* 9(Fall):120–132.

Davis, Nanette J. 1975. *Sociological Constructions of Deviance, Perspectives and Issues in the Field*. Dubuque, IA: W.C. Brown.

Davis, Richard L. 1973. "The Labeling Perspective and Juvenile Delinquency." Unpublished Ph.D. dissertation, University of New Hampshire.

DeCurtis, A. 1992. "Tipper: Dems Send Wrong Message." *Rolling Stone* (September 3):17.

Demone Jr., H. W. 1974. *Directory of Mutual Help Organizations in Massachusetts*, 4th ed. Cambridge, MA: Blue Cross and Blue Shield.

Denes, Magda. 1977. *In Necessity and Sorrow, Life and Death in an Abortion Hospital*. Baltimore: Penguin Books.

Dennis, Richard J. 1990. "The Economics of Legalizing Drugs." *The Atlantic Monthly*, November:126–132.

Dentler, Robert A., and K. T. Erikson. 1959. "The Function of Deviance in Groups." *Social Problems*, 7:98–107.

Dickson, Donald T. 1968. "Bureaucracy and Morality: An Organizational Perspective on a Moral Crusade." *Social Problems* 16(Fall):143–156.

Ditton, Jason. 1977. *Part-time Crime: An Ethnography of Fiddling and Pilferage.* London: Macmillan.

Dominick, Joseph R. 1978. "Crime and Law Enforcement in the Mass Media." Pp. 105–128 in C. Winick, ed., *Deviance and Mass Media.* Beverly Hills, CA: Sage.

Dorner, Gunter. 1976. *Hormones and Brain Differentiation.* Amsterdam: Elsevier.

Douglas, Jack D. 1967. *The Social Meanings of Suicide.* Princeton, NJ: Princeton University Press.

———. 1970. *Deviance and Respectability,* ed. New York: Basic Books.

———. 1971a. *American Social Order, Social Rules in a Pluralistic Society.* New York: Free Press-Macmillan.

———. 1971b. "The Rhetoric of Science and the Origins of Statistical Social Thought: The Case of Durkheim's Suicide." Pp. 44–57 in E.A. Tiryakian, ed., *The Phenomenon of Sociology.* New York: Appleton-Century-Crofts.

———. 1972. *Research on Deviance.* New York: Random House.

———. 1977. "Shame and Deceit in Creative Deviance." Pp. 59–86 in E. Sagarin, ed., *Deviance and Social Change.* Beverly Hills, CA: Sage.

Douglas, Jack D., and P. K. Rasmussen, with C. A. Flanagan. 1977. *The Nude Beach.* Beverly Hills, CA: Sage.

Downs, Donald A. 1989 *The New Politics of Pornography.* Chicago: University of Chicago Press.

Drake, St. Clair, and H. R. Cayton. 1962. *Black Metropolis, A Study of Negro Life in a Northern City.* New York: Harper and Row.

Duff, Robert, and L. K. Hong. 1989. "Management of Deviant Identity Among Competitive Women Body Builders." Pp. 517–530 in D. H. Kelly, ed., *Deviant Behavior, A Text-Reader in the Sociology of Deviant Behavior* 3rd ed. New York: St. Martin's.

Durkheim, Emile. 1895. *The Rules of Sociological Method.* (Edited by George E. G. Catlin, 1938) S. A. Solovay and J. H. Mueller, trans. New York: Macmillan.

———. 1951. *Suicide, A Study of Sociology.* John A. Spaulding and George Simpson, trans. New York: Free Press-Macmillan.

Edelman, Murray. 1964. *The Symbolic Uses of Politics,* Urbana: University of Illinois Press.

Einstadter, Werner, and S. Henry. 1991. "The Inversion of the Invasion of Privacy." *The Critical Criminologist* 3(Winter):5, 7.

Emerson, Robert M. 1969. *Judging Delinquents, Context and Process in Juvenile Court.* Chicago: Aldine.

Erickson, Patricia G., and M. S. Goodstadt. 1979. "Legal Stigma for Marijuana Possession." *Criminology* 17(August):208–216.

Erikson, Kai T. 1964. "Notes on the Sociology of Deviance." Pp. 9–21 in H. S. Becker, ed., *The Other Side, Perspectives on Deviance.* New York: Free Press.

Etzioni, Amitai. 1964. *Modern Organizations.* Englewood Cliffs, NJ: Prentice-Hall.

Farrington, David P. 1977. "The Effects of Public Labeling." *British Journal of Criminology* 17 (April):112–125.

Feldman, Egal. 1967. "Prostitution, the Alien Woman and the Progressive Imagination, 1910–1915." *American Quarterly* 19(Summer):192–206.

Feldman, Saul D. 1975. "The Presentation of Shortness in Everyday Life—Height and Heightism in American Sociology: Toward a Sociology of Stature." Paper presented before The American Sociological Association, Denver, Colorado.

Ferman, Louis, and L. Berndt. 1981. "The irregular economy." Pp. 26–42 in Stuart Henry ed., *Informal Institutions*. New York: St. Martin's.

Fine, Gary A. 1980. "The Kentucky Fried Rat: Legends and Modern Society." *Journal of the Folklore Institute* 27 (May–December):222–243.

Fine, Michele, and A. Asch. 1988. "Disability Beyond Stigma: Social Interaction, Discrimination, and Activism." *Journal of Social Issues*, 44:3–21.

Fink, S. L., J. K. Skipper, Jr., and P. N. Hallenbeck. 1968. "Physical Disability and Problems in Marriage." *Journal of Marriage and the Family* 30 (February):64–73.

Finkelhor, David. 1979. *Sexually Victimized Children*. New York: Free Press.

Fisher, Gary. 1990. "Survivalism." Pp. 129–133 in Stuart Henry, ed., *Degrees of Deviance: Student Accounts of Their Deviant Behavior*. Salem, WI: Sheffield.

Fontana, Vincent J. 1973. *Somewhere a Child Is Crying, Maltreatment—Causes and Prevention*. New York: New American Library, Mentor Books.

Franklin, John Hope. 1956. *From Slavery to Freedom: A History of American Negroes*, 2nd rev. ed. New York: Alfred A. Knopf.

Freeman, Howard E., and O. G. Simmons. 1961. "Feelings of Stigma Among Relatives of Former Mental Patients." *Social Problems* 8 (Spring):312–321.

Freidson, Eliot. 1965. "Disability as Social Deviance." Pp. 71–99 in Marvin B. Sussman, ed., *Sociology of Rehabilitation*. Cleveland: American Sociological Association.

———. 1970. *Profession of Medicine, A Study of the Sociology of Knowledge*. New York: Dodd, Mead.

Friedmann, William. 1972. *Law in a Changing Society*. New York: Columbia University Press.

Frost, Janet. 1990. "Affairs." Pp. 27–29 in Stuart Henry, ed., *Degrees of Deviance: Student Accounts of Their Deviant Behavior*. Salem, WI: Sheffield.

Gable, Richard W. 1958. "Political Interest Groups as Policy Shapers." *Annals of the American Academy of Political and Social Science* 319 (September):84–93.

Gaines, Rick. 1990. "Concealed Handguns." Pp. 123–125 in Stuart Henry, ed., *Degrees of Deviance: Student Accounts of Their Deviant Behavior*. Salem, WI: Sheffield.

Galliher, John F., and A. Walker. 1977. "The Puzzle of the Social Origins of the Marihuana Tax Act of 1937." *Social Problems* 24 (February):367–376.

Gamson, William A. 1975. *The Strategy of Social Protest*. Homewood, IL: Dorsey Press.

Garfinkel, Harold. 1956. "Conditions of Successful Degradation Ceremonies." *American Journal of Sociology* 61(March):420–424.

Garner, Brian, and R. W. Smith. 1977. "Are There Really Any Gay Male Athletes? An Empirical Survey." *Journal of Sex Research* 13 (February):22–34.

Gartell, N., D. Loriaux, and T. Chase. 1977. "Plasma Testosterone in Homosexual and Heterosexual Women." *American Journal of Psychiatry* 13(4):1117–1118.

Geller, Allen, and M. Boas. 1969. *The Drug Beat*. New York: McGraw-Hill.

Gerbner, George. 1978. "Deviance and Power, Symbolic Functions of Drug Abuse." Pp. 13–30 in C. Winick, ed., *Deviance and Mass Media*. Beverly Hills, CA: Sage.

Gergen, David R., and T. Gest. 1989. "Secrets Behind the Gun Lobby's Staying Power." *U.S. News and World Report* (May 8):26.

Gibbons, F. X. 1986. "Stigma and Interpersonal Relations." Pp. 123–144 in S.C. Ainley, G. Becker, and L.M. Coleman, eds., *The Dilemma of Difference*. New York: Plenum.

Giddens, Anthony. 1984. *The Constitution of Society: Outline of a Theory of Structuration*. Cambridge: Polity Press.

Glaser, Daniel. 1971. *Social Deviance*. Chicago: Markham.

Gliedman, John, and W. Roth. 1980. *The Unexpected Minority, Handicapped Children in America*. New York: Harcourt, Brace Jovanovich.

Gluckman, Max. 1969. "Concepts in the Comparative Study of Tribal Law." Pp. 349–356 in Laura Nader, ed., *Law in Culture and Society*. Chicago: Aldine.

Goffman, Erving. 1959. *The Presentation of Self in Everyday Life*. New York: Doubleday Anchor.

———. 1961. *Asylums, Essays on the Situation of Mental Patients and Other Inmates*. New York: Doubleday Anchor.

———. 1963. *Stigma, Notes on the Management of Spoiled Identity*. Englewood Cliffs, NJ: Prentice-Hall.

———. 1971. *Relations in Public*. Harmondsworth: Penguin.

———. 1973. "The Moral Career of the Mental Patient." Pp. 95–105 in E. Rubington and M. S. Weinberg, eds., *Deviance, The Interactionist Perspective* 2nd ed. New York: Macmillan.

Gold, Martin. 1966. "Undetected Delinquent Behavior." *The Journal of Research in Crime and Delinquency* 3 (January):27–46.

———. 1970. *Delinquent Behavior in an American City*. Belmont, CA: Brooks, Cole.

Gold, Martin, and J. R. Williams. 1969. "National Study of the Aftermath of Apprehension." *Perspectus, A Journal of Law Reform* 3 (December):3–38.

Goode, Erich. 1972. *Drugs in American Society*. New York: Alfred A. Knopf.

———. 1989. *Drugs in American Society*, 3rd ed. New York: Alfred A. Knopf.

Gordon, Linda. 1986. "Incest and Resistance: Patterns of Father-Daughter Incest, 1880–1930." *Social Problems* 33(4):253–267.

Gordon, M.T., and L. Heath. 1981. "The News Business: Crime and Fear." Pp. 227–250 in Dan A. Lewis, ed., *Reactions to Crime*. Beverly Hills, CA: Sage.

Gottleib, A. 1986. *The Gun Grabbers*. Washington: Merrill Press.

Gouldner, Alvin. 1954. *Patterns of Industrial Bureaucracy*. New York: Free Press.

Gowman, Alan G. 1956. "Blindness and the Role of the Companion." *Social Problems* 4(July):68–75.

Graham, Hilary. 1981. "Mothers Accounts of Anger and Aggression Towards

Their Babies." Pp. 39–51 in Neil Frude, ed., *Psychological Approaches to Child Abuse*. Totowa, NJ: Rowman and Littlefield.

Graves, William. 1980. "I Want to Make People Laugh." *Mainstream, Magazine for the Able Disabled* 5(June):9 and 15.

Green, Richard. 1987. *The "Sissy Boy Syndrome" and the Development of Homosexuality*. New Haven: Yale University Press.

Greenberg, David. 1981. *Crime and Capitalism: Readings in Marxist Criminology*. Palo Alto: Mayfield.

Greenberg, Jerald. 1990. "Employee Theft as a Reaction to Underpayment Inequity: The Hidden Costs of Pay Cuts." *Journal of Applied Psychology* 75(5):561–568.

Greenwald, Harold. 1958. *The Call Girl, A Social and Psychoanalytic Study*. New York: Ballantine.

Groce, Nora. 1985. *Everyone Here Spoke Sign Language*. Cambridge, MA: Harvard University Press.

Grosswirth, Marvin. 1982. "Medical Menace, Doctors Hooked on Drugs." *Ladies Home Journal* 94 (March):141–144.

Gusfield, Joseph R. 1955. "Social Structure and Moral Reform: A Study of the Women's Christian Temperance Union." *American Journal of Sociology* 61 (November):221–232.

_____. 1963. *Symbolic Crusade*. Urbana: University of Illinois Press.

_____. 1967. "Moral Passage: The Symbolic Process in Public Designations of Deviance." *Social Problems* 15(Fall):175–188.

_____. 1981. *The Culture of Public Problems: Drinking Driving and the Symbolic Order*. Chicago: University of Chicago Press.

Hacker, David W. 1977. "She's Against Gay Rights." *National Observer*, March 12:1, 16.

Hadden, Stuart C. 1973. "Social Dimensions of Jury Decision Making." *International Journal of Criminology and Penology* 1 (August):269–277.

Hahn, Harlan. 1985. "Changing Perceptions of Disability and the Future of Rehabilitation." Pp. 53–64 in L. G. Perlman and G. F. Austin, eds., *Social Influences in Rehabilitation Planning: A Blueprint for the 21st Century*. Alexandria, VA: National Rehabilitation Association.

_____. 1988. "The Politics of Physical Differences: Disability and Discrimination." *Journal of Social Issues* 44:39–47.

Hansell, N. 1976. *The Person in Distress: On the Biosocial Dynamics of Adaption*. New York: Behavioral Publications.

Harris, Richard N. 1973. *The Police Academy: An Inside View*. New York: John Wiley.

Hart, Donna. 1990. "Medical Students on Drugs." Pp. 92–94 in S. Henry, ed., *Degrees of Deviance: Student Accounts of Their Deviant Behavior*. Salem, WI: Sheffield.

Hawkins, Richard. 1984. "Employee Theft in the Restaurant Trade: Forms of Ripping Off by Waiters at Work." *Deviant Behavior* 5:47–69.

Hawkins, Richard, and G. Tiedeman. 1975. *The Creation of Deviance, Interpersonal and Organizational Determinants*. Columbus, OH: Charles E. Merrill.

Henderson, George, and W. V. Bryan. 1984. *Psychosocial Aspects of Disability*. Springfield, IL: Charles C Thomas.

Henry, Stuart. 1976. "Fencing with Accounts: The Language of Moral Bridging." *British Journal of Law and Society* 3(1):91–100.

_____. 1977. "On the Fence." *British Journal of Law and Society* 4(1):124–33.

_____. 1978a. *The Hidden Economy*. Oxford: Martin Robertson.

_____. 1978b. "The Dangers of Self-Help Groups." *New Society* 22 (June):654–656.

_____. 1981. *Informal Institutions*. New York: St. Martin's.

_____. 1983. *Private Justice*. London: Routledge and Kegan Paul.

_____. 1987. "The Construction and Deconstruction of Social Control: Thoughts on the Discursive Production of State Law and Private Justice." Pp. 89–108 in J. Lowman, R. Menzies, and T. Palys, eds., *Transcarceration: Essays in the Sociology of Social Control*, Cambridge Studies in Criminology Vol LV. Aldershot: Gower.

_____. 1990. *Degrees of Deviance, Student Accounts of Their Deviant Behavior*. Salem, WI: Sheffield Publishing Company.

Henry, Stuart, and G. Mars. 1978. "Crime at Work: The Social Construction of Amateur Property Theft." *Sociology* 12:246–263.

Henry, Stuart, and D. Milovanovic. 1991. "Constitutive Criminology: The Maturation of Critical Criminology." *Criminology* 29:293–316.

_____. 1992. "The Constitution of Constitutive Criminology." Paper presented at the American Society of Criminology Meetings, New Orleans (November 5).

Henry, Stuart, and D. Robinson. 1978a. "Talking out of Alcoholism: Results from a Survey in England and Wales." *The Journal of the Royal College of General Practitioners* 28:414–419.

_____. 1978b. "Understanding Alcoholics Anonymous: Results from a Survey in England and Wales." *The Lancet* (February 18):372–375.

Henshel, Richard L., and R. A. Silverman, eds. 1975. *Perception in Criminology*. New York: Columbia University Press.

Hertz, Robert. 1960. *Death and the Right Hand*. Glencoe, IL: Free Press.

Hess, A.G., and D.A. Mariner. 1975. "On the Sociology of Crime Cartoons," *International Journal of Criminology and Penology* 3 (August):253–265.

Hessler, Richard M. 1974. "Junkies in White: Drug Addition Among Physicians." Pp. 146–153 in C. D. Bryant, ed., *Deviant Behavior, Occupational and Organizational Bases*. Chicago: Rand-McNally.

Hibbert, Christopher. 1963. *The Roots of Evil: A Social History of Crime and Punishment*. Harmondsworth: Penguin.

Higgins, Paul C. 1980. *Outsiders in a Hearing World, A Sociology of Deafness*. Beverly Hills, CA: Sage.

Higgins, Paul C., and Richard R. Butler. 1982. *Understanding Deviance*. New York: McGraw-Hill.

Hills, Stuart L. 1971. *Crime, Power, and Morality: The Criminal-Law Process in the United States*. Scranton, PA: Chandler.

Hirschi, Travis. 1969. *Causes of Delinquency*. Berkeley: University of California Press.

Hobson, Laura A. 1976. *Consenting Adult*. New York: Warner Books.

Hollinger, Richard C. 1991. "Neutralizing in the Workplace: An Empirical Analysis of Property Theft and Production Deviance." *Deviant Behavior* 12(2):169–202.

Hollinger, Richard C., and J. P. Clark. 1983. *Theft by Employees*. Lexington: Lexington Books.

Horning, Donald. 1970. "Blue Collar Theft: Conceptions of Property, Attitudes Toward Pilfering, and Work Group Norms in a Modern Industrial Plant." Pp. 46–64 in E. O. Smigel and H. L. Ross, eds., *Crimes Against Bureaucracy*. New York: Van Nostrand Reinhold.

Horowitz, Irving Louis, and M. Liebowitz. 1968. "Social Deviance and Political Marginality: Toward a Redefinition of the Relation between Sociology and Politics." *Social Problems* 15 (Winter):280–296.

Horton, Paul B., and G. R. Leslie. 1965. *The Sociology of Social Problems*, 3rd ed. New York: Appleton-Century-Crofts.

Hough, Henry Beetle. 1974. "Becoming an Alcoholic." Pp. 15–32 in C. H. McCaghy, J. K. Skipper, Jr., and M. Lefton, eds., *In Their Own Behalf: Voices from the Margin*, 2nd ed. New York: Appleton-Century-Crofts.

Hoye, Pamela. 1983. "Mainstreaming vs. Special Education: The Law Demands What's Best for the Child." *Mainstream, Magazine of the Able-Disabled* 8(June):9–15.

Hughes, Everett Cherrington. 1945. "Dilemmas and Contradictions of Status." *American Journal of Sociology* 50 (March):353–359.

Hughes, Graham. 1964. "The Crime of Incest." *Journal of Criminal Law, Criminology, and Police Science* 55(Sept):322–331.

Humphreys, Laud. 1970. *Tearoom Trade, Impersonal Sex in Public Places*. Chicago: Aldine.

———. 1972. *Out of the Closets, The Sociology of Homosexual Liberation*. Englewood Cliffs, NJ: Prentice-Hall.

Ice-T. 1992. "Cop Killer" from *Body Count*. New York: Warner Bros. Records as cited in "Police Boycott Time-Warner to Protest 'Cop Killer' Song," *Law Enforcement News*, 18 (June 30):3.

Illich, Ivan. 1975. *Medical Nemesis*. London: Calder Boyers.

———. 1981. *Shadow Work*. London: Marian Boyars.

Inciardi, James A. 1974. "Drugs, Drug Taking and Drug Seeking: Notations on the Dynamics of Myth, Change and Reality." Pp. 203–220 in J. A. Inciardi and C. D. Chambers, eds., *Drugs and the Criminal Justice System*. Beverly Hills, CA: Sage.

———. 1978 *Reflections on Crime: An Introduction to Criminology and Criminal Justice*. New York: Holt, Rinehart & Winston.

Information Please Almanac, Atlas and Yearbook. 1992. Boston: Houghton Mifflin.

Irwin, John. 1970. *The Felon*. Englewood Cliffs, NJ: Prentice-Hall.

Jackson, Don. 1973. "Dachau for Queers." Pp. 42–49 in L. Richmond and G. Noguera, eds., *The Gay Liberation Book*. San Francisco: Ramparts Press.

Jacob, H. 1984. *Justice in America, Courts, Lawyers, and the Judicial Process*, 4th ed. Boston: Little, Brown.

Jeffrey, Roger. 1979. "Rubbish: Deviant Patients in Casualty Departments." *Sociology of Health and Illness* 1(1):90–107.

Jellinek, E.M. 1960. *The Disease Concept of Alcoholism*. New Brunswick, NJ: Hillhouse Press: College and University Press.

Jensen, E. L., J. Gerber, and G. M. Babcock. 1991. "The New War on Drugs: Grass Roots Movement or Political Construction?" *Journal of Drug Issues* 21:651–657.

Joey. 1973. *Killer: Autobiography of a Mafia Hit Man*." Chicago: Playboy Press.

Johns, Christina. 1992. *The War On Drugs*. Westport, CT: Praeger.

Johnson, Michael P. 1973. "Commitment: A Conceptual Structure and Empirical Application." *The Sociological Quarterly* 14(Summer):395–406.

Justice, Blair, and R. Justice. 1979. *The Broken Taboo*. New York: Human Sciences.

Kando, Thomas. 1973. *Sex Change: The Achievement of Gender Identity Among Feminized Transsexuals*. Springfield, IL: Charles C Thomas.

Kaplan, Abraham. 1964. *The Conduct of Inquiry*. San Francisco: Chandler.

Kasen, Jill H. 1980. "Whither the Self-Made Man? Comic Culture and the Crisis of Legitimation in the United States." *Social Problems* 28(December):129–148.

Katz, Alfred H. 1975. "Some Thoughts on Self-Help Groups and the Professional Community." Paper presented to the National Conference on Social Welfare, San Francisco (May).

Katz, Alfred H., and E. I. Bender. 1976. *The Strength in Us: Self-Help Groups in the Modern World*. New York: Franklin Watts.

Katz, Jack. 1988. *Seductions of Crime: Moral and Sensual Attractions of Doing Evil*. New York: Basic Books.

Kern, Roger. 1991. "The Disabled as Deviant." Unpublished Master's paper, Ypsilanti, MI: Eastern Michigan University, Department of Sociology, Anthropology and Criminology.

Kesey, Ken. 1962. *One Flew Over the Cuckoo's Nest*. New York: Signet, New American Library.

Killilea, Marie. 1976. "Mutual Help Organizations: Interpretations in the Literature." Pp. 37–93 in G. Caplan and M. Killilea, eds., *Support Systems and Mutual Help: Multidisciplinary Explorations*, New York: Grune & Stratton.

King, Michael. 1981. *The Framework of Criminal Justice*. London: Croom Helm.

King, Susan. 1990. "New Wave Culture." Pp. 115–117 in S. Henry, ed., *Degrees of Deviance: Student Accounts of Their Deviant Behavior*. Salem, WI: Sheffield.

Klapp, Orrin E. 1962. *Heroes, Villains, and Fools: The Changing American Character*. Englewood Cliffs, NJ: Prentice-Hall.

Klein, Erica Levy, and K. Kroll. 1992. *Enabling Romance*. New York: Harmony Books.

Klein, Malcolm W. 1974. "Labeling, Deterrence, and Recidivism: A Study of Police Dispositions of Juvenile Offenders." *Social Problems* 22(December): 292–303.

Klein, Mitchell S. G. 1984. *Law, Courts, and Policy*. Englewood Cliffs, NJ: Prentice-Hall.

Klockars, Carl B. 1974. *The Professional Fence*, New York: Free Press.

Knorr-Cetina, Karin, and A.V. Cicourel, eds. 1981. *Advances in Social Theory and*

Methodology: Toward an Integration of Micro- and Macro-sociologies. London: Routledge and Kegan Paul.

Koral, Alan M., and B. McLanahan. 1990. *Employer Compliance with the Americans With Disabilities Act*. New York: Practicing Law Institute.

Kotarba, Joseph A. 1975. "America Acupuncturists: The New Entrepreneurs of Hope." *Urban Life* 4 (July):149–177.

———. 1984. "One More for the Road: The Subversion of Labeling within the Tavern Subculture." Pp. 152–160 in J. D. Douglas, ed., *The Sociology of Deviance*. Boston: Allyn and Bacon.

Kriegel, Leonard. 1974. "On Being Crippled." Pp. 233–246 in C. H. McCaghy, J. K. Skipper, Jr., and M. Lefton, eds., *In Their Own Behalf: Voices from the Margin*, 2nd ed. New York: Appleton-Century-Crofts.

Krisberg, Barry. 1975. *Crime and Privilege, Toward a New Criminology*. Englewood Cliffs, NJ: Prentice-Hall.

Kuhn, Manford H. 1967. "The Reference Group Reconsidered." Pp. 171–184 in J. G. Manis and B. N. Meltzer, eds., *Symbolic Interaction, A Reader in Social Psychology*. Boston: Allyn and Bacon.

LaMarche, Gara, and William B. Rubenstein. 1990. "The Love That Dare Not Speak." *The Nation*, November 5:524–526.

Lauderdale, Pat. 1976. "Deviance and Moral Boundaries." *American Sociological Review* 41:661–676.

Leavitt, David. 1987. *The Lost Language of Cranes*. New York: Bantam Books.

LeGrand, Camille E. 1973. "Rape and Rape Laws: Sexism in Society and Law." *California Law Review* 61(May):919–941.

Lemert, Edwin M. 1951. *Social Pathology, A Systematic Approach to the Theory of Sociopathic Behavior*. New York: McGraw-Hill.

———. 1967 *Human Deviance, Social Problems, and Social Control*. Englewood Cliffs, NJ: Prentice-Hall.

Lemkau, Paul V., and G. M. Crocetti. 1967. "Epidemiology." Pp. 225–232 in A. M. Freedman and H. I. Kaplan, eds., *Comprehensive Textbook of Psychiatry*. Baltimore: Williams & Wilkins.

Letkemann, Peter. 1973. *Crime as Work*. Englewood Cliffs, NJ: Prentice-Hall.

Levi, K. 1989. "Becoming a Hit Man: Neutralization in a Very Deviant Career." Pp. 447–458 in D.H. Kelly, ed., *Deviant Behavior*, 3rd ed. New York: St. Martin's.

Levin, L. S. 1975. "The Layperson as the *Primary*, Primary Health Care Practitioner." *Mimeo*. Cambridge, MA: Yale University.

Levine, Murray. 1988. "How Self-Help Works." *Social Policy* 18(Summer):39–43.

Levine, Murray, and D. V. Perkins. 1987. *Principles of Community Psychiatry*. New York: Oxford University Press.

Levitin, Teresa E. 1975. "Deviants as Active Participants in the Labeling Process: The Visibly Handicapped." *Social Problems* 22 (April):548–557.

Levy, Howard S. 1966. *Chinese Footbinding, The History of a Curious Erotic Custom*. New York: Walton Rawls.

Levy, L. 1976. "Self-Help Groups: Types and Psychological Processes." *The Journal of Applied Behavioral Sciences* 12:310–22.

Lewis, Oscar. 1961. *Children of Sanchez*. New York: Random House.

Lichter, Linda S., and S. R. Lichter. 1983. *Prime Time Crime*. Washington, D.C.: The Media Institute.

Lindesmith, Alfred. 1940. " 'Dope Fiend' Mythology." *Journal of Criminal Law and Criminology* 31(May/June):199–208.

Liska, Allen E. 1987. *Perspectives on Deviance*. Englewood Cliffs, NJ: Prentice-Hall.

Lockwood, Brocton (with H. Mendenhall). 1989. *Operation Greylord: Brocton Lockwood's Story*. Carbondale, IL: So. Illinois University Press.

Lofland, John. 1969. *Deviance and Identity*. Englewood Cliffs, NJ: Prentice-Hall.

Look. 1938. "Tell Your Children." November 22:24–25.

Lorber, Judith. 1967. "Deviance as Performance: The Case of Illness." *Social Problems* 14(Winter):302–310.

Lowry, Ritchie P., and R. P. Rankin. 1969. *Sociology, The Science of Society*. New York: Charles Scribner's.

Luckenbill, David F. 1977. "Criminal Homicide as a Situated Transaction." *Social Problems* 25(December):176–186.

———. 1981. "Generating Compliance: The Case of Robbery." *Urban Life* 10(1):25–46.

Lundman, Richard J. 1980. *Police and Policing, An Introduction*. New York: Holt, Rinehart & Winston.

Lyman, Stanford M. 1974. *Chinese Americans*. New York: Random House.

Lyman, Stanford M., and M. B. Scott. 1967. "Territoriality: A Neglected Sociological Dimension." *Social Problems* 15(Fall):236–249.

———. 1970. *A Sociology of the Absurd*. New York: Appleton-Century-Crofts.

Lynch, Michael. 1983. "Accommodation Practices: Vernacular Treatments of Madness," *Social Problems* 31(2):152–164.

MacAndrew, C., and R. B. Edgerton. 1969. *Drunken Comportment: A Social Explanation*. Chicago: Aldine.

MacKenzie, Norman. 1967. *Secret Societies*. New York: Holt, Rinehart & Winston.

Maclean's. 1990. "Art and Obscenity. The Anti-obscenity Lobby Has Its Day in Court." October 15:74, 78.

Makas, Elaine. 1988. "Positive Attitudes Toward Disabled People: Disabled and Nondisabled Persons' Perspectives." *Journal of Social Issues*, 44:49–61.

Mankoff, Milton. 1971. "Societal Reaction and Career Deviance: A Critical Analysis." *The Sociological Quarterly* 12(Spring):204–218.

Manning, Peter K. 1971. "The Police: Mandate, Strategies, and Appearance." Pp. 149–193 in Jack D. Douglas, ed., *Crime and Justice in American Society*. Indianapolis: Bobbs-Merrill.

———. 1975. "Deviance and Dogma." *The British Journal of Criminology* 15(January):1–20.

———. 1977. *Police Work: The Organization of Policing*. Cambridge, MA: MIT Press.

Margolese, M., and O. Janigen. 1973. "Androsterone/Etiocholanolone Ratios in Male Homosexuals." *British Medical Journal* 3(July):207–210.

Markle, Gerald E., and R. J. Troyer. 1979. "Smoke Gets in Your Eyes: Cigarette Smoking as Deviant Behavior." *Social Problems* 26(June):611–625.

Mars, Gerald. 1974. "Dock pilferage." Pp. 209–28 in Paul Rock and Mary McInstosh, eds., *Deviance and Social Control.* London: Tavistock.

Marsh, Jeanne C. 1983. "Structuring Definition and Response to Rape." Paper presented before the Society for the Study of Social Problems, Detroit, MI.

Marx, Gary T. 1988. *Under Cover: Police Surveillance in America.* Berkeley: University of California Press.

Matza, David. 1964. *Delinquency and Drift.* New York: John Wiley.

———. 1969. *Becoming Deviant.* Englewood Cliffs, NJ: Prentice-Hall.

Mauss, Armand L., and Associates. 1975. *Social problems as Social Movements.* Philadelphia: J.B. Lippincott.

Maxwell, Milton A. 1967. "Alcoholics Anonymous: An Interpretation." Pp. 211–222 in D. A. Pittman, ed., *Alcoholism.* New York: Harper and Row.

Mayhew, Bruce, and R. Levinger. 1976. "Size and the Density of Interaction in Human Aggregates." *American Journal of Sociology,* 82:82–91.

Maynard, Douglas W. 1984. *Inside Plea Bargaining, The Language of Negotiation.* New York: Plenum.

McCaghy, Charles H. 1968. "Drinking and Deviance Disavowal: The Case of Child Molesters." *Social Problems* 16(Summer):43–49.

———. 1976. *Deviant Behavior: Crime, Conflict and Interests Groups.* New York: Macmillan.

McCaghy, Charles H., and J. K. Skipper, Jr. 1969. "Lesbian Behavior as an Adaptation to the Occupation of Stripping." *Social Problems* 17(Fall):262–270.

McNeill, Pat. 1988. "Handicapping the Disabled." *New Statesman and Society* (October 14):26.

Mehta, Ved. 1982. *Vedi.* New York: Oxford University Press.

Meltzer, Bernard N. 1967. "Mead's Social Psychology." Pp. 5–24 in J. G. Manis and B. N. Meltzer, eds., *Symbolic Interaction. A Reader in Social Psychology,* Boston: Allyn and Bacon.

Meyer, Erich. 1981. "The Blind and Social Deprivation." *International Journal of Rehabilitation Research* 4(3):353–364.

Michalowski, Raymond. 1985. *Order, Law, and Crime.* New York: Random House.

Michalowski, Raymond, and E. H. Pfuhl, Jr. 1991. "Technology, Property and Law: The Case of Computer Crime." *Crime, Law and Social Change* 15(3):255–275.

Michigan Judicial Institute. 1991. *The Michigan Prison System.* Lansing, MI: Michigan Judicial Institute.

Mieczkowski, Thomas. 1992. "Crack Dealing on the Street: The Crew System and the Crack House." *Justice Quarterly* 9:151–163.

Mileski, Maureen. 1971. "Courtroom Encounters: An Observation Study of a Lower Criminal Court." *Law and Society Review* 5:473–538.

Milovanovic, Dragan, and S. Henry. 1991. "Constitutive Penology." *Social Justice* 18:204–224.

Miller, Linda. 1990. "Waiting for Tips." Pp. 35–37 in S. Henry, ed., *Degrees of Deviance: Student Accounts of Their Deviant Behavior.* Salem, WI: Sheffield.

Miller, Merle. 1971. "What It Means to be a Homosexual," *New York Times Magazine* January 17:9ff; October 10:67ff.

Millman, Marcia. 1980. *Such A Pretty Face*. New York: W.W. Norton.

Mills, C. Wright. 1940. "Situated Actions and Vocabularies of Motive." *American Sociological Review* 5(December):904–913.

———. 1959. *The Sociological Imagination*. New York: Oxford University Press.

Milner, Christina, and R. Milner. 1973. *Black Players, The Secret World of Black Pimps*. New York: Bantam Books.

Minor, William W. 1980. "The Neutralization of Criminal Offense." *Criminology*, 18:103–120.

———. 1981. "Techniques of Neutralization: A Reconceptualization and Empirical Analysis." *Journal of Research in Crime and Delinquency* 18:295–318.

Missoulian (Missoula, MT). 1992. "Jerry's Kids Say Enough; Now Some Are Jerry's Orphans." August 21:B-4.

Mohr, Richard D. 1988. *Gays/Justice, A Study of Ethics, Society and Law*. New York: Columbia University Press.

Montagu, Ashley. 1979. *The Elephant Man, A Study in Human Dignity*. New York: E.P. Dutton.

Moore, M. H., and R.C. Trojanowicz. 1988. "Policing and Fear of Crime." *Perspectives on Policing*, June, No. 3, Dept. of Justice, National Institute of Justice, Washington, D.C.

Morgan, Robin, ed. 1989. *The Demon Lover, On the Sexuality of Terrorism*. New York: W.W. Norton.

Moss, Louis. 1990. "Guns and Bottle Rockets." Pp. 109–112 in S. Henry, ed., *Degrees of Deviance: Student Accounts of Their Deviant Behavior*. Salem, WI: Sheffield.

Movahedi, Siamak. 1975. "Loading the Dice in Favor of Madness." *Journal of Health and Social Behavior* 16(June):192–197.

Mowrer, O. H. 1971. "Peer Groups and Medication: The Best 'therapy' for Laymen and Professionals Alike." *Psychotherapy: Theory Research and Practice* 8:44–54.

———. 1976. "The 'Self-Help' or Mutual Aid Movement: Do Professionals Help or Hinder?" Pp 44–54 in *Self-help and Health: A Report*. New York: New Human Services Institute.

Natanson, Maurice. 1973. *The Social Dynamics of George Herbert Mead*. The Hague: Martinus Nijoff.

National Commission on Marihuana and Drug Abuse. 1972. *Marihuana: A Signal of Misunderstanding*. Washington, D.C.: U.S. Government Printing Office.

National Commission on the Causes and Prevention of Violence. 1970. *Law and Order Reconsidered*. New York: Bantam Books.

National Observer. 1977. "Views from Readers: On Anita Bryant and 'Gays.'" April 16:12.

National Public Radio. 1991. "Morning Edition." April 23.

Newberger, Eli H., and R. Bourne. 1978. "The Medicalization and Legalization of Child Abuse." *American Journal of Orthopsychiatry* 48(October):593–607.

Newcomb, Theodore M. 1950. *Social Psychology*. New York: The Dryden Press.

Newman, Donald J. 1966. *Conviction: The Determination of Guilt or Innocence without Trial*. Boston: Little, Brown.

Newman, Graeme R. 1975. "A Theory of Deviance Removal." *British Journal of Sociology* 26(June):203–217.

Newsweek. 1990. "Mixed Signals on Obscenity." October 15:74.

———. 1991. "L.A.'s Violent New Video." March 18:53.

New York Times. 1983. "For Homosexuals' Parents, Strength in Community." October 10:16.

———. 1991. "Not Quite a Wedding, But Quite a Day for Couples by the Bay." February 15:A-12.

———. 1992a. "Financier Charles H. Keating, Jr. Sentenced." April 11:1.

———. 1992b. "Clinton Differs with Perot on Hiring." May 30:A-8.

———. 1992c. "For Idle Young in Newark, Pride in a Theft Done Right." August 11:A-1ff.

———. 1992d. "On Stolen Wheels, Newark Youth Defy Authority." August 10:A-1ff.

———. 1992e. "Lift the Ban on Gay Soldiers." August 21:A-19.

NORML (National Organization for the Reform of Marijuana Laws). n.d. *Statement in Support of the Need to Reform Marijuana Laws*. Washington, D.C.

Nuehring, Elane, and G. E. Markle. 1974. "Nicotine and Norms: The Reemergence of a Deviant Behavior." *Social Problems* 21(April):511–526.

Nunnally, Jum C. 1961. *Popular Conceptions of Mental Health; Their Development and Change*. New York: Holt, Rinehart & Winston.

Odgers, Sue. 1978. "Sex on Wheels." *Paraplegia News* 31(April):38–39.

Parker, Donn B. 1980. "Computer Related White Collar Crime." pp. 197220 in G. Geis and E. Stotland, eds., *White Collar Crime, Theory and Research*. Beverly Hills, CA: Sage.

Parker, Jerry, and Pat Lauderdale. 1980. "Political Deviance in Courtroom Settings." Pp. 47–71 in Pat Lauderdale, ed., *A Political Analysis of Deviance*. Minneapolis: University of Minnesota Press.

Partridge, Eric. 1970. *A Dictionary of Slang and Unconventional English*, 7th ed. New York: Macmillan.

Payne, William D. 1973. "Negative Labels: Passageways and Prisons." *Crime and Delinquency* 19(January):33–40.

People Weekly. 1984. "New Hope, Old Anguish." March 19:25–27.

Pepinsky, Harold E., and P. Jesilow. 1984. *Myths That Cause Crime*. Cabin John, MD: Seven Locks Press.

Perrucci, Robert. 1974. *Circle of Madness*. Englewood Cliffs, NJ: Prentice-Hall.

Petrunik, Michael, and C. D. Shearing. 1983. "Fragile Facades: Stuttering and the Strategic Manipulation of Awareness." *Social Problems* 31(2):125–138.

Pfohl, Stephen J. 1977. "The 'Discovery' of Child Abuse." *Social Problems* 24(February):310–323.

———. 1985. *Images of Deviance and Social Control. A Sociological History*. New York: McGraw-Hill.

Pfuhl, Erdwin H., Jr. 1978. "The Unwed Father: A 'Non-Deviant' Rule Breaker." *The Sociological Quarterly* 19(Winter):113–128.

———. 1987. "Computer Abuse: Problems of Instrumental Control." *Deviant Behavior* 8(2):113–130.

———. 1992. "Crime Stoppers: The Legitimation of Snitching." *Justice Quarterly* 9(September):1102–1124.

Piliavin, Irving, and S. Briar. 1964. "Police Encounters with Juveniles." *American Journal of Sociology* 70(September):206–214.

Piven, Frances Fox. 1981. "Deviant Behavior and the Remaking of the World." *Social Problems* 28(June):489–508.

Playboy. 1978. "Playboy Interview: Anita Bryant." May:73ff.

Polsky, Ned. 1967. *Hustlers, Beats, and Others.* Chicago: Aldine.

Ponse, Barbara. 1976. "Secrecy in the Lesbian World." *Urban Life* 5(October):313–338.

Powell, Lyman P. 1940. *Mary Baker Eddy, A Life Size Portrait.* New York: L.P. Powell.

Powis, David. 1977. *The Signs of Crime: A Field Manual for Police.* London: McGraw-Hill.

Primetime Live. 1992. "Welfare Fraud," ABC TV, September 17.

Quinney, Richard. 1969. *Crime and Justice in Society,* editor. Boston: Little, Brown.

———. 1970a. *The Problem of Crime.* New York: Dodd, Mead.

———. 1970b. *The Social Reality of Crime.* Boston: Little, Brown.

———. 1973a. *Critique of Legal Order: Crime Control in Capitalist Society,* Boston: Little, Brown.

———. 1973b. "There's a Lot of Folks Grateful to the Lone Ranger: With Some Notes on the Rise and Fall of American Criminology." *The Insurgent Sociologist* 4(Fall):56–64.

———. 1975. *Criminology, Analysis and Critique of Crime in America.* Boston: Little, Brown.

———. 1977. *Class, State and Crime.* New York: Longman.

Rapoport, David C., and Y. Alexander. 1982. *The Morality of Terrorism, Religious and Secular Justifications.* New York: Pergamon Press.

Reasons, Charles E. 1970. "A Developmental Model for the Analysis of Social Problems: Prostitution and Moral Reform in Twentieth Century America." Paper presented before the Pacific Sociological Association, Anaheim, CA.

———. 1974. "The 'Dope' on the Bureau of Narcotics in Maintaining the Criminal Approach to the Drug Problem." Pp. 144–155 in C. E. Reasons, ed., *The Criminologist: Crime and the Criminal.* Pacific Palisades, CA: Goodyear Publishing Company.

Reiman, Jeffrey. 1979. *The Rich Get Richer and the Poor Get Prison, Ideology, Class, and Criminal Justice.* New York: John Wiley.

Reiss, Albert J., Jr. 1971. *The Police and the Public.* New Haven: Yale University Press.

Reitman, Ben L. 1937. *Sister of the Road. The Autobiography of Box-Car Bertha.* New York: Harper and Row.

Riessman, Frank. 1965. "The 'Helper-Therapy' Principle." *Social Work* 10:27–32.

Richards, Pamela, R. A. Berk, and B. Forster. 1979. *Crime as Play: Delinquency in a Middle Class Suburb.* Cambridge, MA: Ballinger.

Roberts, Simon. 1979. *Order and Dispute,* Harmondsworth: Penguin.

Robins, D. M., C. R. Sanders, and S. E. Cahill. 1991. "Dogs and Their People: Pet-Facilitated Interaction in a Public Setting." *Journal of Contemporary Ethnography* 20(April):3–25.

Robinson, David. 1979. *Talking Out of Alcoholism: The Self-Help Process of Alcoholics Anonymous*. London: Croom Helm.

Robinson, David, and S. Henry. 1977. *Self-Help and Help: Mutual Aid for Modern Problems*. Oxford: Martin Robertson.

Rocky Mountain News. 1988. "Attacks on Gays Rose 42% in '87." June 8:4.

Rodriquez, Octavio. 1974. "Getting Straight: Reflections of a Former Addict." Pp. 83–89 in J. Jacobs, ed., *Deviance: Field Studies and Self-Disclosures*. Palo Alto, CA: National Press Books.

Romano, Mary D. 1982. "Sex and Disability, Are They Mutually Exclusive?" Pp. 64–75 in M. Eisenberg, C. Griggins, and R. Duval, eds. *Disabled People as Second Class Citizens*. New York: Springer.

Rose, Arnold M. 1965. *Sociology, The Study of Human Relations*, 2nd ed. New York: Alfred A. Knopf.

Rose, N. 1987. "Beyond the Public/Private Division: Law, Power and the Family." *Journal of Law and Society* 14:61–76.

Rosenberg, Morris. 1979. *Conceiving the Self*. New York: Basic Books.

Rosenhan, D. L. 1973. "On Being Sane in Insane Places." *Science* 179 (January 19):250–258.

Rosett, Arthur, and D. R. Cressey. 1976. *Justice by Consent: Plea Bargains in the American Courthouse*. Philadelphia: J.B. Lippincott.

Roshier, Bob, and Harvey Teff. 1980. *Law and Society in England*. London: Tavistock.

Ross, Robert, and G. L. Staines. 1972. "The Politics of Analyzing Social Problems." *Social Problems* 20(Summer):18–40.

Rossman, Parker. 1973. "The Pederasts." *Society* 10 (March/April):29–35.

———. 1976. *Sexual Experience Between Men and Boys: Exploring the Pederast Underground*. New York: Association Press.

Rotenberg, Mordechai. 1974. "Self-Labeling: A Missing Link in the 'Social Reaction' Theory of Deviance." *The Sociological Review* 22(August):335–354.

Rubington, Earl, and M. S. Weinberg. 1973. *Deviance, The Interactionist Perspective*, 2nd ed. New York: Macmillan.

———. 1981. *Deviance, Interactionist Perspective*, 4th ed. New York: Macmillan.

Russell, Diana E. H. 1982. *Rape in Marriage*. New York: Macmillan (Collier).

Rychtarik, R. G. 1986. "Behavioral Assessment of Coping Skills in Spouses of Alcoholics." Paper presented to 94th Annual Meeting of the American Psychological Association, Washington D.C. Cited in Levine (1988).

Safilios-Rothschild, Constantina. 1970. *The Sociology and Social Psychology of Disability and Rehabilitation*. New York: Random House.

———. 1976. "Disabled Persons' Self Definitions and Their Implications for Rehabilitation." Pp. 39–56 in G. L. Albrecht, ed., *The Sociology of Physical Disability and Rehabilitation*. Pittsburgh: University of Pittsburgh Press.

Sagarin, Edward. 1969. *Odd Man In. Societies of Deviants in America*. Chicago: Quadrangle Books.

_____. 1975. *Deviants and Deviance, An Introduction to the Study of Disvalued People and Behavior.* New York: Praeger.

Sanders, William B. 1977. *Detective Work, A Study of Criminal Investigation.* New York: Free Press.

San Francisco Examiner. 1991. "Bruce Hilton AIDSWEEK." March 10:B-4.

Sataloff, J., R. T. Sataloff, and L. A. Vassallo. 1980. *Hearing Loss,* 2nd ed. Philadelphia: J.B. Lippincott.

Scarpitti, Frank R., and E. C. Scarpitti. 1977. "Victims of Rape." *Society* (July/August):29–72.

Scheff, Thomas J. 1964. "The Societal Reaction to Deviance: Ascriptive Elements in the Psychiatric Screening of Mental Patients in a Midwestern State." *Social Problems* 11(Spring):401–413.

_____. 1966. *Being Mentally Ill: A Sociological Theory.* Chicago: Aldine.

_____. 1968. "Negotiating Reality: Notes on Power in the Assessment of Responsibility." *Social Problems* 16(Summer):3–17.

_____. 1979. "Reply to Comment by Horwitz." *Journal of Health and Social Behavior* 20(3):305.

Schmid, Alex P., and J. de Graff. 1982. *Violence as Communication, Insurgent Terrorism and the Western News Media.* Beverly Hills, CA: Sage.

Schostak, John F. 1983. *Maladjusted Schooling: Deviance, Social Control and Individuality in Secondary Schooling.* London: The Falmer Press.

Schur, Edwin M. 1971. *Labeling Deviant Behavior, Its Sociological Implications.* New York: Harper and Row.

_____. 1973. *Radical Nonintervention, Rethinking the Delinquency Problem.* Englewood Cliffs, NJ: Prentice-Hall.

_____. 1979. *Interpreting Deviance: A Sociological Introduction.* New York: Harper and Row.

_____. 1980. *The Politics of Deviance: Stigma Contests and the Uses of Power* Englewood Cliffs, NJ: Prentice-Hall.

_____. 1984. *Labeling Women Deviant: Gender, Stigma, and Social Control.* New York: Random House.

Schutz, Alfred. 1945. "On Multiple Realities." *Philosophy and Phenomenological Research* 5:533–576.

Schwab, John J., and R. B. Schwab. 1973. "The Epidemiology of Mental Illness." Pp. 58–83 in Gene Usdin, ed., *Psychiatry: Education and Image.* New York: Bruner/Mazel.

Schwartz, Charlotte Green. 1956. "The Stigma of Mental Illness." *Journal of Rehabilitation* 22 (July/August):7–29.

Schwartz, Howard D. 1988. "Further Thoughts on a 'Sociology of Acceptance' for Disabled People." *Social Policy* 19:36–39.

Schwartz, Howard, and J. Jacobs. 1979. *Qualitative Sociology, A Method to the Madness.* New York: Free Press.

Schwartz, Richard D., and J. H. Skolnick. 1964. "Two Studies of Legal Stigma." Pp. 103–117 in Howard Becker, ed., *The Other Side, Perspectives on Deviance.* New York: Free Press.

Scott, Marvin B., and S. M. Lyman. 1968. "Accounts." *American Sociological Review* 33(February):46–62.

Scott, Robert A. 1965. "Comments About Interpersonal Process of Rehabilitation." Pp. 132–138 in Marvin B. Sussman, ed., *Sociology and Rehabilitation*. Washington, D.C.: American Sociological Association.

———. 1969. *The Making of Blind Men*. New York: Russell Sage.

———. 1970. "The Construction of Conceptions of Stigma by Professional Experts." Pp. 255–290 in Jack D. Douglas, ed., *Deviance and Respectability, The Social Construction of Moral Meanings*. New York: Basic Books.

———. 1972. "A Proposed Framework for Analyzing Deviance as a Property of Social Order." Pp. 9–35 in Robert A. Scott and Jack D.Douglas, eds., *Theoretical Perspectives on Deviance*. New York: Basic Books.

Secord, Paul F., and C. W. Backman. 1964. *Social Psychology*. New York: McGraw-Hill.

Seidman, David, and M. Couzens. 1974. "Getting the Crime Rate Down: Political Pressure and Crime Reporting." *Law and Society Review* 8:457–493.

Shaskolsky, Leon. 1973. "The Legal Institution: The Legitimizing Appendage." Pp. 294–337 in L. T. Reynolds and J. M. Henslin, eds., *American Society, A Critical Analysis*. New York: David McKay.

Shaw, Colin. 1969. "Television and Popular Morality: The Predicament of the Broadcasters." Pp. 117–127 in Paul Halmos, ed., *The Sociology of Mass Media Communicators*. Sociology Review Monograph No. 13. University of Keele.

Sheley, Joseph F. 1980. "Is Neutralization Necessary for Criminal Behavior?" *Deviant Behavior* 2:49–72.

Shover, Neal. 1984. "The Official Construction of Deviant Identities." Pp. 66–74 in Jack D. Douglas, ed., *The Sociology of Deviance*. Boston: Allyn and Bacon.

Shuey, Chris. 1978. "The Nuke Fight Escalates." *New Times Weekly* (Phoenix, AZ) 10(December 6–13):3, 25.

Sidel, Victor W., and R. Sidel. 1976. "Beyond Coping." *Social Policy* 7(September/October):67–69.

Sieh, Edward W. 1987. "Perceptions of Inequity and Employee Theft." *British Journal of Criminology* 27(2):174–190.

Simmel, Georg. 1903. *Conflict and the Web of Group Affiliations* (1955) Kurt Wolff; Reinhard Bendix, trans. New York: Free Press.

———. 1950. *The Sociology of Georg Simmel*. Kurt H. Wolff, ed. and trans. New York: Free Press.

Simmons, J. L. 1969. *Deviants*. Berkeley, CA: Glendessary Press.

Simon, David R. and D. S. Eitzen. 1990. *Elite Deviance*, 3rd ed. Boston: Allyn and Bacon.

Simpson, Ruth. 1977. *From the Closet to the Courts, The Lesbian Transition*. New York: Penguin.

Skolnick, Jerome H. 1966. *Justice Without Trial: Law Enforcement in a Democratic Society*. New York: John Wiley.

Smythe, Dallas W. 1954. "Reality as Presented by Television." *Public Opinion Quarterly* 18(Summer):143–156.

Spector, Malcolm. 1977. "Legitimizing Homosexuality." *Society* 14(July/August): 52–56.

Spector, Malcolm, and J. I. Kitsuse. 1977. *Constructing Social Problems*. Menlo Park, CA: Cummings.

Spong, John Shelby. 1988. *Living in Sin? A Bishop Rethinks Human Sexuality*. New York: Harper Collins.

Spradley, James P. 1970. *You Owe Yourself a Drunk*. Boston: Little, Brown.

State Press (Arizona State University). 1980. "'Alibi Service' Provides $20 Substitute Roommate." January 23:8.

Steinmen, Richard, and D. R. Traunstein. 1976. "Reducing Deviance: The Self-Help Challenge to the Human Services." *The Journal of Applied Behavioral Sciences* 12:347–362.

St. James, Margo. 1987. "The Reclamation of Whores." Pp. 81–87 in L. Bell. ed., *Good Girls/Bad Girls: Feminists and Sex Trade Workers Face to Face*. Seattle: Seal Press.

Stoddard, Kenneth. 1982. "The Enforcement of Narcotics Violations in a Canadian City: Heroin User's Perspectives on the Production of Official Statistics." *Canadian Journal of Criminology* 23(October):425–438.

Sudnow, David. 1965. "Normal Crimes." Pp. 174–185 in E. Rubington and M. S. Weinberg, eds., *Deviance, The Interactionist Perspective*, 2nd ed. New York: Macmillan.

Sullivan, Robert E. 1990. "Despite Losing the Spotlight, the Effort to Legalize Drugs Is Still Making Gains." *Rolling Stones* November 15:5.

Sutherland, Edwin H. 1937. *The Professional Thief, By a Professional Thief*. Chicago: University of Chicago Press.

———. 1950. "The Diffusion of Sexual Psychopath Laws." *American Journal of Sociology* 56(September):142–148.

Sutherland, Edwin, and D. R. Cressey. 1978. *Criminology*, 10th ed. Philadelphia: J.B. Lippincott.

Sykes, Gresham M. 1958. *The Society of Captives, A Study of a Maximum Security Prison*. Princeton: Princeton University Press.

———. 1972. "The Future of Criminality." *American Behavioral Scientist* 15(3):403–419.

Sykes, Gresham M., and D. Matza. 1957. "Techniques of Neutralization: A Theory of Delinquency." *American Sociological Review* 22(December):664–670.

Taber, Merlin, H. C. Quay, H. Mark, and V. Nealey. 1969. "Disease Ideology and Mental Health Research." *Social Problems* 16(Winter):349–357.

Tannenbaum, Frank. 1938. *Crime and the Community*. Boston: Ginn and Company.

Taylor, Laurie. 1972. "The Significance and Interpretation of Motivational Questions: The Case of Sex Offenders." *Sociology* 6:23–29.

———. 1984. *In the Underworld*. London: Basil Blackwell.

Taylor, M. 1982. *Community, Anarchy and Liberty*. Cambridge: Cambridge University Press.

Tempe Daily News/Tribune (Tempe, AZ). 1987a. "Institution Abuse Called Worse Than 'Cuckoo's Nest'." March 3:A-3.

———. 1987b. "Court Nominee Admits Past Marihuana Use." November 6:A-1.

———. 1987c. "Clamor forces Ginsburg out." November 8:A-1.

_____. 1991. "Americans Just Say No to Morals. Survey Says." April 29:A-1, A-3.

Terry, W. Clinton, III, and D. F. Luckenbill. 1976. "Investigating Criminal Homicides: Police Work in Reporting and Solving Murders." Pp. 79–95 in W. B. Sanders and H. C. Daudistel, eds., *The Criminal Justice Process: A Reader.* New York: Praeger.

Thoits, Peggy A. 1985. "Self-Labeling Processes in Mental Illness: The Role of Emotional Deviance." *American Journal of Sociology* 91(2):221–249.

_____. 1986. "Social Support as Coping Assistance." *Journal of Consulting and Clinical Psychology* 54:416–423.

Thorsell, Bernard A., and L. W. Klemke. 1972. "The Labeling Process: Reinforcement and Deterrent." *Law and Society Review* 6(February):393–403.

Thrasher, Frederic M. 1936. *The Gang.* Chicago: University of Chicago Press.

_____. 1963. *The Gang,* abridged ed. Chicago: University of Chicago Press.

Time 1974. "Lefty Liberation." January 7:85.

_____. 1975a. "Armed Forces: Homosexual Sergeant." June 9:18–19.

_____. 1975b. "Male and Female." June 16:73.

_____. 1985a. "AIDS: A Spreading Scourge." August 5:50–51.

_____. 1985b. "AIDS: A Growing Threat." August 12:40–47.

_____. 1991a. "Let's Change the Subject." March 4:17.

_____. 1991b. "Scandal in Phoenix." February 18:44.

_____. 1991c. "More Spontaneous Eruptions." February 18:62.

_____. 1991d. "Dr. Death Strikes Again." November 4:78.

_____. 1992a. "The Jock as Fallen Idol." April 6:60.

_____. 1992b. "Abortion, The Future Is Already Here." May 4:26–32.

Toby, Jackson. 1957. "The Differential Impact of Family Disorganization." *American Sociological Review* 22(October):505–512.

Toch, Hans. 1965. *The Social Psychology of Social Movements.* Indianapolis: Bobbs-Merrill.

Toffler, Alvin. 1970. *Future Shock.* New York: Bantam Books.

Tracy, G., and Z. Gussow. 1976. "Self-Help Health Groups: A Grass Roots Response to a Need for Services." *The Journal of Applied Behavioral Sciences* 12:381–396.

Trice, Harrison, and P. M. Roman. 1970. "Delabeling, Relabeling, and Alcoholics Anonymous." *Social Problems* 17(4):538–546.

Troyer, Ronald J., and G. E. Markle. 1983. *Cigarettes, The Battle Against Smoking.* New Brunswick, NJ: Rutgers University Press.

Truzzi, Marcello. 1968. "Lilliputians in Gulliver's Land: The Social Role of the Dwarf." Pp. 197–211 in M. Truzzi, ed., *Sociology and Everyday Life.* Englewood Cliffs, NJ: Prentice-Hall, Inc.

Tucker, Bonnie P. n.d. *The Americans With Disabilities Act.* College of Law, Arizona State University.

Tucker, James. 1989. "Employee Theft as Social Control." *Deviant Behavior* 10(4):319–334.

Turk, Austin T. 1976. "Law as a Weapon in Social Conflict." *Social Problems* 23(February):276–291.

Turner, Henry A. 1958. "How Pressure Groups Operate." *Annals of the American Academy of Political and Social Science* 319(September):63–72.

Turner, Ralph H. 1972. "Deviance Avowal as Neutralization of Commitment." *Social Problems* 19(Winter):308–321.

Unitarian Universalist World. 1976. "Coalition Opposes Anti-Abortion Plan." February 15:1–2.

Up Against the Law Collective. 1974. "Police Corruption." *Up Against the Law* 2:21–35.

U.S. Department of Justice. 1992. *Criminal Victimization in the United States, 1990*. Washington, D.C.: Bureau of Justice Statistics.

U.S. News and World Report. 1978. "Uncle Sam's Computer Has Got You." April 10:44–48.

———. 1980. "The Push-Button Criminals of the '80's." September 22:68–69.

Vander Zanden, James W. 1983. *American Minority Relations*, 4th ed. New York: Knopf.

Vandivier, Kermit. 1987. "Why Should my Conscience Bother Me?" Pp. 103–123 in D. M. Ermann and R. J. Lundman, eds., *Corporate and Governmental Deviance*, 3rd ed. New York: Oxford University Press.

Van Maanen, John. 1978. "The Asshole." Pp. 221–238 in P. K. Manning and J. Van Maanen, eds., *Policing: A View from the Street*. Santa Moncia CA: Goodyear Publishing Company.

Varni, Charles A. 1972. "An Exploratory Study of Spouse-Swapping." *Pacific Sociological Review* 15(October):507–522.

Vattano, A. 1972. "Power to the People: Self-help Groups." *Social Work*: 17:7–15.

Vose, Clement E. 1958. "Litigation as a Form of Pressure Group Activity." *Annals of the American Academy of Political and Social Science* 319(September):20–31.

Wall Street Journal. 1987. "Retailers' Losses." May 15:41.

Warren, Carol A.B. 1974a. *Identity and Community in the Gay World*. New York: John Wiley.

———. 1974b. "The Use of Stigmatizing Social Labels in Conventionalizing Deviant Behavior." *Sociology and Social Research* 58(April):303–311.

———. 1980. "Destigmatization of Identity: From Deviant to Charismatic," *Qualitative Sociology* 3(Spring):59–72.

Warren, Carol A.B., and J. M. Johnson. 1972. "A Critique of Labeling Theory from the Phenomenological Perspective." Pp. 69–92 in R. A. Scott and J. D. Douglas, eds., *Theoretical Perspectives on Deviance*. New York: Basic Books.

Watson, Lyndon. 1978. "Awakening of the New Minority." *Paraplegia News* 31(May):20.

Weber, Max. 1962. *Basic Concepts in Sociology*. New York: Philosophical Library.

Weigert, Andrew J. 1981. *Sociology of Everyday Life*. New York: Longman.

Weinberg, Martin S. 1968. "The Problems of Midgets and Dwarfs and Organizational Remedies: A Study of the Little People of America." *Journal of Health and Social Behavior* 9(March):65–71.

———. 1981. "Becoming a Nudist." Pp. 291–304 in E. Rubington and M. S. Weinberg, eds., *Deviance, The Interactionist Perspective*, 4th ed. New York: Macmillan.

Weitz, Rose. 1989. "Uncertainty in the Lives of Persons with AIDS." *Journal of Health and Social Behavior* 30:270–281.

———. 1993. "Living with the Stigma of AIDS." Pp. 222–236 in Delos H. Kelly, ed., *Deviant Behavior: A Text-Reader in the Sociology of Deviance*, 4th ed. New York: St. Martin's.

West, Donald J. 1977. *Homosexuality Re-Examined*. Minneapolis: University of Minnesota Press.

Westley, William A. 1970. *Violence and the Police: A Sociological Study of Law, Custom, and Morality*. Cambridge, MA: MIT Press.

Whitam, Frederick L. 1975. "Homosexuality as Emergent Behavior." Paper presented at the 46th annual meeting of the Pacific Sociological Association, Victoria, British Columbia, April 17–19.

———. 1977a. "The Homosexual Role: A Reconsideration." *The Journal of Sex Research* 13(February):1–11.

———. 1977b. "Childhood Indicators of Male Homosexuality." *Archives of Sexual Behavior* 6(2):89–96.

———. 1983. "Culturally Invariable Properties of Male Homosexuality: Tentative Conclusions from Cross-Cultural Research." *Archives of Sexual Behavior*. 12(3):207–226.

———. 1984. "A Cross-Cultural Assessment of Early Cross-Gender Behavior and Familial Factors in Male Homosexuality." *Archives of Sexual Behavior* 13(5):427–439.

———. 1991. "Childhood Cross-Gender Behavior of Homosexual Females in Brazil, Peru, the Philippines and the United States." *Archives of Sexual Behavior* 20(2):151–170.

Whitam, F., and R. Mathy. 1986. *Male Homosexuality in Four Societies*. New York: Praeger.

White, J.V. 1982. "Privacy in the Information Society." *Vital Speeches of the Day* 48(March):313–315.

Whiting, Leila. 1977. "The central registry for child abuse cases: rethinking basic assumptions." *Child Welfare* 56 (January):761–767.

Wilde, William A. 1969. "Official News: Decision Making in a Metropolitan Newspaper." Unpublished Ph.D. dissertation, Northwestern University.

Wilkins, Leslie T. 1965. *Social Deviance: Social Policy, Action, and Research*. Englewood Cliffs, NJ: Prentice-Hall.

Wilkinson, Paul. 1977. *Terrorism and the Liberal State*. NY: John Wiley.

Williams, Linda S. 1984. "The Classic Rape: When Do Victims Report?" *Social Problems* 31(April):459–467.

Williams, Terry. 1992. *Crack House: Notes From the End of the Line*. Reading, MA: Addison-Wesley Publishers.

Winick, Charles. 1964. "Physician Narcotic Addicts." Pp. 261–279 in H. S. Becker, ed., *The Other Side, Perspectives on Deviance*. New York: The Free Press.

———. 1978. *Deviance and Mass Media*, ed. Beverly Hills, CA: Sage.

Wiseman, Jacqueline P. 1970. *Stations of the Lost, The Treatment of Skid Row Alcoholics*. Englewood Cliffs, NJ: Prentice-Hall.

Wong, L. S., and B. K. Alexander. 1991. "Cocaine-Related Deaths: Media Coverage in the War on Drugs." *Journal of Drug Issues* 21:105–119.

World Almanac and Book of Facts. 1990. New York: Scripps Howard.

Wrong, Dennis H. 1961. "The Oversocialized Conception of Man in Modern Sociology." *American Sociological Review* 26(April):183–193.

―――. 1968. "Some Problems in Defining Social Power." *American Journal of Sociology* 73(May):673–681.

―――. 1979. *Power, Its Forms, Bases and Uses*. New York: Harper and Row.

Yablonsky, Lewis. 1959. "The Delinquent Gang as a Near Group." *Social Problems* 7(Fall):108–117.

Yarrow, Marian Radke, et al. 1955. "The Psychological Meaning of Mental Illness in the Family." *Journal of Social Issues* 11(4):12–24.

Yinger, J. Milton. 1965. *Toward a Field Theory of Behavior, Personality and Social Structure*. New York: McGraw-Hill.

Yollin, Patricia. 1991. "Painting the Town Lavender." *Image, San Francisco Examiner* March 10:18–29.

Young, Jock. 1971. "The Role of Police as Amplifiers of Deviancy, Negotiators of Reality and Translators of Fantasy." Pp. 27–61 in S. Cohen, ed., *Images of Deviance*. Baltimore: Penguin.

Zukav, Gary. 1979. *The Dancing Wu Li Masters, An Overview of the New Physics*, New York: Bantam Books.

Zola, Irving K. 1972. "Medicine as an Institution of Social Control." *Sociological Review* 20:487–504.

―――. 1975. "Helping One Another: A Brief History of Mutual Aid Groups." Mimeo. Waltham, MA: Department of Sociology, Brandeis University.

Author Index

Subject Index